Acclaim for Henry Petroski's

PAPERBOY

"*Paperboy* delivers as a pleasant trip though an America that has faded into history, with a tour guide who shares with us both the eyes of a young boy and the wisdom of a grown man."
—*Civil Engineering*

"Petroski . . . can see the poetry in a bicycle." —*The New York Sun*

"An unlikely combination of mathematical brain power and a more irrational curiosity. . . . Petroski not only can put science in laymen's terms, but also can do so without killing its magic."
—*The Christian Science Monitor*

"Petroski . . . asks us to see the extraordinary in the ordinary."
—*Chicago Tribune*

"*Paperboy* is a masterpiece of navigation, a marvelous blend of scenic asides and commitment to the course—and to the ultimate satisfaction of being able to harvest the fruits of a future that were tended to well by the truths and honor of a tender and treasured past."
—*The Boox Review*

"The book is a joy to read for anyone who enjoys a good story, not just working on a challenging project." —*CE News*

HENRY PETROSKI

PAPERBOY

Henry Petroski is the Aleksandar S. Vesić Professor of Civil Engineering and a professor of history at Duke University. He is the author of nine previous books.

BOOKS BY HENRY PETROSKI

The Book on the Bookshelf

Remaking the World

Invention by Design

Engineers of Dreams

Design Paradigms

The Evolution of Useful Things

The Pencil

Beyond Engineering

To Engineer Is Human

Paperboy

PAPERBOY

PAPERBOY

Confessions of a Future Engineer

HENRY PETROSKI

VINTAGE BOOKS
A DIVISION OF RANDOM HOUSE, INC.
NEW YORK

FIRST VINTAGE BOOKS EDITION, APRIL 2003

Copyright © 2002 by Henry Petroski

All rights reserved under International and Pan-American
Copyright Conventions. Published in the United States by Vintage Books,
a division of Random House, Inc., New York, and simultaneously
in Canada by Random House of Canada Limited, Toronto.
Originally published in hardcover in the United States by Alfred A. Knopf,
a division of Random House, Inc., New York, in 2002.

Vintage and colophon are registered trademarks of Random House, Inc.

Map used with permission. Copyright © Hagstrom
Map Company, Inc., N.Y., Lic. No. H-2200.

The Library of Congress has cataloged the Knopf edition as follows:
Petroski, Henry
Paperboy: confessions of a future engineer/Henry Petroski—1st ed.
p. cm.
1. Petroski, Henry. 2. Civil engineers—New York (State)—
New York—Biography. 3. Paper boys— New York (State)—New York—
Biography. I. Title
TA140.P43 A3 2002
974.7'243043'092—dc21
[B] 2002038100

Vintage ISBN: 0-375-71898-2

Book design by Robert C. Olsson

www.vintagebooks.com

Printed in the United States of America
10 9 8 7 6 5 4 3 2 1

To my family, then and now

Contents

vii

List of Illustrations

PAPERBOY

1

ALL YOU NEED IS A BIKE

On my twelfth birthday, our family moved from the city that we knew to the suburbs that we did not. We traded a world of curbs, sidewalks, and stoops for one of driveways, lawns, and porches. But the city savvy developed on the streets of Brooklyn would not be enough to comprehend all at once the backyards and basements of Queens, especially for a young boy. I would have to learn a new geography, a new language, and a new way to behave and occupy myself. It wouldn't happen all at once, and in the process I would become a young businessman and lay the foundations for becoming an engineer, all in an era when technology was growing increasingly attractive, important, and humbling to me and to the country.

On the drive from the old to the new house, my father repeated what he had been saying for weeks: that we were moving up in the world. We were leaving behind an icebox for a refrigerator, a bathtub for a shower, a party line for a private phone, the subway and trolleys for buses and a car. I kept waiting for him to say "and a tricycle for a bicycle," but the words never came. How could I expect him and my mother to worry about my single birthday wish with all the other things on their minds? We had lived among boxes for

3

the last week or two, and our meals had become increasingly unbalanced as we cleaned out the cupboard and emptied the icebox. Last night we had had only canned vegetables. Since everything was on the moving truck, this morning we had all sat cross-legged on the bare kitchen floor around the coffee ring my father had brought home last evening, the only fresh food we had had for days. After I listened to a spirited rendition of "Happy Birthday, Dear Henry," I halfheartedly blew out the twelve mismatched candles on the cake that we ate with the last quart of milk from the icebox. My present that year would be moving into our new house, I guessed. My wish would remain unfulfilled.

I rode silently with my siblings in the backseat of the car, each of us cradling something special in our lap. My brother, Bill, held his dog, Blackie, and a box of caps for the guns he wore in holsters at his side. (My brother's given name was William, but we always called him Billy or Bill.) My sister, Marianne, whom we called Mary, cradled in the frills of her party dress what must have been a dozen dolls. Skippy, our other dog, lay at my feet as I opened and closed a birthday card from which a clown popped up to taunt me. It was winter, and last week's snow had all but disappeared, save for the dirty piles in the shade of the parkway's retaining wall. I daydreamed of Skippy pulling me in a dogsled, away from my family and their set ways. But without my own ways or means or wheels, I was still very much dependent upon them. A bicycle, I knew, would take me a long way toward my goal, but in the rush of the move it looked like my birthday was going to pass without any presents.

None of us children had yet seen the place our parents had bought. Like our house in Brooklyn, the new one had been purchased from a couple whom my father knew from his days as a bachelor. He was not an adventurous man, and so he reacted to offers rather than made them. When his old landlords suggested that he buy a house from them, he agreed, even to their price. Had they not moved ever upward by capitalizing on the appreciation of their real estate holdings, my father might never have taken the initiative to buy a house like this himself. We were grateful he was sentimental and kept in touch with old landlords. It enabled us to move from a row house to a tract house.

I came out of my daydreams on what seemed a street of extraordinary beauty, which our father said was ours. Though the trees lining it were bare of leaves, their branches arched over it as the ceiling did in St. Patrick's Cathedral, which we had visited once after a Thanksgiving Day Parade. The trees were planted as regularly among the driveways as the columns in St. Pat's were among the pews. The houses were set way back from the street, like side altars from the nave. There was a privacy that we had not known on our treeless street in Brooklyn. Except in winter, it was difficult to see the houses for the trees.

Many of the houses on our new street had exposed front yards whose lawns ran to the sidewalk, but the grass in front of ours and of several of our closest neighbors was hidden behind thick hedges. The walkway to our front door was flanked by two enormous blue spruce trees, which concealed the entrance from everyone but those who approached it head-on. The house was not vulnerable to strangers; it was a fortress within which we could retreat.

The house's distinctive style of a red-brick bottom and a brown-and-white timber-and-stucco top was English Tudor, we were told. In fact, it shared an elevation and a floor plan with virtually all of the neighboring houses. Their individuality came mostly in how the second story was wrapped. Some were shingled and some were sheathed in clapboards, with the color of the shingles or siding often providing the house's main distinguishing feature. The area today is described as "a rather homogeneous semisuburban district, largely made up of conservatively styled brick homes." On our street there was little brick above the first floor, as if the material were too heavy for the builders to carry up to the second.

My father had parked the car at the curb, and we stood for a moment at the front gate, my sister's hand on its unfamiliar mechanism. We were caught between awe and adventure. The dogs could run free, my mother told us, and we let them go. We stood mesmerized by the tableau. Before us was not a sinuous yellow-brick road,

The new house in Cambria Heights

but a gray concrete walkway running straight as an arrow between the spruces to the front door. The house loomed also above some shrubs, seeming to dare them to try to overtake it, which they almost would in time. If this was not exactly a castle, it was our home, and we were all anxious to explore it. I showed Marianne how the latch on the gate worked, and swung it open.

We passed single-file between the trees, Mary showing her exuberance by running ahead. Billy advanced with his hands on his six-shooters, looking from side to side. I moved at a pouty pace, resigned to walk instead of ride a bike for the rest of my life. My mother looked over my head, something she would not be able to do in another year, and my father lingered by the gate, closing it behind him and looking up at the trees.

As we approached the porch, which I would try to but never

fully succeed in calling that, I saw several newspapers folded in a curious way sitting under the bushes beside the stoop. They were recognizable to me as papers only by their columns of type and bold headlines. In shape they resembled the makeshift flyswatters my father fashioned in the summer out of the papers he brought home from work in the evening, but these did not need a strong hand to hold them together. They had been soaked by rain and looked heavy, like wrung-out wash ready to be hung on a clothesline. I pointed out the litter to my father, and he commented that it looked like several days of the local paper, which the previous owners must have forgotten to stop delivery on. When the paperboy came to collect later that afternoon, my father paid him for the week but told him we did not want the paper delivered anymore.

It must have been easy for the paperboy to miss the porch, I thought, for it was much smaller than our stoop in Brooklyn. But there was little need for it to be larger, for it would be used only by the rare solicitor and the even rarer guest. It certainly would not be used by roomers my parents had inherited with the rooming house we had just left behind in Brooklyn. They had paid the second mortgage, my father told us. Whatever they did, we children had always had to compete with the roomers for the attention of our parents, and we had been looking forward to now having them all to ourselves. Or at least my brother and sister may have been, for I was already looking ahead to exploring the neighborhood on my own, even if it had to be on foot. But first I did want to see our new house.

The heavy, thick front door opened into a phone booth of a vestibule. Its far wall, not five feet away, was set at an angle and contained a modest arched opening. Through it we entered the living room, which was almost as long as the house was wide. The front wall, which faced east, was interrupted by a window of three casements, and high on the north wall were two glass-brick windows flanking a large mirror. The glass bricks provided some degree of privacy from the neighboring house, which was not ten feet away. The mirror, I would later deduce, was located exactly where one would have hung an expansive landscape over a mantel. We had no picture so grand, so perhaps it was better that we had no mantel.

Among my most vivid memories of my father remains the one of him standing before that mirror combing his hair in the morning sun that streamed through the casement windows. Old pictures show that he had had a handsome head of hair as a young man, but by his mid-forties his hairline had begun to recede and he was thinning badly. This gave my father a lot of forehead, making his round face seem longer than it was. He wore rimless octagonal glasses, with the small nick in one corner long forgotten and no longer seen by him or by us. He had worn glasses for so long that they had impressed grooves into his temples and craters into his nose. The symmetry of his face was usually broken by a pipe, which drew down the right corner of his mouth—his left in the mirror—and his pipe's smoke usually wafted about him. He himself did not waft, for he was heavy on his feet and his hands fell clumsily on everything but a comb.

Instead of drawing his hair across his balding pate, he combed it straight back, as if not wanting to make himself appear to be other than he was. On many an occasion, I would watch him combing his hair long after it had been optimally arranged. He was not really looking in the mirror, I am sure. I suspect that this morning, for an instant, he saw neither himself nor his older son standing on the stairway behind him. Was he thinking about the house, or perhaps about the fireplace that he would have opted for had he been the original owner? Might he have had some shelves built on either side, in lieu of the glass bricks? But buying the house now had left no budget for improvements. Without roomers, he would have to take a second job just to pay the mortgage. Perhaps he was trying to see into the future, to imagine what he would look like when he burned the mortgage.

Today, not a minute into our tour of the house, my father was already in another world, lost in the mirror that in years to come would reflect the flash in countless family photographs. We all had the most difficult time remembering that the best vantage point for family photos was not necessarily the most advantageous, or flattering. I continued to watch my father in the mirror from across the room, from the stairway that led up to the second floor. Bill and Mary were already upstairs, choosing their rooms; my mother had gone to the kitchen. I was waiting for my father, to give him the pleasure of showing us what we could see for ourselves.

The stairway on which I was standing was on the south side of the living room, rising from a small landing and hugging the outside wall. In the wall was a recess, an alcove like those that hold statues in a church, but shallower. It was an inexplicably extravagant detail in a house without frills. The sound of children running up the stairs had called my father out of his trance, and he turned to join me. A dozen or so stairs led up to a second small landing, lit by a single-casement window. Through it we could see that the house of our neighbors to the south was about fifteen feet away, the wider space allowing for a driveway. At the very top of the stairs was a squarish hallway, with five doors set jamb-to-jamb around it. One led to the bathroom that served the three bedrooms. The fifth door would normally have opened into a linen closet, but in this house it opened onto a stairway that led up to an attic.

Bill and I would share a bedroom, something that we were used to doing. Mary's room, which she would have to herself, was minuscule. The master bedroom was the largest, of course, but even it was not extravagant and it had neither a walk-in closet nor a private bath. Behind its shrubs and arboreal fortifications, our new house had looked huge from the gate. In fact, most of its rooms were smaller than those we had left behind, as we would see when our furniture was moved in. Instead of the twin beds my brother and I had expected to use, our new bedroom would accommodate only a single double bed, which we had to share. Nevertheless, this was now our house and our home in the suburbs, and we had not yet even seen the rest of the downstairs.

Family portrait, with author behind flash in mirror

Retracing his steps down to the living room, our father led us through it and past the mirror into the dining room, a feature our house in Brooklyn did not have. There we had always eaten in the middle of the kitchen, which was large and square and the center of all activity. In this house, the kitchen was separated from the dining room by a swinging door, which when left open was either in the way of the kitchen cabinets or jutting out into the dining room, ready to intercept a running boy.

The new kitchen was diminutive, seeming even smaller than my sister's bedroom. Looking in from the dining room, I saw a white refrigerator in one corner, and on the wall opposite it, behind the door, some built-in cabinets flanking a window above the sink. A large butcher-block counter filled a space where I would have expected to see a stove. Beneath the counter, in a kneehole, nestled a flimsy stool. The room seemed to have no place left for a kitchen table. And where was the stove?

Entering the kitchen and turning back toward the dining room, I saw that the room was L-shaped. There was more floor space to the right of the doorway than I first thought, and in this space sat the stove. It was enormous, like no stove I had ever seen. In our old house, and in houses of friends and relatives, stoves were inconspicuous things, either coal-gray cast iron or white enamel edged in black. This stove was bright red, with chrome trim, knobs, and lever-like handles that looked like they opened a refrigerator rather than an oven door. The stove actually had two ovens, plus a warming well on top, and its edges and corners were softly curved, like those of the streamlined cars and trucks of the time. In fact, the stove appeared to be coming out of the wall the way the hood and fenders of a too-long fire engine poked out from under the overhead door of a too-short firehouse. If I waited long enough, would this major appliance begin to wail and move out, as if answering an alarm?

The stove was a Chambers, and a top-of-the-line model, we were told. To me, it seemed that the previous owners of the house must have left this incongruous thing behind because they could not get it out of the door. I could not imagine how it had been installed in the first place, unless the house was built around it. Now, the stove being set off in its own space dictated where everything else in the kitchen was located, as if in obeisance to the great red god. Instead of opening against the wall, the refrigerator door opened out into the middle of the room. It was also a good distance from the sink, an inconvenient arrangement when it came to defrosting the ice-cube compartment. With our heavy old kitchen table and chairs moved into it, the room would be suited neither to cooking, eating, nor movement among the appliances. But I could imagine my mother being sold on the house by the stove alone, even if she had to live with a crowded, undersized, and poorly arranged kitchen. It was what it was.

My mother kept no mirror in the kitchen, and I don't remember ever seeing her look into the one in the living room. She wore glasses, though not self-consciously, and stood tall, even though she was not. Whenever she did primp up, she must have done so in the privacy of the bathroom or bedroom. She wore her hair in a permanent wave and her mouth in a permanent purse. Loose lips sink ships, she knew even before the war.

Many a time I would come into the kitchen from the dining room or from the side door and find my mother engrossed in whatever she was doing, talking about it to herself, telling herself what she had to do next in the process of her task. At first I thought this odd behavior, but I have since caught myself talking audibly to my own self when engaged fully at something, especially a task that I am enjoying alone. I like to think that my mother wanted to share her pleasure with someone, but she thought no one was around at the time.

In spite of its difficult geometry and its loneliness, the kitchen remained her favorite room. It would be, at least when no one else was home, her office, her study, her space, her place of business. It was where she would sit and compose grocery lists, where she would stand and prepare food. Fixing a meal there was not for her a chore to be endured, it was a creative opportunity to be enjoyed. In her kitchen, she would revel in the transformation of raw ingredients into delicious and attractive dishes, an accomplishment I would now liken at the same time to chemical engineering and to fine art. When my father daydreamed of mantels, did my mother dream of hearths? That is hard for me to say, for she remains a circumspect woman who has always worn an apron over her heart.

By floor plan and by her plan, the kitchen would again be our home's hub of activity, for it was where our mother presided. We had entered the house this first time through the front door, but we would seldom use that as our entrance. The side door was our access point. From the side stoop—there was never any pretension in calling it a porch—an anodized aluminum storm door opened under a brown-and-white enameled aluminum awning onto a three-by-three-foot landing, and it was a single step up from that to the second door, which led into the kitchen. Opening it put one face-to-face with the Chambers, its chrome front bumper edging into the right-of-way.

Now that we were all crowded into the kitchen, my father said we should go downstairs to the basement. There, we saw immediately, the previous owners had left a bar and bar stools—fixtures then as common in suburban basements as oil burners and oil tanks—probably because the bar itself, like the stove, seemed impossible to remove from its space. Like a sailboat built of lumber passed easily in through the basement windows, this requisite suburban-basement symbol of urbanity was beached where it was built.

Bill and Mary jumped on the bar stools and pushed off from the edge of the bar to spin themselves around. Mary was a ballerina, she informed us, her hands held in prayer above her head. Billy, who got his stool spinning too fast, was thrown off by the centrifugal force. He picked himself up and tried again, this time with some restraint. He took out his cowboy guns and shot up the place. Both Bill and Mary began to get dizzy, and so dropped to the floor.

The basement floor was covered with white-flecked black asbestos tile, set on the bias with every other black square cut on the diagonal and mated with half of a white floor tile. The overall effect presented a compromise between the starkness of the yellow walls and the ostentation of the bar. Overhead, pocked acoustical ceiling panels had been nailed across the bottoms of the floor joists. Still, the basement was not what could be considered a fully finished rumpus room. An exposed steel I-beam spanned the width of the house, supported by two painted but otherwise unadorned cylindrical steel columns, forming an invisible curtain where the ceiling and floor tiles ended abruptly. The machinery of the house—the oil burner, oil tank, hot water heater, and laundry tubs—lay beyond, all exposed on the far side of what seemed to me then to be a large open space but must have been no more than about twenty-five feet square.

As much as the bar stools excited my siblings, the back of the basement captured my imagination. Here, on a bare concrete floor and beside unpainted foundation walls, was what made the house work. The oil burner sat like a Buddha in its own space, immobile yet giving. Out of its corpulent body arms reached in all directions, ready to take the warmth of that body to the rooms of the house. This heating system was at the same time like the one in our Brooklyn basement and different. That was steam heat and this was hot water, I learned from my father, who offered it as another way that we were better off. Hot-water heat didn't make the banging noise that steam heat did. He showed me how to look through the little glass window of the oil burner to see the fire burning inside.

As much as the sight of the furnace warmed my heart, my father tried to direct my attention to the other side of the basement. While I had been looking at the furnace, Bill had discovered a door concealed in a short stretch of wood paneling beside the bar. I had noticed the paneling painted yellow with black trim, but I thought it just an aborted project. Now I saw that the door itself concealed a shallow closetlike space in which the meters for water, gas, and electricity were located, as well as the fuse box. The main water supply pipe for the house projected out the side of this closet at about bar level, and a small wooden shelf had been built to fit over it and conceal it. The shelf's disproportionately deep fascia, painted yellow, was ornamented with a wooden boss, painted black, into which the pipe head fit. The bar had been positioned directly in front of this shelf, which must have served to hold liquor bottles the way I had seen them arranged behind the bar in saloons in Brooklyn. Anyone sitting at our bar faced the one semifinished section of the basement and could ignore the fact that the tile floor stopped just short of the house's machinery. Unlike in the saloons, there were no mirrors behind this bar, and so adults could drink in the basement oblivious to the mechanical and electrical support system out of their view.

To me, at twelve, the kitchen and basement and their appurtenances, rather than the living room and bedrooms of our new house, seemed its most important parts. The kitchen was a grand chemistry laboratory. The basement revealed the structural bones and mechanical organs of the house. It was these kinds of things that fascinated me, that would shape my mind, that would prepare me for becoming an engineer.

But my father had not brought us down to the basement to show off the house's innards. Bill and Mary had caught on and were giggling on the bar stools, to which they had returned. My mother had remained standing at the foot of the stairs, ready to return to her own mechanical room. My father finally said bluntly that my birthday present was somewhere in the basement. Where? All I really wanted was a bicycle, as I had been letting him know for months, but there was none here.

In all my exploring, I had overlooked a large corrugated-cardboard box that lay flat but now no longer inconspicuous on the floor, askew to the lines both of the tile and of the walls. I had assumed it was something left by the old residents. I finally realized that my father's focus was clearly on this box. It was about the size of a baby-crib mattress, which was not the size or shape of anything that I had been wishing for. In my fixation on the patterns and shapes and things in the basement, I had not read the obvious clue on the box, the single word "Schwinn." The box held not something fully formed but an unassembled bicycle lying on its side.

In my joy I forgot to thank my father looking over my shoulder and my mother standing on the stairs. One part of me wanted to open the box carefully and slowly, to savor the discovery; another part wanted to rip the box apart, to touch its contents. Removing the tenacious large staples that held the top closed would require a tool of some kind, but there was nothing in the empty house to use. My father never carried tools in the car, except for the tire iron and lug wrench, neither of which would do. The carrying handles that had been cut into the sides of the box seemed to provide an entree, and I pulled on them as if they would trigger perforations. My progress being slow, in spite of my movements being fast, my father took over. His meaty hands, which I had seen tear his hometown phone book in two, opened the box immediately, as if it were a tiny one of cornflakes. Now exposed, the parts of the maroon-colored bicycle lay nestled among themselves, like the parts of an Erector set. Today I would liken the order in the box to a Picasso portrait of a bicycle.

I had never even ridden a two-wheeler, but as a child in Brooklyn I had learned the exhilaration of wheels: riding my first tricycle along the sidewalk in front of our apartment, exploring Prospect Park on a pair of roller skates, hurtling down the great slope below the park on a homemade scooter. The sensation of rushing down a hill always gave me at the same time a visceral thrill and a mortal fear, and I suspected that I could reproduce either or both sensations on a bike. I finally thanked my father and yelled my thanks up to my mother for the greatest birthday present ever. I saw in my brother's eyes that he was already looking ahead to his own twelfth birthday, if not an earlier one.

My bicycle needed first to be assembled, but my father was not the one I wanted to see do it. I admired him greatly for his sharp mind and strong arms. He could name the forty-eight states in alphabetical order, in order of population, and in contiguous order, beginning either with Maine in New England or with Washington in the Pacific Northwest. At family weddings and reunions, he could defeat any of my uncles at arm-wrestling, and it was he who could hold the most cousins on his shoulders and in his arms. But he seemed incapable of following the instructions for screwing a nut onto a bolt, and whatever thing his hands tried to fix always seemed to have worked better broken. Anything plastic broke between his thumb and second finger. Nothing seemed to fit within his fist. In his hands a wrench stripped pipe threads, a hammer bent nails, a screwdriver gouged wood and scratched metal. If my father assembled my new bicycle, I feared, it would immediately look like a used one.

Fortunately, the moving truck arrived before my father could touch the bike, and he was called upstairs to oversee the unloading. Bill and Mary followed him, leaving me alone with the separate parts of the bicycle but with no tools to put them together. I read the assembly instructions slowly and carefully, as if I would be tested on them in school. After a short while my father came back downstairs carrying his toolbox. I held my breath. The toolbox, he said, was always the last thing to be loaded on a moving truck so it could be the first thing unloaded, just in case. He said he was sorry that he could not work on the bicycle right then, because he had to check the condition of the furniture and show the movers where it belonged. He and I could assemble the bicycle as soon as they were through. I resumed breathing, and wondered if I could get the bike put together before he returned.

My father's toolbox had always attracted and repelled me at the same time. It was a long gray metal one, big enough to hold two full-size saws—rip and cross-cut—in place under its lid. It had a removable tray, which was subdivided into smaller compartments to hold different tools and parts the way a cash register's drawer is divided to hold different denominations of bills and coins. The tools my father kept in the box were an indiscriminate assortment of ones he had inherited from his own father and specialized ones bought for odd jobs that never saw a second use beyond taking up space in the toolbox.

Without question, the most distinguishing feature of my father's toolbox was its disorder, though that may be too precise and mis-leading a description of a jumble of tools and hardware staples that had never been in order. Wrenches, pliers, screwdrivers, planes, hammers, awls, chisels, files, and putty knives were mixed together with nails (bent and straight), brads, tacks, staples, used cotter pins, washers, bolts, nuts, screws, wire, and string, which was tangled amid pencils, crayons, chalk, razor blades, oil cans, sawdust, wood shavings, and scraps of anything and everything. The smaller com-

partments of the removable tray were distinguished from the large
space in the bottom of the box only in being filled with a jumble of
smaller items.

In the chaos of the toolbox I found an adjustable crescent
wrench, a pair of pliers, and some screwdrivers. I proceeded to follow the instructions and assemble the bicycle. It was a standard
Schwinn model, with balloon tires and a coaster brake whose name,
New Departure, seems decades ahead of its time in its utopian language of commerce. The most difficult part of assembling the bicycle had been done at the factory. The rear wheel was already
mounted on the bike frame, the brake set in place and the sprocket
connected by the chain to the larger front sprocket, which in turn
was connected to the pedal cranks. In my head, I sang a mechanical
version of "the foot bone's connected to the ankle bone"—the rear
wheel's connected to the sprocket, the sprocket's connected to the
chain, the chain's connected to the front sprocket—though the
rhythm did not sound quite right.

The main parts to be attached to the bike were the pedals themselves, the handlebars, the front fender, the front wheel, and the
seat. Getting the handlebar shaft into the sleeve above the fork was
the trickiest part of putting together the bike, and yet it seemed to
me to be the most critical. If the handlebars did not hold firmly to
the fork assembly, I feared I might lose control and crash into a
lamppost or oncoming car.

The mechanism to connect the handlebars to the fork was
immensely clever, I thought, and I tried to understand it. The shaft
of the cylindrical post was cut in two at an angle, the way the
butcher sliced salami and my mother string beans. The two halves
of the shaft were strung together on a long bolt. When the bolt was
loose, the pieces could be aligned into a straight shaft and slid into
the hub of the frame above the fork. When the bolt was tightened,
the two halves of the shaft were forced to slide along the fault and
thus move sideways, pushing hard against the inside of the casing
into which they fit.

As much as I admired this inner mystery of the machine, I had to leave the theory behind and apply it. I tightened the bolt that held the handlebars with considerable consternation, worrying throughout the process that I might strip its threads or break the shaft, as my father had done with so many nuts and bolts that he had overtightened. The memory of a bolt head on my sister's baby carriage coming off in the jaws of his pipefitter's monkey wrench haunted me, and the balance between something being too tight and too loose would often freeze me in the slush of indecision. With the handlebars finally attached with what seemed like the right tightness, I quickly slid the plastic grips over the ends of the tube, remembering the time my little brother fell on my tricycle's exposed handlebar end, hurting his eye. I worried at the time that he would lose the eye or have to wear glasses. He had to have the eye washed out every evening with some solution in an eyecup and had to wear a black patch on the other eye for weeks. It seemed odd to cover up his good eye, until my mother explained that that was so his hurt eye would not get lazy.

Next I attached the bicycle seat to the frame, repositioning the galvanized shaft several times in the maroon tube before deciding that it was neither too far in nor too far out for my feet to reach the ground without resting flat on it. Again, I wrestled throughout this process with the question of when to stop turning the wrench tightening the bolt that squeezed the clamp that fixed the height of the seat.

With the handlebars and seat in place to my satisfaction, or rather to my hope, I next had to turn the bike upside down and rest it on the three points of the handlebar grips and seat. I worried about scuffing these parts and first laid out on the floor some odd pieces of cardboard packing. With great care and considerable effort, I turned the heavy bike carcass over.

The idea of using the seat and handlebars to form a tripod on which the bike rested seemed like a brilliant concept to me, something that was an extra feature of the machine. I was fascinated by the fact that it required no extra or special parts and did not diminish the bike's primary function. I pondered but could not decide

whether such a feature was fortuitous or by design. My admiration
for such simple mechanical pleasures, if they can even be called
that, no doubt marked me as an engineer in the making as surely as
technology and politics would conspire four years later to push me
toward engineering school.

With the bike upside down, I proceeded to attach the pedals.
The pedals, I discovered, had to be screwed into the crank in different directions on either side of the bike. I admired the neatness
of this detail, which I assume was developed by clever bicycle
mechanics, like Wilbur and Orville Wright, who noticed that with
conventional threads left pedals were likely to work their way loose
with use. Fitting them with left-handed threads solved the problem, though to this day some cycle-theorists disagree on why.

I was not interested in theory at the time, and I proceeded to
attach the front wheel. I had to remove the nuts the first time I put
them onto the axle, because I forgot to put the fender stays on first.
My father would be coming back down into the basement any
moment, I kept thinking, and so I rushed to finish. On my second
attempt, I put the inner washer outside the fender stays, and so had
to undo that arrangement too. On my third attempt, I got everything in the right order.

The seemingly simple assembly of the front wheel turned out to
be complicated because I was unfamiliar with the multiple combination of parts and the several adjustments that had to be performed on the single axle. The inner, cone-shaped nuts that held
the ball bearings in just the right place had to be tight enough to
eliminate any rattle or any wobble in the wheel but could not be so
tight on the bearings as to impede the balls turning in their race.
The slotted fender stays had to be adjusted so that the fender did
not rub against the tire, and the wheel had to be centered so that it
did not rub against either the fender or the tines of the fork.
Though I got all the parts in the right order, it took some doing to
get them in the right adjustment. And in the process I introduced
some scratches on the fork.

I was unsure about how much to tighten the bolts against the fork. It occurred to me that the factory-assembled rear wheel might give me a clue, and so I loosened one of the nuts holding it to the frame. In doing so, I was surprised to find that the innermost washer was not flat but serrated or ridged, like the edges of the pie crusts that my mother made. The ridges of the washer clearly made for a better grip between the axle and the bicycle frame—certainly a desirable feature when hitting bumps, potholes, and curbs—but the washer had been pressed into the frame so hard that it broke the paint and bit into the steel beneath. What must have been a pristine paint job before the wheel was attached was now crushed and indented. The damage had been hidden beneath the washer and would be hidden again when I retightened the nut, but it pained me to know that the scars would remain there for the life of the bike. I tried to torque the nut so that the ridges of the washer fell into the same valleys as before, but there was no way I could be sure I was doing so.

That something had to be marred to be assembled properly bothered me as much as the simple tripod pleased me. The part-by-part perfection of the bicycle in its shipping carton, unassembled, was in sharp contrast to its blemished wholeness. Still, the potential had become reality—now defying gravity, standing upside down on its handlebars and seat, its wheels up in the air, out of place—put together by a boy just turned twelve. For a moment, I watched the front wheel rotate slowly all by itself, the unbalanced air valve seeking six o'clock.

With as much care as I had taken, and though some of the bike's scars were not of my doing and were necessary by design, I wished that they hadn't happened. Were they a punishment for my impatience and impertinence in not waiting for my father to help me? My fear of his denting or scratching the bike may have deprived him of a pleasure. But, knowing what he must have of his own hamhandedness, I may also have saved him the anxiety of tightening the handlebar shaft into its sleeve or the nuts onto the axle. I thus rationalized my transgression while righting the bicycle.

Doing this alone was not an easy task, especially since I wanted to lift it fully off its tripod and turn it without touching anything but the rubber-tired wheels to the floor. (I estimate that the bike weighed perhaps fifty pounds to my ninety-one.) With strength fired by will, I grasped the bicycle by the top of the frame and pulled it up and toward me, letting the steel tubing rotate in my hands as if it were part of a jungle gym. As my hands reached the zenith of their arc, I let the bike fall down on its tires, which caused the whole thing to rebound like a bouncing rubber ball. With the bicycle in its natural position, I lowered its kickstand and stepped back to admire the machine that I had assembled. It was in its resting pose: body leaning to the left; front wheel and handlebars canted farther left. Steeped in the cowboy movies of the time, I saw it as a horse pawing the ground and looking at its tail, full of contentment and only a little curiosity about itself. I walked around the steed, whose seat was a saddle and whose handlebars were reins, and thought about mounting and riding it for the first time.

I could hear the movers upstairs continuing to bring things in through the front door, the noises of furniture being placed down and moved, like a deep dull thunder rumbling in the distance, signaling rain. In fact, it had already begun to rain lightly outside, as I could see through the windows set high in the basement wall and hear in the drainpipes beside them. I could not take my initial ride on my new bike outside in the rain, I thought, and so I considered the basement space. Except for the bicycle box now leaning against the side wall, the bar against the front wall, the stairs against the other side, the two steel poles at the tile limit, and the furnace beyond them, the basement floor was largely unobstructed.

I had installed the seat low enough so I could mount the bike with only a little trouble, my legs straddling the boy's bar and the soles of my Keds barely touching the floor as I moved the bike back and forth through a few inches of play. A two-wheeler with 24-inch wheels would probably have fit me perfectly, but my parents had bought me a full-sized 26-inch bike. I'm sure they thought that I would grow into it, the way I grew into too-large shoes and shirts.

A Schwinn, fully assembled

For once, I was ecstatic at being outfitted with something too large. Anything smaller would have been humiliating.

I nudged the kickstand backwards with some difficulty, nicking the paint on the bottom rail of the frame. I felt the bicycle inch forward in reaction to the backward momentum of my leg. But I was unprepared for the weight of the bike and the bite of its front wheel, which turned suddenly to the side and locked on a white asbestos tile, grabbing the floor as a pencil eraser does a misspelled word. My body hurtled toward the handlebars and at the same time fell to the side. My left foot hit the floor hard and my knee buckled under the unexpected weight of the bike falling, but I caught myself and it just before we fell over completely.

I righted the bike with a new respect for the thing's mass, and then mounted it again. This time I was ready for it, and I held the handlebars tightly and square to the frame, my legs prepared to fight the floor. I pointed the bike straight at the oil burner, planning to pass to the right of the steel pole, and then to turn left around it well before the furnace. I pushed off with the toes of both feet and the bike surged forward. I lifted my feet onto the pedals and began to crank, tentatively at first but then moving with the rhythm I had learned on my tricycle, and the bike's movement went from wobble to smooth. The wheels felt frictionless on their axles and the sideways sway of the machine was being quickly tamed. I went past the column and then steered into a fifteen-foot circle on the basement floor. I could hardly have made a complete circuit when I heard someone coming down the stairs. It was my father, grinning ear to ear.

2

THERE ARE 1,809,849 OF US!

W E HAD MOVED from Park Slope, one of the westernmost sections of Brooklyn, to Cambria Heights, one of the easternmost reaches of Queens. As the crow flies, it was no more than a dozen miles. By car, it was about a half hour's drive via the Belt Parkway, or an hour with the traffic lights on Linden Boulevard. In every other way, it was a move of incalculable distance and interminable duration.

Geographically, Brooklyn and Queens are both indisputably on Long Island, but Brooklynites ignored the fact. To them, living on Long Island meant living beyond the last subway stop. Mostly it meant living in Nassau or Suffolk County, which constituted 85 percent of the island's area, but it also meant living in the more remote sections of Queens. To our old friends in Brooklyn, we had definitely moved "out to the Island." But we were not so sure. If only a stone's throw from Nassau, the county that seceded in 1899 just after Greater New York was formed, we were ourselves still within the city limits.

In the 1950s, Queens was the fastest-growing of New York's five boroughs, adding on the order of 50,000 residents per year to the 1,550,849 counted in the last census. Some parts of Queens, called

areas, sections, localities, neighborhoods, or communities, depending on where the speaker learned to talk New York, actually lost
population in the ensuing years, often to make way for the construction of highways, which at first accommodated the growth but
in time fueled it. Cambria Heights was home to some twenty thousand residents, with little room for future growth, there being
barely a handful of vacant lots in its two hundred or so oblong
blocks. Its population grew mostly as young families with kids, like
ours, moved into a house sold by an older couple with an empty
nest.

Before Cambria Heights was developed in earnest, which meant
as long as natural gas was not piped into the area, it had been
known as Kerosene Hill, after the fuel that the community burned
for heat. The origin of the present name is uncertain. Some say it
came from a local family; others say the name referred to the Cambria Title Savings and Trust Company, the Cambria County, Pennsylvania, institution that owned the land, and possibly also the
company that supplied the kerosene. Old Kerosene Hill commands
the third-highest elevation on Long Island, but at fifty feet above
sea level that is hardly remarkable. If library services tell us anything about a community's development, it is significant that in 1930
Cambria Heights rated little more than a bookmobile stop. Two
decades later, a sub-branch of the Queens Borough Public Library
was opened in a rented storefront, a reflection of the postwar
expansion. The community got a branch post office in 1950, just
four years before my family acquired its new address.

Our house dated from the boom era, but local history and soci-
ological significance were of little interest to me on moving day.
The movers and their truck were gone by early afternoon, and our
furniture was more or less arranged as it would be until my parents
moved to their next house, almost twenty years later, long after I
left home. By midafternoon my brother and I had filled our respective bureau drawers with clothes and put our toys, jigsaw puzzles,
and comic books away in the closet, his on the right side and mine
on the left. That was the last time there would be order in the room.

Billy and I were an odd couple. In looks, and perhaps in ways, he favored my father and I my mother, we were told. His idea of order was a jumbled toolbox, mine a partitioned silverware drawer. He liked to dress up in cowboy clothes, perhaps some of the same ones I had outgrown, while I had come to feel comfortable in dungarees, as we all called blue jeans. He kept a cap gun under his pillow and liked to fire it; I craved silence in which to assemble model airplanes and study baseball cards. He was almost two and a half years younger than I, and already before we left Brooklyn we had begun to form separate friendships with our separate classmates. On our first days in Cambria Heights, we were temporarily without classmates and so necessarily thrown together.

It had stopped raining. I was ready to take my bicycle outside, with Billy's help. Our mother urged us to wait for our father before trying to get the bike out of the basement. I worried that he would be more careless than we in carrying it up the stairs, manipulating it around the tight space of the landing at the top and taking it out the side door onto the driveway. Bill and I debated the pros and cons, even as we struggled with the bike up the basement stairs.

To us, the driveway was one of the great features of our new house, because it led directly from the street to the backyard garage. In Brooklyn, our backyard was landlocked, and my father had to rent a garage that was a good five blocks' walk from our home. Not only was renting the garage an added expense, but also the long walk to the small structure beside an alley, which required a truck driver's skill to maneuver into and out of, made for many a poor start for weekend excursions, even when it was not raining.

Unfortunately, though our new driveway was perfectly straight between curb cut and garage door, both the driveway and the single-car garage itself were very narrow, as if designed for the cars of the thirties, not those of the postwar years. It may still have been a cinch to drive our 1948 Dodge into the garage, but, once in, it was difficult to squeeze out through the driver's door, which banged up against the exposed wooden studs, full of nails from which left-behind yard tools and snow shovels were hung.

My father, a heavy but not obese man, would quickly learn to empty the car of passengers before entering the garage. He would then angle the car into the far right corner of the structure and pull up just far enough so that he could open his door into the hollow between two studs, thus giving himself an extra couple of inches through which to exit. He would also learn to angle his body just right to get out without losing his glasses.

In time, the far right corner of the garage became the repository for old newspapers. As are the places for a lot of things around a house, this one for the papers was an accident of history. The papers that we had noticed beside the front stoop had been brought into the house by Marianne. Neither my mother nor my father had the time or desire to read the damp rags, and so they lay unopened on the kitchen floor.

In Brooklyn, old papers had been collected in a shack out back until I had a wagonload to take to the junk dealer, who bought them for as much as twenty-five cents a hundred pounds. My mother assumed that we would do the same in Cambria Heights, and so she threw the papers out onto the driveway, from which they were to be taken to the garage. When I later found them, I carried the papers still unopened to the garage and tossed them in the far right corner, which was the emptiest. When my father brought newspapers home from work, they came to be collected in the garage also. The folded papers were pushed to the side, and a pile of flat papers was started in the corner, where the pile could lean against the two walls as it rose. At first, the pile was low enough so that the car bumper passed right over it. Before long, the pile had grown so that it arrested the bumper short of the back of the garage. With the bumper touching the papers, the car just fit into the garage so the door could be closed. Fortunately, in this position the driver's door opened between two studs, and so the feel of the bumper against the papers became a convenient parking gauge.

My bike's position in the garage came to be leaning up against the right-hand wall, its left handlebar sticking out like a feeler for the car. This naturally added to the complications of putting the car away, for it limited how far to the right my father could actually angle it. If I did not put the bike far enough forward, its handlebar could be clipped by the car's mirror, knocking the bike down and wedging it between the car and the wall. I had to be sure to push the bike far enough up toward the pile of papers so that the car's right fender could fit under the left handlebar. This all made entering the garage a new adventure each time it was done, and my father had to compromise between hitting my bike and hitting his head on the handle of a rake. Backing out of the garage without bringing the bike out too proved to be very tricky indeed. Like driving a nail, parking the car in the garage never seemed to be perfectly reversible: It always went in easier than it came out.

Even when the car cleared the garage door safely, my father could not breathe easy. The southern edge of the driveway was only six inches or so from the property line, and the neighbors had installed a tall wooden fence right up to it. Backing out of the garage, especially from an angled position within it, required taking care not to continue to drift to the left into this fence. Yet, farther down the driveway, the car had to get pretty close to the same fence in order to clear the mature yews that flanked the side entrance to the house. And then the vehicle had to be steered in a corrective mode to get back on course to miss an old gatepost.

Clearing the fence and gatepost safely must have given my father a sense of accomplishment and relief that he would not have to deal with the neighbors, but in his exhilaration he was usually headed on a course for their lawn. To correct his course, he often oversteered and so backed into our hedge, stopping only when the noise of the scratching branches reached a certain pitch. Pulling forward snapped the branches through their bend, but only after their pruned tips had gouged the right side of the car. Since my father always entered the car from the driver's side, he did not have to look at the scratches, but they were a constant irritant to me, for I dreamed of someday taking friends for a ride in the car. The hedges were trimmed regularly, but no matter how far back the branches were cut, my father could find them.

From the side door of our house to the sidewalk, the driveway had two narrow concrete tracks divided by a grass median. This was an extravagant feature I would ponder often when mowing the lawn, for it presented an annoying detail that because of its crest was difficult to cut neatly. Though the median's breadth was not wide by grass standards, it just exceeded the capability of our lawn mower and so took two passes to be fully cut. But the presence of the grass down the middle of the drive did keep oil from dripping onto the concrete. We did not have to lay cardboard down under the crankcase when the car was left in this part of the driveway the way we did when it was in the garage. It was in the nature of a car to drip oil, we thought, and it was accommodated the way a dribbling or leaking baby was. When the car was parked on the fully paved portion of the driveway between the garage and the median's end, an area that doubled as a patio when we had a charcoal grill in the backyard, an old newspaper or piece of cardboard would usually be placed beneath it to protect the concrete.

Having gotten my new bicycle safely out of the basement, I tried to ride it in a circle on the driveway in front of the garage, but the space was much narrower than that downstairs. So my brother and I walked the bike down the driveway and into the street. Unlike our street in Brooklyn, this one was silent and empty. There, cars and trucks had constantly interrupted our stickball games and honked behind us when we were on our roller skates and scooters. Here, there was little traffic, at least on this Saturday afternoon, and there also were no parked cars for some distance up and down the street. No one on the block, I would come to realize, had more than one car, and when it was not being driven it was in the driveway or the garage.

I mounted my bike near the curb and showed Billy how I could straddle the crossbar and still touch the ground with the toes of my Keds. I pushed off with him holding the rear fender and running alongside, and I left him behind as I picked up speed. Soon I was riding in extended ovals and figure eights up and down the street, proud that I had mastered the machine. Bill wanted me to let him ride the bike, but I told him his legs were too short and so he would not be able to reach the pedals to apply the brakes. I told him he might fall and hurt himself again. He rubbed his eye and watched from the driveway.

Before long, some other boys on bikes came down the street and rode in circles at a cautious distance from me, perhaps seeing that I was not as steady on my new bike as I imagined I was. We all rode in silence for several minutes. In time, the oldest-looking of the boys rode up beside me and asked if I had just moved in. I said yes, that morning, while continuing to ride around in the street. He told me he lived in the house on the corner, and he pointed to one of the four. I said I lived in this house, and as soon as I pointed I realized that I was stating the obvious. After a silence, the boy told me his name was Jim Wall, and he asked me mine.

Jim was about my height, but he was even thinner than I. His face was long and pale, and his eyes were narrow and blue. His nose was sharp, and he had dark hair parted to the left, with a wave kept in place with a heavy coating of pomade. He wore a red-plaid flannel shirt and dungarees that were still bright blue. His shoes were black oxfords. They looked like dress shoes, though not especially shiny ones. He told me that the kids in the neighborhood played stickball on the cross street. He said I should come out and play in the afternoons, and maybe we could be friends. What grade was I in at school, he asked. Seventh, I said, and was surprised when he told me that he was only in sixth. He looked to me almost old enough to be in high school. What school did I go to, he asked. I realized that I did not know. The Catholic school, I said.

Our family had moved on a Saturday so that my father would not have to take a day off from work and we kids would not have to miss a day of school. We had gone to school as usual on Friday, as if it were just another day. I don't recall telling my teacher or any classmates that I would not be back, for fear they might ask me to tell them about a house I had not yet seen. They all seemed to know that something was up, however, and said unusually long goodbyes at the end of the day. My mother's plan was for us to start at our new school on Monday, without missing a beat, but things did not go as planned.

In Brooklyn, all three of us—Bill, Mary, and I—had attended St. Thomas Aquinas, the Catholic school just down the block, barely fifty yards from our old house, and we assumed that we also would attend a nearby parochial school in our new neighborhood. That was also my parents' expectation, but it was only after my mother walked us the eight blocks to Sacred Heart School on Monday morning that we learned in the principal's office that it could not be. The "transfers" that she had been given by the secretary at St. Thomas could not be honored by Sacred Heart.

St. Thomas, like many of the larger parochial schools in Brooklyn, had half grades, designated A and B, that started anew each fall and each spring. Generally speaking, children born early enough in the year entered 1A in the February of the academic year in which they would turn six and would continue in 1B the next September. Had my brother and I stayed at St. Thomas we would have entered 5A and 7A, respectively, at about the time we moved. Sacred Heart did not have the same system, and all students began a new A grade each September, and the subsequent B grade each February. This presented a dilemma as to what grade my brother and I might be put into in the new school. Would we be put back or advanced a half-grade? The preference of Sacred Heart would have been the former; my mother preferred the latter. The matter turned out to be somewhat moot, for the school was full to capacity in all the higher grades.

Sacred Heart School had opened its doors only a few years earlier, and that was only a dozen or so years after the parish itself was founded, with its earliest services held in a tent. But Cambria Heights was now home to so many Catholic families with children that the school was unable to accommodate all the new kids who were moving into the neighborhood. We were told that we had to go to the public school just a few blocks farther from our home.

Sacred Heart had room for only my sister. She was born in the latter part of the year and so was on Sacred Heart's more usual grade schedule and did not present a problem to the system. At six, Mary was only half my age, and so I did little with her but walk her to school and pose with her for family pictures. Now I would not even go to the same school as she. Bill and I could only be put on the waiting list.

With Mary left at Sacred Heart, my mother walked Billy and me over to PS 147. (Whether PS stood for Public School or Primary School was to be debated in our house until the end of the school year.) We were registered that morning in grades five and seven and introduced to our respective classes just after lunch. I had attended a public-school kindergarten in Brooklyn, and family lore reminded us annually that on the first day I walked out of the room unnoticed during nap time and retraced my steps home, where I was accustomed to napping. My mother took me back to school immediately, and I was told that now that I was a big boy I had to take my naps on the mats with the other boys and girls at school. I never again ran away from school, but my one offense was not expunged from my record at home. Nor, evidently, was the example of my escape far from my brother's mind.

Whether because the school was new to him or because the classroom was not equipped with a crucifix over the blackboard, Billy did not like public school at all. My mother told us that the other children laughed at him for wearing a white shirt and tie to class, something we had been required to do and had gotten accustomed to at St. Thomas. He went to school reluctantly for a month or so, but conditions did not improve for him. So he traded on my bad example and threatened to run away from school if he had to continue in public school. He furthermore claimed that he would run away from home itself if my mother tried to force him to continue at PS 147. My mother took Billy seriously and pleaded his case to the principal's office in Sacred Heart. She, and Bill, must have been convincing, for the school did find a space for him in fifth grade in March that we had been told in February did not exist. Where the vacant seat was located, I could not imagine.

The parochial-school classrooms I had known in Brooklyn were tightly furnished with desks bolted to the floor. In some rooms they were arranged in rows of six and eight, held in place as rigidly as the forty-eight stars on the flag. (When Alaska and Hawaii were admitted to the Union five years later, I was annoyed that the flag was changed and its neat rows and columns of stars disrupted.) Other rooms were fitted with double rows of double desks, making it possible to fit even more pupils onto the same floor area. In St. Thomas Aquinas, there had barely been space in the aisle around the periphery of the room for us to stand for rhythm band, when we played cymbals, sticks, and triangles, or to line up for spelling contests, eye examinations, and class pictures. This rigid geometry of the parochial-school classroom made the rejection by Sacred Heart understandable and acceptable to me. I had become accustomed to classrooms of fixed desks, and I imagined that if every seat was occupied there certainly would be no more room for even one more pupil, knowing as I did that he could not sit in the aisle. It did not occur to me until much later that Bill might have been accommodated because a student could leave as well as arrive in the middle of the school year, thus vacating a seat.

The public-school classroom that I accepted to be my fate was altogether different. There were fewer students, and they were seated at large tables that could be moved into different configurations. There was open floor space in the back of the room, which made entering and exiting easy, and there were large cabinets along the back wall, full of supplies of paper, paint, and paste in quantities sufficient to last for years.

Since I joined the class in the middle of the school year, I was not integrated into the established seating plan. Rather, I was seated out of alphabetical order at the odd table in the room, a table separated by a noticeable distance from the main array. There was another boy already sitting at this table, and he had clearly been segregated from the rest of the class. He looked older, had blond hair tending toward white, which made his hint of a stubbly beard look glinty, and he smelled different from any boy I had known in Brooklyn. His name was Lenny Scott, and I soon learned that he was just biding his time until he was old enough to drop out of school. What I smelled was the faint odor of a horse stable.

The teacher and the other students must have known that I was showing up in their classroom the second week in February only because there was no room for me in the Catholic school, and so they held me at arm's length, the way they did Lenny. I didn't care, because I soon grew to like Lenny and became accustomed to his horsy odor. I began to hang out with him during recess, which we spent in a corner of the schoolyard by ourselves, usually talking about bikes and horses or wondering why the windows in the courtyard were covered with heavy wire screens. I said it was probably so balls would not break them; Lenny said it was to protect them from rocks. One day he asked me if I would like to see the horses he took care of at Belmont Park, the racetrack, and I said sure. After school he led me to the bicycle rack, where he parked the bike he rode to school. I never brought my own bike because I did not want it scratched or stolen, something that would happen at a public school, I was sure. Our plan was for me to get a ride with Lenny and for us to stop by his house on the way to my house, where I would drop off my books and tell my mother where I was going. I would also pick up my bike there and we would ride on to Belmont, which was about a mile north.

Lenny's bicycle was different. It was not a Schwinn or any other make familiar to me, and it was of an unusual dusty rose color, something I would expect for a girl's model. But his bike did have a boy's crossbar. Its white-walled balloon tires were dirty and, being caked with mud and straw, looked much larger than normal. The bike had a luggage rack of massive proportions, to which were tied countless cords and ropes, and onto which Lenny secured his lunch box. The handlebars were adjusted to a straight-up position, so that when Lenny held them it looked as if he were holding ski poles. The faded red-and-yellow plastic streamers on the ends of the handlebar grips ruined that image, though, for when he first mounted his bike they draped around his hands like the wig on the fist puppet Johnny that Señor Wences performed with on Ed Sullivan's Sunday evening television show. As Lenny's bike gained speed, the streamers flamed out of each fist as if from the mouth of a fire-eater. There was a horn tank built into the frame of the bike, and on the front fender was a light that was faired into it. Though the bike had clearly been ridden a good deal, everything on it worked.

Lenny told me to sit facing forward on the horizontal part of the handlebars and place the inside edges of my sneakers on the part of the threaded front axle projecting out from either side of the fork. It was not easy to hold my balance at first, but by the time we were out of the schoolyard I had gotten the hang of it, anticipating the changes of speed and direction. After we had ridden along the sidewalk for a while, I felt the bike bounce easily off the curb onto its underinflated tires, which made for a very soft and smooth ride, the way Lenny wanted it to be. I learned only later that it also made the bike much harder to pedal, especially with an extra load.

His house was not far from school, but it was in an area that I had yet to explore. The houses were attached and did not have large front yards. The arrangement reminded me more of Brooklyn than of Cambria Heights. He stopped in front of one of the middle houses on the block and asked me to wait for him to drop off his lunch box and tell his mother where he was going. I heard him climb a flight of stairs and then heard a door open and close. It was quiet for several minutes, but then I heard someone shouting and saw one of the upstairs windows open and a woman's head stick out, look down at me, and disappear inside. When Lenny came back downstairs, slowly, he spoke with less assurance. He told me that his mother had said that he couldn't take me to the stables because it was a long bicycle ride through heavy traffic, and anyway the horses were too dangerous.

He seemed to be embarrassed that our plans were ruined, and he offered to ride me home. I told him that was not necessary; I could walk home from there. Lenny was not at school the next day, and, except on one occasion, I never saw him again. I figured he turned sixteen. I rode my bike by his house on several occasions after school, but I was always afraid to encounter his mother. His bike was never in front of his house, where, he'd told me, he chained it to the fence when he wasn't riding it. Late one afternoon, I did see him approaching from the distance, but when I began to ride toward him, he turned around and rode fast in the other direction. I chased him for several blocks, but I couldn't keep up with him. He seemed to be heading toward the racetrack. After that day, I stopped looking for him.

Age was something of which all the kids I knew were keenly aware but about which we were terribly ignorant. Our dog Skippy must have been well past sixteen in human years, each of which we knew equaled seven dog years. Nobody questioned what this actually meant, we just struggled with trying to remember whether to multiply or divide our ages by seven to figure out how old we were in dog years. In Brooklyn, Skippy had served as part watchdog and part pet. Like the dog Skippy who got his picture in the newspaper for barking until he woke a household to warn them of a fire, our Skippy was "long on brains but short on pedigree." Her tail was curled into a tight spiral, hinting of the "Alaskan husky" heritage our uncle swore she had. For us, her main claim to fame was that she was the mother of Blackie, the runt of the litter. Some of Blackie's toes grew out of the sides of his back legs. The loose toes dangled when he walked and made him look very vulnerable, and so we had kept him as a pet.

But now my bike was my new pet, and my mother recognized this. I spent so much time with it, keeping Skippy away lest her claws scratch its fenders, that I began to ignore her. At first, the dogs had continued to get plenty of attention from Bill and Mary, but Skippy became increasingly listless. One day, while we were at school, Blackie and Skippy both disappeared, and neither my brother nor I, on bike and on foot, could find them anywhere in the neighborhood. Our mother did find Blackie at the ASPCA pound the next morning, but Skippy, she told us, was lost for good. I imagined that she must have tried to find her way back to Brooklyn; I didn't know then that it was cats and not dogs that did that sort of thing.

Our mother told us that we didn't need a watchdog in Cambria Heights the way we had needed one in Brooklyn. She was not afraid to be home alone, either during the day when we kids were at school or at night when my father worked late. With Skippy gone, Blackie became increasingly lonely, we kids being occupied with school and homework. He was better during the summer, but he too would eventually get "lost." I wondered how old my bicycle would be in bike-years before it had to be let out to pasture. Dogs got buried, I knew, but what happened to dead bikes?

If I had been attending a Catholic school, I would have been preparing during religion period for receiving confirmation, a sacrament whereby young boys and girls reaffirm their faith in God and pledge to be soldiers for the faith. The Catholic students attending public school were expected also to be confirmed, so they had to get prepared for it by some other means. There was an agreement between the public and parochial schools to reserve Wednesday afternoons for such activities. Those students who did not attend any religious instruction at that time remained in school and participated in arts and crafts projects. We Catholic students, who were dismissed with students of other religions at two o'clock, went over to Sacred Heart for our "released time" instruction.

There were a lot more Catholics attending PS 147 than I would have guessed, as was evident when we assembled in the schoolyard in preparation for walking the few blocks to the church. My age group of students must have numbered fifty or more, though it was hard to count because we were not arranged neatly in classes the way we were for filing into school or for fire drills. We were led down the middle of the street, as if marching in a parade, but there was not nearly the order expected of a parade. In fact, there were no lines or rows or columns of any kind. The amorphous crowd of students was not especially loud or unruly, perhaps because they generally did not know each other, but I remember being embarrassed because we were being herded like sheep along a route we should easily have been able to negotiate by ourselves. On these weekly walks I could usually be found near the head of the pack, because that way I would reach our destination quickest and thus suffer embarrassment for the least possible time. I could not hide in the middle of the crowd, because I was among the tallest students in my grade. I was also wearing a tie and good slacks, because we were going to church.

The other students were all dressed casually, in colored shirts and dungarees. Even the adults who brought us to the church, where nuns took over, were dressed individually, not like the nuns. Whenever students from Catholic schools went to church on school days, they naturally wore uniforms, and they looked more as if they belonged. The regular colors of their clothes went with the regular geometry of the church itself. The pews and columns and windows were all repeated up and down the aisles, and the uniformly dressed children fit right into the pattern. Now, there was no pattern, and the children clashed with the church.

When the priest in the pulpit spoke, however, all the children listened as if they were hearing his words for the first time. What I heard were aspects of religion and the church that were very familiar to me from my years in Catholic school. The preparation for confirmation that I was being forced to attend seemed to be designed for public-school students who were exposed to religious instruction only on these Wednesday afternoons, there being no such thing as Sunday school in our church.

Because the instruction was familiar, my eyes and mind usually wandered on those afternoons. I stared at the pews, with their hard seats and padded kneelers, and got absorbed in following the grain of the oak into cul-de-sacs. I liked the way the kneelers could be turned up when we had to stand and then rotated back into place when we had to kneel, but I did not enjoy the sound they made during mass. When we were seated, we could move the kneelers up and down with our feet, balancing them dead center on the toes of our shoes. Invariably, some boy, thinking he had achieved perfect balance, would lower his toes, leaving the kneeler still like a coin on its edge. It would stay in place for an instant, but the pressure of all the gazes, or a fidget in the pew ahead to which it was attached, would disturb the unstable equilibrium. The crash of steel-cleated oak on the terrazzo floor would bring a nun flying down the aisle, her habit forming wings, looking for the culprit, whom she seldom found. When we stood to file out at the end of the session, some of the students would walk on the kneelers, but if I did that I would appear to be even taller than I was, and that was something I did not want to be.

I looked at the back of the pew in front of me and thought about the angle at which it was built, like a chair's back, and how smooth its solid wood felt when we sat down against it. The grain was pronounced, but what we saw was not what our hands felt. The top of the pew ended in a polished roll of wood, like a handrail on a stairway. It was comfortable and convenient to hold when we rose to stand, but I had to stoop down to keep holding it when I was standing up.

When I was seated and looked down, I watched the shoes of the children in the pew ahead. The shorter children, whose feet did not touch the floor, swung their legs back and forth, as if they were trying to pump a swing that would not budge. Taller children threw their feet under the pew and rested their shoes on their toes. I inspected their soles. No matter how shiny were the tops of their shoes, the bottoms were black with the dirt of the street, spotted with thumbtacks, chewing gum, oil, and grease. Even the newest pair of shoes had the soles soiled in the walk to church. I puzzled over the mysteries of original sin and the black spots of mortal and venial sins that marked our own souls, but it never seemed to be possible for me to comprehend anything beyond the metaphor itself. I was easily distracted by other, more tangible things.

Oblivious to their soles, the soon-to-be-confirmed continued to fidget with their feet, pumping them up and down, moving them back and forth, crossing and uncrossing them, as if they had to go to the bathroom. None of the children in the pews before me were tall enough for their feet to reach the kneeler behind them, the way adults' feet sometimes did when kneeling at Sunday mass. There, I always tried to get the kneeler down before the man in front of me got it dirty with his shoes extending back into my pew's space. When we were standing, I watched how other people stood, some on their right foot, some on their left. I watched them flex their knees when we had been standing a long time, and I watched them scratch one leg with their opposite shoe, or polish the shoe tops on the backs of their trousers, without seeming to think about what they were doing or where they were.

I looked at the heavy lighting fixtures hanging from the ceiling of the flat-roofed church. I knew nothing of Galileo at the time, but like him I watched the chandeliers swing from the end of their chains in the spring breeze coming in through the opened stained-glass windows. Unlike Galileo, who saw in the pendulum the principles of dynamics, I worried that the swinging would work the heavy fixture loose from the ceiling. I tried to avoid, as much as possible, sitting under a chandelier.

There were no prayer books or hymnals to read in the pews, and the altar was too far away for me to see enough detail to study it. Like many of the other boys, I began to crack my knuckles in the cavernous church, quietly at first, but then increasingly more loudly until some nun indicated that I should stop. In time I learned to crack my knuckles surreptitiously with one hand, by bending my crooked fingers back above the knuckles and then rolling them forward to make a tight fist. The noise was like a small string of ladyfingers exploding on the Fourth of July. The sound frustrated the nuns, who could not see anyone putting his hands together and so made blanket threats to the assembled heathens.

As part of the sacrament, I was to choose a confirmation name, which I understood was to be added to the names I already had. Since I had been given a middle name at baptism, the whole idea was confusing, but I complied and took the name Joseph, which was that of two of my uncles—one my godfather—not to mention the husband of Mary, the mother of Jesus. Whether a confirmation name had any legal force was never discussed. I do not recall if anyone ever recorded my choice; I certainly do not remember filling out or receiving any piece of paper documenting it.

The name Joseph, being chosen when I was confirmed, obviously does not appear on my birth certificate or baptismal certificate. These show my name to be Henry Raymond Petroski, the first being also my father's name and the second that of his youngest brother. My father's middle name was Frank, and so I was not properly a Junior, though I often had identified myself as Henry Petroski, Jr., on my school composition books and assignments. No one seemed to care what I called myself or how I signed my name.

Generally, though, before I was confirmed, I identified myself properly as Henry R. Petroski. After I took Joseph as my confirmation name, I began to identify myself as Henry R. J. Petroski, but increasingly as I grew older the monogram HRJP annoyed me by its length and its awkward look and its cacophony. Since I did not care for the name Raymond, I dropped it and began to call myself Henry J. Petroski. It is this unofficial name that is on my official high school and college diplomas, on my early technical publications, and on my professional engineer's license and seal. My driver's license, which alone required a birth certificate to obtain, identifies me as Henry Raymond Petroski, but I signed it simply Henry Petroski, the form of my name that I have used consistently ever since I realized how confused I was about what my name really was.

My name was seldom called in seventh grade, and so what it really was was of little consequence then. In my anonymity, I did not find public school to be disagreeable. In fact, it provided opportunities not found in Catholic school. One day the whole of PS 147 was taken to Field Day, an event that needed no explanation to my fellow seventh-graders, but of which I as a newcomer knew nothing. Field Day was held at some high school stadium, and each student was expected to participate in at least one track-and-field event. There was no prearranged registration procedure, but those who had taken part in previous Field Days already knew what they were good at and in what they would compete. When my teacher found me sitting alone in the stands watching the races, he asked me what event I would like to take part in, and I told him it didn't matter to me. This response automatically registered me for the next event, the 220-yard dash, and I had to get down on the track immediately. I toed the starting line, imitating the rest of the kids, but I got off to a slow start. I was not used to formal starts. I had been used to running only in hide-and-seek and stickball games, and occasionally to flee a pursuer, but I had been accustomed to winning races around the block in Brooklyn. I had prided myself in being fast in my Keds, but here in Queens I had come to rely on my bike when I really wanted to move.

Though the race must have taken no more than thirty seconds or so for us twelve-year-olds to run, it seemed to me to last for a much longer time, certainly enough time for me to reflect upon my position in the race and in the universe. My Brooklyn speed seemed to have deserted me, for here I was looking at the heels of these public-schoolers whose backs I stared at in class. I didn't want to be left behind, and so I called upon my swiftest legs to carry me through the pack and into a neck-and-neck race with the leader. As we approached the ribbon at the finish line, we ran faster but time ran slower. In my mind, the final twenty yards took as long to cover as the first couple of hundred. I saw my opponent out of the corner of my eye but wanted to waste no motion in turning to look at him. From my perspective, I passed him just before the ribbon, and my chest touched it first. The teachers at the finish line saw it differently. My opponent, from a rival seventh grade, was ruled the winner, and I was congratulated for taking second place. I swore it was fixed, but I had no recourse but to take myself back into the stands and watch the rest of the races.

My classmates, who had all but ignored me when I sat in the back of the room, first with Lenny and then by myself, had cheered me on when they saw me gaining in the race. Now they treated me like one of the regulars, and they began talking immediately about how our class could take the 220 at the next Field Day.

By the time the school year drew to a close, I was more or less integrated into the seventh grade at PS 147, even having been moved up into alphabetical order in homeroom. I took as a further indication of my acceptance the citizenship citation I was given in the last week of school. It said at the bottom, where a parent had to sign, that it was granted by my classmates, teachers, and principal. It was printed within an official-looking green border even fancier than that on the hundred-dollar bill my father once brought home from the bank:

CODE FOR CITIZENSHIP

PUBLIC SCHOOL NO. 147, QUEENS

1. I will be courteous and polite to all at all times.
2. I will play fair keeping the rules. I will be a good loser or a generous winner.
3. I will be tolerant and stand by the truth regardless of my likes or dislikes.
4. I will try to gain and keep good health; protect the health of others and guard their safety as well as my own.
5. I will work in friendly cooperation to keep things in good order in our school and community.

These all seemed to be reasonable rules to follow, and I carried the certificate home inside a notebook, so that it would not get bent. My mother proudly signed it in her best hand.

After a rough start in PS 147, my citizenship had been recognized as good, my running had been declared remarkable, my scholarship had been graded excellent, and I was promoted from 7-2 to 8-1, the highest-track eighth grade. My homeroom teacher let me know this in the hallway, but he suggested that I not make much of a fuss about it in front of the other students, for only two others in the class would be moving up with me. I felt proud and left school for the summer looking forward to returning to public school for eighth grade, even if I would know only a few of my new homeroom classmates.

My mother, in the meantime, having learned the value of persistence and waiting lists, had arranged for me to attend Sacred Heart in the coming year. This meant that I would not have to trudge the few blocks on Wednesday afternoons to attend religion classes. Overall, I figured it would be an advantage to go to Sacred Heart, which was closer to home, even though I did not know where I would sit or who any of my classmates would be.

3

SUMMER DRIZZLES IN
ON LONG ISLAND

Summers in the suburbs were sluggish. Without school to occupy our days, and with the days themselves longer, we looked for things to do. In Brooklyn, the Police Athletic League—the children's PAL—closed off entire blocks to traffic during the day, painted lines for games on the streets, and opened up the fire hydrants on the hottest afternoons. There, there were enough kids on the single block and its friendly environs to make for a crowded affair, and the variety of activities scripted throughout the day by the PAL counselors was enough to keep even the most hardened city kid happy. In the much less densely populated Cambria Heights, there were not enough young kids on any single block, whose curbs were cut with a driveway every forty feet or so, to justify such an extravagant impediment to traffic flow, light as it was.

Cambria Heights, like most sections of Queens, is laid out on a grid of oblong blocks. One side of the grid is cut off on the bias by the Cross Island Parkway, which runs roughly north-south across most of the island. The Cross Island defines the easternmost boundary of Cambria Heights, of Queens, and thus of New York

City at this location. The westernmost boundary of the community is Springfield Boulevard, whose name evoked for me the image of a field of green fed by water trickling down from the slopes that buttressed the heights. The northern- and southernmost boundaries of Cambria Heights sounded less bucolic. They were, respectively, 114th Avenue and 121st Avenue, the latter coinciding with Francis Lewis Boulevard for the stretch where it ran alongside Montefiore Cemetery.

Most of the houses were located on the streets, which ranged in number from 217th to 238th Street. The principal arteries ran mostly east–west and were called, in diminishing order of importance for vehicle traffic, boulevards, avenues, roads, drives, and terraces. For example, on the northern fringe of Cambria Heights there were, in succession, a 114th Avenue, a 114th Road, a 114th Drive, and a 114th Terrace. I played my first game of Monopoly in the backyard of a schoolmate who lived on 114th Terrace, a street so short that its name barely fits on the map.

What made my visit to my friend's house most memorable was not landing on Boardwalk and Park Place on his patio, but finding his address, which was 229-05 114th Terrace. When he first told it to me, the numbers seemed to be out of order or wrong. In the form I had quickly gotten used to in Cambria Heights, an avenue number was always the prefix, so that a house with the address 115-68 229th Street would be south of 115th Avenue. There was no 229th Avenue in Cambria Heights, I knew, and so where was my friend's house? It was only when he gave me directions and I rode my bike into the unfamiliar northern hinterland that I saw how the long blocks there, in the fuzzy area between Cambria Heights and Queens Village, were oriented at right angles to those around my house and everywhere else I had theretofore explored. The word clue at the end of a Queens address was as important as the string of numbers that preceded it. Once I had caught on to the cumbersome house numbering system, it seemed to be as logical as a map grid, and I was as embarrassed that I had had to ask for directions to the house as I was that I had to ask the rules of Monopoly once I found it.

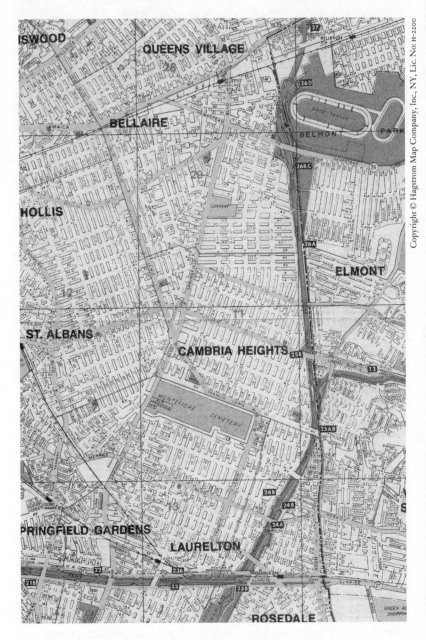

Cambria Heights and environs

It is for historical reasons that streets in Brooklyn and especially in Queens do not line up from area to area. When the counties were young and consisted of numerous independent towns and villages, the distance between them made the random orientation of their streets of little concern. It was only when towns began to grow together that their grids clashed like tectonic plates. This was not necessarily seen as an undesirable thing, and some new towns purposely aligned their streets differently than their neighbors to assert their independence and emphasize their boundaries. On a map of the boroughs or viewed from an airplane approaching La Guardia Airport from the southwest, Brooklyn and Queens neighborhoods, in sharp contrast to those of Manhattan, appear to be stitched together like a crazy quilt.

The impression is strikingly different at ground level and close to home. Except for the minor anomalies like the one where I played Monopoly, the vast majority of streets in Cambria Heights were as uniform as the bricks in a walk, and the houses on them were as regularly spaced as cookies on a baking sheet. In fact, the core streets were so similar that, at first, a bike ride up and down a few of the blocks around my house could lead to total confusion about whether I was near 115th Avenue or 116th Road on 225th or 226th Street. The confusion was removed when I looked at the house numbers or when I was under a street sign on a lamppost at a corner. Being displaced but seldom disoriented on such a grid led not to adventure but to ennui, and so randomly riding around close to home was not something I was drawn to do.

The kids who lived near our corner ate dinner early, whether or not the man of the house was home from work, and afterward we played in the streets until dark, even in the drizzling rain. When it got too late to play ball or ride bikes, we gathered under the streetlight on the corner and talked about what we would do the next day. The lamppost was a graceful structure. It had a broad, sculpted cast-iron base, a more slender fluted shaft, whose diameter diminished ever so slightly as it rose—emphasizing its height—and an ornamental bracketed arm that cantilevered out over the street and terminated in a decorative lamp housing. The lamp bulb appeared to come on dimly at first and then gradually glowed more and more brightly as the sun set.

Under the light, we used chalk to draw on the street a stylized gallows and stepping-stones—blank spaces really—leading to a game of Hangman. The kid playing the executioner would think of a word to be guessed—each letter represented by a stepping-stone—and the challenger called out letters one by one. Each correctly guessed letter was printed in its place; an incorrect guess resulted in a part of a stick figure being hung from the gallows. First a circle head, then a line neck, then an oval body, then two stick arms, two stick legs, and two stick feet—the final one sealing the victim's doom. The guessing aspect of the game was not unlike *Wheel of Fortune,* but without the prize money or the chance to buy a vowel.

On occasion, the streetlight under which we played itself attracted our attention. Inside the base of the lamppost was a timer that with a great mechanical commotion turned the light on and off automatically, but it had to be attended to twice a year to be reset for standard or daylight saving time. Whenever we found an access panel left loose after a resetting, we explored the mechanism inside. We always did so rather gingerly with a stick or twig, for fear of the fate that befell a boy on 223rd Street, who was electrocuted.

We were less timid in attacking the lamp itself. The bulb hung down inside a faceted glass globe that was the first line of defense against the bulb's being broken. We threw at it rocks and pieces of metal that had fallen off passing cars, trying to shatter the globe and then the bulb inside. On occasion the same missile went straight through the globe and into the bulb, creating a shower of glass and an instant hero. We threw at the lamp mostly out of boredom, but the activity also provided a form of competition to identify a winner, something we seemed constantly trying to do. An ancillary benefit was that invariably someone would report the streetlight being out, and eventually the Broadway Maintenance service truck would come. A workman would climb up a telescoping and revolving ladder to replace the broken parts. We watched the mechanical show from a respectful distance, and this gave us something else to do on a slow, hot summer afternoon.

Why there was this propensity to destroy things was not something that we reflected upon under the glow of the streetlight. I did not think about it even when alone at home in the dark after bedtime. We never discussed whether it was a sin to do what we were doing; we just did it as if it were instinctive, like a dog chasing a cat. We certainly had no idea of rebelling against technology or society or culture. The streetlight was simply a thing that was there for our use and entertainment, and it attracted us the way a flame does moths. The artifact itself was neither good nor bad nor indifferent. The same might have been said of us kids, but it was certainly not true of our behavior.

In time, the cast-iron lampposts were replaced with sleek new aluminum ones, also with an access panel in the base but with nothing but a couple of wires inside. The machinery to turn the lights on and off was replaced by an electric eye located atop the lamp housing, and the lamp itself was protected behind a shallow, shatterproof plastic shield. In place of an incandescent bulb was a mercury-vapor lamp that started up like a bad fluorescent light, with a loud and grating buzzing sound, and that continued to hum while operating. For a few evenings we watched and listened to the light turn itself on and then for a few weeks we tried unsuccessfully to break its plastic cover. After acknowledging that it was unbreakable, we ignored the lamp structure, except when we captured someone's sneakers, tied their laces together, and tossed them like a bola at the lamppost's arm. They stayed up there until a bulb had to be replaced. Then a crewman dropped them to the sidewalk, where they remained until the truck drove off. When it was not the target of mischief, the eerie yellowish-green to blue color of the light above us was as plain as the geometry of our streets.

Linden Boulevard, as if an east–west axis, more or less bisected our community. Linden, the only named street that was wholly within Cambria Heights, was lined with namesake trees. It was the local shopping street and the route of the bus that took us to Jamaica, where the department stores were. Jamaica was also where our fathers caught the subway on to Brooklyn and the City, as everyone in New York called Manhattan, where most of them worked. The bus that ran along Linden Boulevard was designated the Q4, but in one of our earliest attempts at off-color humor we called it the 4Q. Walking by a line of commuters, one boy would ask another, "What bus is this?" The answer, "4Q," prompted the further response "4Q2," giving us no end of satisfaction that we had used an obscenity in front of adults. And technically we could not get in trouble for it, because we were only talking about bus numbers. When we rode the bus and saw a police car beside it, we got an equally great sense of hilarity by asking loudly of a friend hanging out the window behind us, "What's a penny made of?" The response, "Dirty copper," broke us up.

We didn't try that from the exposed seat of a bicycle, but bike riding nonetheless became one of our most enjoyable summer occupations. "Do you want to ride bikes?" became the default greeting between my new best friend, Jim Wall, and me. We would spend many a day riding to the fringes of Cambria Heights, often ending up at a candy-store soda fountain drinking chocolate egg creams or malted milks, or at the Carvel stand, eating dipped soft ice cream cones or drinking thick shakes. A trip to Carvel was a special event, because it was located in Elmont, which was across the parkway that everywhere else in America would have been described as a city or a county line. Here it was both.

Where Jim's money came from I cannot say, but I know mine came from a modest allowance of twenty-five cents a week, supplemented by two-cent deposits claimed on soda bottles found along the parkway, plus whatever my childless aunt slipped me on our frequent visits to her home in Lynbrook.

Aunt Jean and Uncle Joe lived in a two-story stucco house on a small and neat dead-end street off Cherry Lane. My aunt was a large-boned woman whose face and arms were blotched by eczema.

The sun was her enemy, because it brought out the contrast in her skin, and so she seldom went out of the house without a hat. At the same time, gardening was her first love and her gift, and she risked her skin for fresh vegetables. She didn't curse the sun, because it ripened her tomatoes as well as darkened her skin, but she railed against most things that were man-made and therefore deliberate. Nothing escaped my aunt's scorn, and she disliked nothing so much as having someone even suggest how she should lead her life.

I had many aunts and uncles, but it was only this one, my mother's sister, who lived close by and whom we saw on a regular basis. Aunt Jean, whom my parents called Jenny or Jay, was my mother's oldest sister and reminded her of this whenever they had a disagreement. The trouble might involve something as simple as remembering whether as kids they walked home from school together or not. My aunt sometimes berated my mother in front of us kids. Somehow, I gathered, being older was more important than being right. But hard feelings never lingered; they vanished in the time it took to make a phone call on Monday morning.

The sisters had come down together from their hometown in upstate New York to find work in the city at the height of the Depression. My mother worked as a pastry cook in Schrafft's, and she often mentioned it when we ate in a restaurant. Aunt Jean worked in the Hattie Carnegie hat factory, attaching flowers and ribbons to Easter bonnets, as I understood her description of what she did. They lived together until my mother married my father and Aunt Jean married Uncle Joe. He was thin, stern, and taciturn, and for years the only Protestant I knew.

Uncle Joe was as frail-looking as Aunt Jean was strong. He had thin hair on a balding head, and he wore wire-rim glasses whose temple pieces pinched on his face like a paper clip on a too-thick pile of papers. He was a man of few words and hence a man of mystery. We children were often warned not to cross our uncle. He would grow livid when we talked back to our mother or father, and we lived in mortal fear of him.

Still, it was to Aunt Jean and Uncle Joe's that we always went on holidays, and it was with them alone that we exchanged Christmas presents. All the rest of my mother's family remained upstate, some three hundred miles away. Most of my father's family lived in New Jersey or Pennsylvania. One of his brothers did live in Brooklyn and one of his sisters in Bayside, but we saw their families only infrequently and didn't exchange presents with them at all.

Lynbrook was well beyond Elmont and Valley Stream, so solidly in Nassau County that it was definitely out on Long Island. But in fact Lynbrook was only about six miles from Cambria Heights, and the route my father drove almost every Sunday afternoon had become etched in my mind. So too had the etymology of the town's name—a transposition of the first and second syllables, an anagram, of Brooklyn—which my father remarked on every time we passed the town sign. The name was chosen in 1894 by its residents in honor of the beloved urban borough that so many of them had left for the rural area then known as Pearsalls Corners. (If it was so beloved, why did they leave it, I often wondered.) Pearsalls Corners had grown up around a major crossroads—a place known still in Lynbrook as Five Corners; main roads and railroads terminated there in the late nineteenth century. Back then the bicycling craze that swept America brought many a cyclist to Pearsalls Corners, which was known as the starting point for hundred-mile races.

It was not two weeks into our first summer with a bike before Billy and I conceived not of a race beginning at Five Corners but of an expedition ending not far from there—at our aunt's house, whose location we had memorized. We planned to do it all on our own and unannounced, lest it be forbidden and we have nothing else to do. For much of the distance, I rode my bicycle with my brother sitting sidesaddle on the crossbar. We must have respected the danger of the adventure, for we rode mostly on the sidewalks of the heavily trafficked streets that had looked much safer from the backseat of a car. Since time was such an abundant commodity for us, we were in no rush and stopped regularly to look in store windows and to buy sodas. We stopped for lights and walked the bike across busy intersections.

When we did arrive at our aunt's, to our surprise we were not greeted with the joy we found on weekend visits, nor were we showered with the multiple quarters that not only supplemented our allowance from our parents but often dwarfed it. Rather, we were scolded for our recklessness, and after a long and silent lunch were sent home without a penny. The trip back seemed much longer, even if we rode faster, and at its end we were greeted by another angry woman. My brother and I played together even less frequently after that adventure, and I had to promise not to ride my bicycle such long distances without permission.

Nevertheless, I was intrigued by the idea of distance and how much of it I could cover on my bike. Our Dodge's odometer always became the focus of attention when its numbers registered a full house or better, and the turning over from a string of 9s to one of 0s was a much more important event than the change of a digital calendar at the end of the millennium would be. With the odometer's red digit, we could compare with great precision, to the tenth of a mile, different routes to my aunt's or to the beach. On my bike, however, I could measure distance only in blocks, which came mostly in two sizes. The long blocks, which separated the streets called avenues and roads, were about ten to the mile; the short blocks, which separated the streets called simply streets, were about twenty-five to the mile.

To know more precisely how far I traveled on my bicycle, I wanted to install an odometer on it, and so I went to price one at Sam's Cycle Shop, which was just two blocks from my home. Other than vegetable and fish stores, which did it all the time, Sam's was one of the few shops on Linden Boulevard that spilled its merchandise out onto the sidewalk. In front of Sam's were used bicycles arranged like motorcycles parked at the curb, except facing out rather than into it. Inside the shop were tiers of new bicycles on racks along the side walls and, in the rear, a small glassed-in display counter, in which were arrayed the accessories I coveted and dreamed of installing on my bike. I fixed my eyes on the odometer, a pillbox of a machine with a slotlike window against which were pressed the 0s that I wanted to turn into 9s.

Sam himself reminded me of an odometer, for his face seemed to be crafted out of numbers. His eyes were flattened 0s, his nose an elongated 4, his ears longish 9s. His hair and wrinkled skin concealed other numbers—3s, 6s, 7s, 8s—the way they might be disguised in a game on a restaurant place mat or in a puzzle in the Sunday comics. His mouth was filled with spaces between teeth through which part numbers and prices came. When I asked Sam how much the odometer cost, his face moved like a cash register's display and he whistled through his teeth a number larger than I wanted to hear. Without my aunt's quarters, I knew I was short. As he watched me count out an inadequate amount of coins from the pocket in my dungarees, he asked me where I lived. When I told him just two blocks away, he asked me if I would like to do odd jobs for the odometer. He said he needed a hand around the shop.

My first job at Sam's was to sweep out the store and to bring to him on the dustpan any small parts I found in the debris. I was also responsible for bringing the bikes in from the street at closing time and rolling them out again when the store opened in the morning. At first, I came and went throughout the day, but soon I began to hang out at Sam's, and he began to give me more tasks, especially in the workshop, which was entered through a low swinging door behind the counter. Among the things I spent hours doing was separating the various small parts that had become mixed up in the many bins and drawers that surrounded his workbench. Unlike my father's toolbox, which had lots of different items that were hard to arrange because they were hard to classify in mutually exclusive lots, Sam's workshop had only a small number of distinct bicycle parts, but each part was present in multitudes.

As a poet can see a world in a grain of sand, so an engineer, even a budding one, can see a bicycle in a ball of steel. The movement of my fingers separating lock nuts from wheel nuts, spoke nipples from needle valves, and hubcaps from bearing cones became my mechanical mantra. An engineer before my time, and alone with the parts of the whole, I came to a new appreciation of the bicycle as the sum of its parts. Before a tin tray of items as pied as a printer's drawer of used type, I played the devil to Sam's god, reordering the universe of parts into little tin drawers. We worked together back to back in silence, I taking parts of haste and carelessness apart and he putting things together with patience and care. There was very little conversation between us, except when Sam told me what he wanted me to do next or I asked him what something was called or what it did. I also asked him how much accessories cost and how long I had to work for a particular one.

One afternoon, when I had put the last ball bearing in its place, Sam gave me my first task of synthesis. Over by the door—he pointed—there was a bicycle wheel mounted on a fork set upside down into a hole centered in a square wooden tabletop. The wheel could not be turned freely, for it rubbed against the fork's tines. It was a wheel that had been left in the shop for realignment, and it was my task to tighten the three dozen spokes in such a way that the wheel was brought into trueness. I was given a spoke wrench, of which I had seen many in my division and classification of the parts in the tin drawers. But I had never used the simple and clever tool that fit around a spoke nipple and allowed it to be tightened with the same motion that is used to tighten a wing nut.

I approached the problem of integrating the loose spokes into a taut wheel as if it were the task of lacing up a shoe. I chose to start with the spoke that was farthest away from my chest, which I pressed up against the wheel to steady it. With my arms extended to their fullest, I tightened the first spoke and then went to the next one and did the same thing. I progressed around the wheel, alternating spokes on either side of the starting one, which to me was a very satisfyingly methodical and analytical approach. As I worked, I got a feel for the wrench and the tension of the spokes. But it was difficult to keep track of where I had started and where I had gone; I hadn't thought at the outset to use the air valve as a marker. I probably circled the wheel several times, feeling that I was adding incremental finishing touches to a job of care and enjoying my communion with the machine part before me. When I came out of the trance into which the wheel had put me, I realized that it was not true but only more systematically and geometrically warped out of plane. The wheel was as askew as a sprung cookie sheet.

Sam must have known what I would do and had been doing, but he waited for me to discover my own error and waited for me to call him to the table in an act of supplication. Silently, he walked over, took the wheel in his hand, spun it with great force, and watched it rub loudly against the fork only a few times before coming to a stop. Deftly, he took up the butterfly of a wrench and caused it to light on the slender petals of the steel flower. Sam showed me how to loosen a spoke where the wheel rubbed and tighten an opposite one, working always in a pattern that was diametrically opposite to the one I had used. In less than a minute he had righted what I had wronged, he had wrought what I had warped, and I begged to be given another chance with another wheel. He said there was no other to be aligned that day, but maybe there would be the next day. Right then, a customer had come into the shop and needed help, and Sam left me alone to consider how much I did not know.

I straightened up the workplace and left in silence. On the way out Sam's front door, I ran smack into a beat-up delivery basket on a beat-up old bike left leaning against the store's brick front because it had no kickstand. The bike fell over and the basket was given a further realignment, which could not easily be fixed with any tool I had seen in Sam's workroom. As I was picking the bicycle up to stand it back against the wall, a boy of fifteen or sixteen—the customer—came out of the store and told me not to worry about the basket because he had just bought a replacement. In his hands he held a well-formed galvanized-steel delivery basket. At about eighteen by fourteen by twelve inches deep, it was large enough to hold bags of groceries and parcels, I thought. I had seen many a bike with an open-topped cage like this used for carrying orders from the Chinese restaurant and the grocery store to customers who had called them in on the telephone.

It would not do to turn the bike over onto its natural tripod of seat and handlebars for the operation of replacing a basket that sat over the front wheel. So the boy asked me if I would straddle the bike and hold the handlebars steady while he took off the rusty, disfigured basket and installed the clean, rectilinear one. He had borrowed a screwdriver and a box wrench from Sam, and he was going to make the change right there in front of the cycle shop. I admired the deftness with which he fastened the new support brackets one at a time onto the front axle without altering the position of anything else attached to it.

As he worked at a task he had clearly performed before, the boy and I talked about the basket. I asked him what store he worked for as a delivery boy, and he told me he didn't work for a store exactly. What he delivered was the newspaper, the *Long Island Press.* He told me that it didn't take more than an hour or so each day and that he made lots of money doing it. I asked him how old a kid had to be to deliver papers, and he told me that a twelve-year-old could get a work permit.

The idea of a regular job for pay, rather than for bicycle accessories, appealed to me. I had earned at Sam's the odometer, plus a speedometer, headlight, rearview mirror, horn, and other bells and whistles that I once had wanted so badly. Now I was actually beginning to remove some of them from my bike because I thought it had gotten too cluttered and would look better stripped down. The bike still appeared almost new, but it was acquiring an increasing number of small rusting scratches on its frame and handlebars and shallow dents in its fenders, not a few of which had come from installing, adjusting, and removing the accessories I had earned at Sam's. My bike was no longer a pampered pet.

The paperboy had told me the location of the *Press* circulation office, where he said I could go to see if any routes were becoming available. He told me to go to the office at a certain time on a cer-

tain day, because it was only then that the district circulation manager would be sure to be around to talk with. Although the manager
would not be there the next morning, I rode my bike to the *Press*
office anyway to see exactly where it was and what it was like. To
get to the office, I had to cross Springfield Boulevard, something I
had done only once or twice before, because it was on the fringes of
a neighborhood that my friends thought was dangerous and better
avoided. Andrew Jackson High School, which was known for frequent gang fights, was not far on the other side.

The office was on a small triangular block bounded by Colfax
Street, Murdock Avenue, and 212th Street. It was at the common
intersection of three neighborhoods—Cambria Heights, Queens
Village, and St. Albans—whose blocks are oriented at roughly 120
degrees to each other. It was St. Albans that my friends expressed
concern about, but their worry confused me.

Cambria Heights had originally been part of St. Albans, a village that grew up around the golf course from which it took its
name. Dating from the early twentieth century, the development of
St. Albans attracted upscale residents, including celebrities like
Babe Ruth. The golf course did not survive the Depression, however, and it eventually became the site of the St. Albans Naval Hospital, beside whose lush grounds the Q4 bus passed on its way to
and from Jamaica.

In the 1950s, St. Albans was known to us mostly as a very affluent
black community, the home of Brooklyn Dodgers Jackie Robinson
and Roy Campanella. Many of the houses that I glimpsed from the
bus were far more grand than those in Cambria Heights. I saw no
reason to worry about riding my bike through the neighborhood,
even though I had really only viewed a small slice of it from the bus
window. But I saw on my latest excursion that the area beside
Springfield Boulevard was occupied by much more modest homes
and row houses, making it look more like Brooklyn than Cambria
Heights or the St. Albans I thought I knew.

The *Press* office was in the middle of a small group of store-
fronts, which collectively sat on the triangular block like a wedge of

cheese on a cutting board. On the pointed corner was a dry cleaner's, and between the other two corners was the entrance to a drugstore. The newspaper circulation office seemed hardly that. It was closed—the *Press* was an afternoon daily—but I could see through the undecorated windows that it was furnished with little more than bare wooden benches placed against the walls, with another counterlike bench dividing the floor space into two unequal parts. There were no chairs and there was no desk. The walls were unadorned, save for a few calendars and notices, and the only object that broke the straight lines of the place was a large round trash barrel, from which overflowed torn newspapers and snaking steel wires. Made of cardboard with a metal rim, the barrel was not unlike the one into which the movers had packed my mother's dishes. The blank newsprint in which they had been wrapped could not be fitted back into the volume from which it was unpacked; now the barrel held old rags in our basement.

I rode around the pointed corner of the block to look at the back of the place, but there was nothing to distinguish it from the back of any other store, other than an inordinate number of cigarette butts in the gutter. I rode around to the front again. The *Press* office looked like an abandoned shell of a store that had gone out of business. But there were no signs on the windows advertising a final sale. In fact, there were no signs on the storefront at all.

I rode back home, carefully checking the distance on the odometer, the last accessory I would remove from my bike. The counting device was attached to a small bracket that fitted onto the front-wheel axle. The outside nut had had to be undone to allow the bracket to be slipped on, and I had found it difficult fitting everything onto the axle and getting the fender stays and wheel realigned during the installation. On the side of the odometer facing the bicycle was a gearlike wheel that had arms like a starfish. This star gear meshed with a pin attached to one of the spokes of the bicycle wheel, and with each revolution of the wheel the pin struck the gear and advanced it one sprocket. The odometer was calibrated to the twenty-six-inch wheel of my bicycle, and it mea-

sured the linear distance traveled essentially by counting the number of revolutions of the wheel, the same principle as that of the
long-handled wheeled device that police use to measure distances
at accident scenes. The distance from the *Press* office to my home
measured 0.8 mile, something I could cover easily in less than five
minutes.

On the afternoon that the circulation manager was to be there, I
again rode over to the *Press* office. This time the storefront had a
couple dozen bikes in front of it, all rather beat-up. Few had fenders, chain guards, or kickstands. None had a seat through which
bare metal did not show. One bike's seat was all bare metal, like a
tractor's. Most bikes had bent and rusted delivery baskets, with only
a few having newer baskets like the one I had helped the paperboy
install in front of Sam's. The bikes were not in formation the way I
lined up the used ones on Linden Boulevard. Most were lying on
their sides on the ground, fallen steeds on a battlefield. A few bikes
were leaned up against the storefront window or the utility pole in
front of it. Given their numbers, it was nearly impossible to pass
through the carnage of bikes. The people in the neighborhood
must have gotten used to walking on the other side of the street
when the *Press* boys were in the office.

I parked my own bike, using its kickstand, beside the drugstore.
I stepped gingerly over the other bikes, like a football player trying
to negotiate a tire course during a coordination drill. I learned that
the papers were late arriving that afternoon, which explained why
several groups of boys were sitting around the office playing cards
and, as I had seen when riding up the street, several other groups
were smoking, pitching pennies, and playing handball against the
wall behind the office. The camaraderie was strong, I sensed, and I
thought I would enjoy being part of any of the groups, except the
smokers. My father's pipe repelled me, and I thought that the cigars
he smoked stank.

Behind the bench dividing the room stood a lone adult with an
older boy, and they seemed to be going over some record books. My

unfamiliar face caused the boy to nod in my direction and draw the man's attention to where I stood at the counter. He was a man younger than my father, but much heavier. He was, in fact, fat. His hair was black, thick with hair cream, and combed into a pompadour in front, back on the sides, and overlapping in back of the head. He wore a matte black suit, a soiled white shirt, and a shiny black tie holding together a too-small collar. He looked like a type that I would later associate with being a chauffeur. I did not understand what men like him did when they passed middle age, because I never saw an older version of them, but in their young adulthood they seemed to have enough confidence, arrogance, and leisure time to last forever.

The man asked me what I wanted. When I told him I wanted a paper route, he introduced himself as Mr. Vitalis, the circulation manager, and told me I had come to the right place but at the wrong time. Unfortunately, there were no routes available at the moment. He turned some kind of form over and told me to write my name and phone number on the back of it. Sometimes he needed a new boy fast when an old one got ill or suddenly quit. My name would be put on a list, and I would be called if something turned up. In the meantime, he said, I should get a work permit and be ready to post bond. He gave me some papers that explained the rules of being a *Press* boy and told me to show them to my parents.

That weekend, I showed my mother and father the information and told them that I wanted to be a paperboy. They asked me if I really wanted to deliver papers every day. I told them I enjoyed working at Sam's, but would prefer to be my own boss and work for money. My mother agreed to take me to Jamaica to get a work permit, and my father promised to provide the forty-dollar bond that had to be posted before I could be assigned a route. With the paperwork all in order and the bond arranged, I waited for a phone call from Mr. Vitalis.

It was only the middle of July. School did not start until mid-September, so there was plenty of summer left. A group of us played stickball on 115th Road, the wider and less trafficked of the intersecting streets defining the corner on which Jim Wall lived, and we rode our bikes. Our riding was aimless, and we often progressed down the street in overlapping circles as if we were practicing the Palmer method of penmanship between the curb lines. Thunderstorms drove us into Jim's basement, where there was an old kitchen table and chairs, but we rode right through the light drizzles, the raindrops evaporating off our shirts flapping in the wind. When it got too hot and humid, we took our shirts off and rode bare-chested.

Since I had acquired all the paraphernalia I had once so badly wanted for my bike, I had stopped working at Sam's, which gave me even more time to kill. A form of two-man stickball became the favorite pastime for Jim and me. To play it, we needed a parking lot with a blank wall on which we could draw a strike zone in chalk. Once drawn on the vertical wall, it usually lasted for months, needing only a touching up every now and then with some fresh chalk. The one of us who was up stood a couple of feet from the wall, in an imaginary batter's box, while the other pitched from about thirty feet away. Balls and strikes were called, just as in a real game, and each batter got three outs. There were agreed-upon foul lines, and parking lanes, curbs, fences, and roofs defined singles, doubles, triples, and home runs. When a ball was hit, the pitcher became the fielder. If he caught a ground ball, he could get an out by throwing the ball into the strike zone. A fly ball caught was an automatic out. Runners advanced as in a normal ball game, and balls, strikes, outs, runners, runs, and the score were all kept track of in our heads. A disputed pitch was settled by the presence or absence of chalk on the ball; a disputed hit by the flip of a coin.

One of the best places to play two-man stick was in the Safeway parking lot, on Linden Boulevard and 219th Street, about twelve blocks from home. All we had to do was carry a stickball bat across our handlebars and a rubber ball in our pocket. The bat was usually sawn off an old mop or broom that one of our mothers had discarded. When there were no old ones around, it was very tempting to saw the handle off a good broom, but we knew this was a grievous offense. Instead, we used electrician's tape to mend a cracked bat and played a softer game than we had hoped to.

The ball we used in stickball was of the pink rubber kind, preferably a brand-new Spalding, bought just before the game. Spaldings, pronounced *spaul-deens* in the New York area, were expensive, costing about nineteen cents. But the newer the Spalding, the more firmly its powdered surface could be gripped, the farther it could be hit, the better it bounced, and the livelier the game.

Naturally, as strikes were the aim of every pitcher, so home runs were the goal of every hitter. If the ball went on the roof behind the pitcher, it had to be retrieved by us getting up there by whatever means possible. This usually meant climbing a chain-link fence beside the building and pulling ourselves up onto the roof, where we often found several other Spaldings and lesser balls, perhaps abandoned there because they were old and soft, or because some boys had grown tired of playing. They were now hard and cracked and bleached by the sun. Irregardless, as many a New Yorker would say, we retrieved them for reserve. No store proprietor liked the idea of kids on his roof, and so whenever we got up there we walked slowly and softly and made the most of the opportunity.

The roof on which our Spaldings most frequently landed was over the very candy store where we bought them. What we kids called a candy store our parents called a cigar store. Either name was a misnomer, or at least an oversimplification, for the small mom-and-pop corner establishments sold not only candy and cigars but also everything else—from newspapers, magazines, and comic books to rubber balls, batteries, and novelties. It was at the soda fountain in this store that we spent our allowances on syrupy Cokes and cherry Cokes, on egg creams and malted milks, and on the chocolate sodas with vanilla ice cream that we called black-and-whites. At the counter with the cash register, we bought candy bars and baseball cards. The store's layout was usually long and narrow, but the proprietor's gaze always reached into the farthest, darkest corner when kids came in to look at the latest comics or bounce the Spaldings in pairs to select the best one.

One afternoon, Jim asked me if I wanted to smoke a cigarette, and I said I didn't know. I didn't want to say to him that I didn't like it when my father smoked. He said we could buy a pack of Lucky Strikes at a candy store close to our home and smoke them in the empty lot across the street. I said we weren't old enough to buy cigarettes, but he assured me he could get them. He knew from experience that if he went into the store when there were no other customers, the woman behind the counter would sell them to him. It was only when there would be a witness to the transaction that she would obey what we believed to be the law, since then it wouldn't be just her word against some kid's. Our plan was for me to go inside and act as if I was looking at the comic books and come out when there was no one else in the store but the woman. Then Jim would go in right away, head directly for the cash register, and buy the cigarettes immediately.

It worked exactly as he said it would, and we went across the street to smoke. Since there were no parks in Cambria Heights, its few vacant lots became our great refuges. They usually were thickly overgrown with weeds and bushes that we could hide among. The lot across from the candy store stretched from 229th Street to 230th and was about the size of four residential lots put together, which would have made it about 160 by 80 feet, which was a gigantic space of green for our neighborhood. Jim led me along paths which only he could see to the middle of the veritable jungle, where there was a hollow under a circle of tall, thick bushes. The ground was bare of grass, so popular must the place have been for kids to squat and smoke and do whatever else I was not yet privy to.

I was surprised to find two younger kids already there. Jim said that they were okay; they were his cousins and he had told them to wait for us in this place. As we sat under the bushes among the empty beer cans and crushed cigarette packages, Jim opened the pack of Luckies like a pro. He unpeeled the red strip that cut through the cellophane and separated the top from the rest of the package. He then used a fingernail to lift up a corner of the foil and tore it neatly along one side of the blue tax stamp, so that he could reclose the top neatly and tightly after he had removed the cigarettes. He turned the open pack upside down and tapped it firmly across the loosely crooked fist of his left hand, causing a few of the cigarettes to project a small amount from the rest of the pack. He pushed most of the protruding cigarettes partway back into the pack and with his fingertips grabbed the one that remained sticking up and handed it to one of his cousins. Then in a single grasp he removed three more cigarettes, one of which he offered to me.

I had no choice but to take it in front of these kids who were no more than ten years old, and so I imitated them in the way they held the cigarette deep between their curled fingers and covered their mouth with their hand when they put the butt to their lips. Theirs was a much different style from that of my Aunt Jean, who held her fingers straight, with the cigarette between their extremities, and covered only the very center of her mouth when she puffed. Her hand looked like a priest's blessing the congregation; ours looked like we were hiding something.

Jim struck a match and began to light up. The kids did the same, and then handed the book of matches to me. I had used matches many times in lighting firecrackers on the Fourth of July, but I had never struck a match with a cigarette in my mouth. I held the cigarette tightly between my stiffened lips and put the lighted match to its end. The match was burning down to my fingertips, and so I dropped it and stomped it out in the dirt. Jim asked me if I had ever smoked before, and I had to admit that I had not. He told me I had to draw—suck—on the cigarette to get it to light, and I did so with the next match. The cigarette's end glowed, and I felt a wooziness in my head that I had never before experienced. Fortunately, I did not inhale, and so the sensation passed quickly. I held the cigarette in imitation of my co-smokers, but the puffs I released from my

mouth seemed to me to be of a different color and to meet a wall of
air that the others' cut right through. It would be a while before I
got the hang of smoking.

In the meantime, I rode my bike and waited for a call. It came
early one midweek morning in late July, and my mother woke me
from bed to tell me to come to the telephone. It was Mr. Vitalis, who
said that he needed a new paperboy to start a route that coming
Sunday. I told him I was ready to do it, and I would report to the
Press office that afternoon with my working papers and bond.

4

CLOTHES CAN MAKE OR
BREAK THE BOY

THERE IS A LONG and rich tradition of boys selling newspapers in America. During colonial times, Benjamin Franklin enjoyed the outdoor work of carrying the *New-England Courant* to its customers. As early as 1761, the *New-York Mercury* advertised for "a nice boy to deliver papers to city patrons. He will not be employed for more than two hours every Monday." Many a paperboy was bitten by the bug and welcomed the opportunity to work much longer hours.

At twelve years of age, Thomas Alva Edison, known in his boyhood as Al, got permission from his mother to sell papers on the regional train. He was a "news butch" on the extension of the Canadian Grand Trunk Junction Railway into the thumb of Michigan, making daily runs between Port Huron, where his home was, and Detroit. Butches like Al sold not only newspapers and magazines but also guidebooks, candy, fruit, sandwiches, coffee, tea, cigars, soap, towels, and various and sundry other necessities for the traveler. Robert Louis Stevenson, after a train trip in the American

West, reported that the butches also sold washbasins and "tinned eatables, mostly hash or beans or bacon."

Some news butches earned an unsavory reputation by having false bottoms in their goods trays under which they stashed "Paris packages," girlie books that sold for a dollar but were not to be opened until the patron left the train. The boys were known by all to be an aggressive lot, looking above all else to make a sale—any sale. The reputation was captured by a Thomas Nast cartoon captioned with the dialogue:

> *News Butch:* "Rock candy, rock candy, sir?"
> *Passenger:* "No, no, go away. I don't have any teeth."
> *News Butch:* "Gumdrops, sir?"

Civil War news sold newspapers, and so when Al Edison saw crowds gathered around Detroit bulletin boards eagerly reading about the Battle of Shiloh, he devised a scheme to expand his sales. He gave free subscriptions to telegraph operators for sending the news headlines ahead to be posted at stations between Detroit and Port Huron, and he secured ten times the number of papers that he normally sold on the run home. As he had expected, the headlines preceding him created a great demand for the elaboration provided in the papers that he carried. Instead of selling the usual two papers at the first stop, Utica, he sold thirty-five. His supply of a thousand papers was going much faster than he had anticipated, and so he quickly raised the price from five cents to ten. By the time he reached Port Huron, he had only a few papers left, which he sold for twenty-five cents apiece.

While working as a news butch, young Edison had long layovers in Detroit, where he read and sought out ways to occupy himself. The offices of the *Detroit Free Press,* the paper that he hawked, provided him an opportunity to secure some old type and printing supplies, which he put to good use on the train, setting up a small printing plant in the baggage car. He wrote and printed his own *Grand Trunk Herald,* a weekly that had as many as five hundred subscribers paying eight cents a month for it. Young Edison was not one to waste time, and so he also set up a chemical laboratory in the baggage car to carry out experiments during slack periods. Unfortunately, an explosion cost him his rent-free space and, reportedly, also his hearing. The business of chemicals, like the newspaper business, was not without risk, but young boys were willing to take the risks.

In the early part of the twentieth century, the most prevalent means of delivering newspapers in the United States was the "boy method." By the 1930s, a newsboy or carrier handled more than 80 percent of all newspapers sold in America, and in most cities a paper route had a cash value. For a new boy to get a route he had to buy it from a carrier with an established list of subscribers who was willing to sell it. The transaction was strictly between the two boys, who could be as young as eleven or twelve years old and as old as sixteen or seventeen, though sometimes an adult circulation manager or supervisor gave advice about the value of the route under negotiation or brokered the deal. In some cases, the newspaper itself had a special fund from which new paperboys could borrow to help raise the capital for the purchase of a well-established route. On rare occasions, a young boy could start a new route from scratch by getting his family, relatives, friends, and neighbors to subscribe.

In my case, I was lucky to live in the right place at the right time. Cambria Heights in 1954 was a community of upwardly mobile, or at least upwardly striving, families, most of whom did not require or expect their children to work to earn money. Jim Wall and his brothers and cousins, as far as I know, never held a job throughout their teenage years. Although Jim's mother worked, his family seemed also to have some source of income connected with his father's early death, which was never talked about. Jim was not a conspicuous consumer, but his brothers and their cousins, who lived only two blocks away, were. They seemed always to have new clothes and toys and spending money for the Good Humor man, who kept as regular a schedule in his truck as the mailman did on his feet. No kid I knew on our block had a job—summertime, part-time, or any other time.

Because of such changing circumstances and economic prefer-ences, paper routes in Cambria Heights did not have a cash value. They were not bought and sold but just transferred from the old carrier to a new one over the course of a few days, under the over-sight of the manager in charge of the circulation office and respon-sible for making sure the *Press* was delivered without interruption. As I would later learn, Mr. Vitalis, who oversaw the transfer of my route, often had to beat the bushes to find carriers on short notice because an existing carrier was moving out of the area or going away to school. Since it was so difficult to find boys, many of the routes in the circulation district were double routes. It was easiest for Mr. V to cover a route by asking the boy who had the adjacent one to double up on the number of papers he carried until a new boy could be found. In more cases than not, the doubling-up became permanent, as twice the number of papers to deliver also meant twice the amount of money to be made.

The overwhelming majority of paperboys took routes to make money. Some wanted to earn money just for its own sake. Others had more specific goals, such as buying a new bike or fashionable clothes. Only a small portion of the paperboys worked to help their families or, in even rarer cases, to support themselves. Which boy worked for which purpose was never discussed among us. All boys were equal in the *Press* office, at least with regard to the economics of the operation.

My reason for wanting a paper route was partly monetary and partly to keep busy during the summer. As I had learned working at Sam's, the idea of a regular schedule of activity appealed to me. It gave me a fixed fulcrum about which to balance my days. I liked being part of something bigger than myself. I liked the fact that I could count on the *Press* being delivered to the circulation office each day, and that each day my customers could count on my deliv-ering the *Press* to them. I liked having to pick up and deliver a defi-nite number of papers. It was something that I could start and finish every day with a sense of satisfaction. I liked having a daily goal, even if it was one that was as ephemeral as a newspaper.

My love of a fixed reference in my life was something that my friends, who seemed to do everything—from playing stickball to riding a bicycle to spending money—on an ad hoc basis, could not understand. So we did not discuss my wanting to tie myself down to the obligation of being a paperboy while I was considering it, and we did not ever speak of my being a paperboy after I became one. I would just disappear each afternoon around three-thirty or four o'clock and reappear under the streetlight after supper.

The route that Mr. Vitalis offered me covered 231st and 232nd Streets between Linden Boulevard and 121st Avenue. Had I known at the time that it was very near Montefiore Cemetery and that I would often have to ride my bike by the northeast corner of it in the darkness of winter, I might have waited for another opportunity. But I didn't. The delivery area I was offered was designated Route 12 territory, and since it was in Circulation District 58, it was known as Route 5812 on all official documents of the *Long Island Press*, of which I saw surprisingly few.

On the Thursday before I was to take over the route, I went to the *Press* office to meet the boy who was relinquishing it and to learn the ropes from him. Mr. Vitalis introduced him to me as Don, but he told me later that his name was Dan, Daniel Healey. He showed me how he went to the counter to "draw" his proper number of papers, double-counting them in front of the older boy who was called the stationmaster and acted as an office manager. When he had checked and double-checked that exactly seventy-four papers had been drawn, Dan took them over to one of the belly-high benches set against the wall and put them down on the shelf below. On top of the bench, arranged as neatly as the sheets and covers on a freshly turned-down bed, lay his delivery bag. But unlike crisp, clean sheets, the canvas *Press* bag was limp and dirty-looking, threadbare and torn, a result of many months of its being stuffed and emptied of freshly printed newspapers daily—rain or shine.

Each day the bag had been filled with newspapers folded for delivery but never bound with rubber bands or protected in plastic bags. Unlike the plastic-bagged newspapers delivered today from a moving car to the foot of the driveway, in mid-1950s Cambria Heights, at least, the *Long Island Press* was delivered unprotected to the door by the practiced hand and arm of a paperboy. To do so from a bicycle moving swiftly along the sidewalk, the boy had to prepare his papers well, and this was done before leaving the *Press* office.

From the lower shelf, Dan took a good handful of papers and put them on the bench just in front of his bag. He grabbed the top paper and folded it in a motion that was way too fast for me to follow. The folded paper was placed in the bag and the action repeated again and again, like on an assembly line. But this line didn't move. The folding process proceeded at a mechanical pace interrupted only when the pile of papers on the bench was gone and Dan had to bend down to bring another handful up, readying in the process the top one for folding. I became accustomed to his paper-hat trick but without understanding it. I figured I would master it before Sunday by practicing at home.

The papers in the bag stood neatly in staggered rows, like choirboys in a Christmas pageant. Though his *Press* bag seemed to me to be totally full, Dan continued to pack papers into it, squeezing a newly folded one between two that had been flattened like pursed lips. The heavily stitched seams of the bag were stretched seemingly to breaking, but the bag was remarkably elastic and tolerant of abuse. I asked Dan how he had learned to fold and pack, but all he could tell me was that he'd just learned it the way I would learn it. I asked him how the papers held together, but he said he could not show me now that his bag was full.

The *Press* bag was also heavy, weighing perhaps as much as thirty pounds, but the veteran paperboy handled it with ease and carried it before him—its long, wide strap slung like a limp canvas yoke over his shoulders—out to his bicycle, which was lying on its side on the concrete. In his only request for help, Dan asked me to hold the bike up and the handlebars steady while he placed the bag in the basket, or rather onto it. The bag was so swollen with the Thursday papers that it would not fit inside the wire cage. One edge of it rested on the basket's bottom and another was supported by the rim. The bag would remain that way until enough papers had been removed and delivered for it to settle into its more secure place. With the bag loaded, we rode off. Dan delivered the route, and I observed, riding at a respectful distance behind on my no longer new bike with its brand-new basket, which I was eager to use.

What I saw of the route that I was to take over in three days went by as quickly as the papers had been folded and packed into the bag. Dan rode along the sidewalk on one side of the street, taking papers one by one out of the bag and throwing them at what appeared to be random houses. Now and then he would stop and dismount his bike, leaning it against a tree, to walk up onto the stoop—he didn't call it a porch, and neither could I still bring myself to do so—and throw the paper between the screen door and the front door of the house. This was called "doorknobbing," he told me, and he did it because the woman in the house wouldn't take the paper otherwise. Besides, she gave him a fifteen-cent tip each week.

The entire route could not have taken more than half an hour to cover, even with the special delivery procedures. At the end of the route, my mentor gave me a couple of sheets of two-holed loose-leaf paper filled with the addresses of the subscribers and the special delivery requirements. He told me that he would collect from his customers for the last time on Friday and Saturday, but he did not want me to accompany him on those days. He also notified me that if I used his route list to collect from his customers he would break my nose.

Sunday morning, I would be on my own. There was to be no introduction of me to the customers; I would have to introduce myself when I collected the next weekend. I would have to assume that the subscribers would take my word for it that I was the new *Press* boy, and hope that Dan would not pull a fast one on me. I had never broken anyone's nose.

For the next two days, I studied the route list as I would a multiplication table or a list of populations for a geography test. Apart from the house numbers of the subscribers being in the order in which Dan had ridden his bicycle down one sidewalk and up the opposite one—the even numbers ascending and the odd descending—there was no discernible order to the numbers on the list. They seemed to come in clumps of two, three, and four, but then random numbers would be skipped. How nice and easy it would have been if all the houses subscribed to the paper, or maybe just every other one on the block. Since they didn't, I thought I had to commit the list to memory. I began to write it out over and over on small shirt-pocket-sized slips of paper, topped by the little cross and sometimes even the holy-family monogram, JMJ, that the nuns had taught us to put on important papers, like tests and letters to pen pals in heathen countries. I made separate daily and Sunday lists, since not all subscribers took both editions. On my first day on the route, I planned to take a good copy of the Sunday list with me, like a crib sheet, just in case my memory failed me. I also planned to stuff a second copy in my back pocket, in case I lost the first.

The papers were supposed to arrive at the *Press* office by 4:30 a.m. on Sunday morning, and so on Saturday night I set my alarm clock for 3:30. I went to bed just after sunset, counting papers instead of sheep, but I tossed and turned and did not fall into a deep sleep until well past midnight. It was hard to get up; my mother had to call to me to shut off the alarm clock. My father, who had fallen asleep in his chair watching a movie on television, had offered to drive me to the *Press* office to pick up the papers and then to drive me along the route this first day, but I told him I could do it myself. He did not insist on helping me, for which I was grateful. I tried to tiptoe past him on my way to the kitchen, but he awoke as I approached. He smiled. I proceeded into the kitchen, where my mother had already started cooking me bacon and eggs. She and my father stood together by the red stove as I ate, proud that their son was growing up, was going to work. After eating, under the pretense of wanting to brush my teeth, I went back upstairs to get an extra route list. "Be careful" and "Good luck," they called after me, as I went out the side door and into the quiet dark.

There was no moon, and the streets were pitch black between streetlights, some of which were out. I had never ridden my bicycle in such darkness, and the weak headlight I had mounted under my basket was small comfort against anything that might want to attack me from the side or rear. As I pedaled down 115th Road toward Springfield Boulevard, I heard sounds from my bike that I thought would warn all burglars that I was coming and would wake up the sleeping people in every house that I passed. The tires hissed loudly on the damp asphalt, the fenders creaked on their bent stays, the chain meshed menacingly with the sprockets, the crank clicked on the loose kickstand with every revolution of the pedals, the seat squeaked with the pumping of my legs, and the red reflector rattled on the fender behind me. The bike that had been new less than six months before now sounded like the Spike Jones band tuning up. The noises bounced off the night and crashed against my ears.

There was one noise that I could not identify. It was a dampened click, click, click in synchrony with my pedaling. I stopped pedaling and coasted, but the sound continued. Thuddy compared to the other noises, it was difficult to hear at first, but once I had begun to hear it, it was the sound that became the loudest and that annoyed me the most. Many of the others were sounds that I could identify and that I knew were fixable with a screwdriver, wrench, or grease. Others, like the hiss of the tires, though they could not be eliminated, were tolerable because they were soft and steady. This odd sound was regular but intermittent, small but incessant, like that of a dripping water faucet. I slowed the bike to listen more carefully, but the noise correspondingly slowed and softened. Stopping the bike stopped the noise, as if it were playing hide-and-seek with me. I could not find it; I could not diagnose it. I was sure Sam could.

Thoughts of noises and darkness and ignorance ended when I

got to the *Press* office. There was a bright streetlight mounted on
the utility pole located right in front of the storefront, and it
showed that the sidewalk was already littered with bicycles, like
steeds asleep in a concrete pasture. The office itself was quiet, and I
was informed immediately that the papers had not yet arrived, a
condition that I learned a paperboy had to get used to. The boys
were sitting around the room atop their empty bags, saving their
places for the folding ritual, waiting like a bomber crew for a mis-
sion to begin. Some of the older boys were smoking, something I
had been told was not to be done in the office and was not done
when the circulation manager was around. He was certainly not
expected to pop in this early in the morning.

A few of the boys recognized me as the new kid and asked me to
show them my bicycle. Flattered by the attention, I led them outside, and the whole lot of boys seemed to follow. As I walked
proudly over to my bike, several of the boys grabbed me from
behind. They held me by the arms while other boys grabbed my
kicking legs. Still others unbuckled my belt and pulled down my
dungarees, dragging off one of my sneakers in the process. One boy
threw my pants up in the air toward the utility pole, where they
caught about midway up on one of the climbing spikes. My other
sneaker was torn from my foot, and the pair were tied together and
flung up at my pants, catching on another spike. With this accom-
plished, I was let go, though some boys shouted to take off my
underpants. Others ran around me flipping the straps of their *Press*
bags, like damp gym towels, at my legs and my behind. I had
nowhere to go; I was being initiated into the fraternity of paperboys.

Someone took the brand-new bag that I had purchased on Friday out of the brand-new basket that I had bought and installed at
Sam's earlier in the week. The bag had emblazoned in red letters
across its front, in an open Gothic typeface, *Long Island Press,* and
the wire cage of the basket glinted under the streetlight. One of the
boys threw the bag into the gutter and walked on it and scuffed it in
a puddle, making it look dirty and used before it had held a single

paper. Another boy burned a hole in the *o* with his cigarette, though others did not seem to approve of that. Still others pushed the bike from one to the other, as if it were a wheeled medicine ball, letting it fall on its side or crash into the brick wall or rumble off the curb, disfiguring the basket and the fenders. Once, the bike was heading straight for the large storefront window, and a boy ran after it to stop it, bringing it down hard on its side in the process. The harassment ended abruptly when the *Press* truck was heard backing up behind the office with the morning's papers. I was left standing in my socks and underwear with my pants and shoes halfway up a utility pole and my initiated *Press* bag another three rungs farther up, where it had been thrown as a final insult. Under the glow of the streetlight, I could see clearly the task before me.

I had climbed plenty of high fences to get into schoolyards and to retrieve balls from roofs, but there was no foothold on the lower eight feet of the utility pole to get started up it. I climbed onto the seat of one of the bicycles leaning against the pole and reached for the lowest spike sticking out of it. I was able to reach it and, by swinging from it, grasp the next one up with my other hand. I pulled myself up, wrapping my bare legs around the pole to get extra leverage, feeling my legs being badly scraped and filled with splinters from the pole. After my feet were firmly set on the lowest spikes, I could climb hand over hand like a lineman. I climbed past my pants to reach the bag, which I slung over my shoulder. I picked up my pants and sneakers on the way down and stuffed them into the bag. When I was on the ground again, I pulled the largest splinters from my thighs, put on my dungarees, and worked at getting the knots out of the laces of my Keds. When once again fully dressed, I walked into the office to draw my papers.

Many of the boys had already left with their papers. Those who remained were scattered around the room, with their backs to the door. They faced the benches along the walls, folding their papers and packing their bags in silence. After I came in, the silence continued for a moment, but then a half-dozen or so of them yelled and shouted greetings, as if I were an old friend, and several came over to make sure I knew the ropes of getting my right count of papers. Among them was the boy I had met at Sam's. He now told me his name was Vinnie, and he showed me to the counter, where I drew my papers. He reminded me to double-check the count before I took them away.

The Sunday paper was much larger than the previous Thursday's, and my count was given to me twice, for the paper came in two parts. The main part contained the news, sports, and classified sections, which had been printed just that morning. The rest of the paper, the comics, magazine, and features sections, each set of which was known collectively as an insert, had been delivered and assembled earlier in the week. The main section looked like Thursday's paper, with its black-and-white front page, that I had watched my predecessor fold, pack, and deliver; the insert had the color comics as an envelope of sorts, with *Mary Worth* and *Mutt and Jeff* headlining "New York's Best Comics," by the *Press's* own declaration. The insert was actually used as a bright outer covering for the entire paper when sold on the newsstand, but that was not necessary for home delivery to subscribers.

The boys still in the *Press* office had just about finished folding and packing their papers, which in most cases filled two bags. I saw that the papers were folded differently from last Thursday's paper, with the comics filling the center of the paper tube the way the jelly filled a napoleon. One boy who was still folding papers told me the whole 116-page paper was too thick to fold in the usual fashion. He showed me that he was folding the main section as if it were a regular daily paper and then stuffing the rolled-up comics-clad insert into the middle. It was a doubly challenging way to fold, and he advised me against trying it my first day.

Rather, he said, I should walk my route and deliver the papers flat, placing them under the corner of a doormat or inside the door to keep them from blowing away. He said that I should assemble the entire paper in the *Press* office, putting the comics inside the main section, and pack the papers flat into my delivery bag. I was relieved to learn that I would not have to try to fold my papers, a process I had not yet been able to master, in spite of two days of practice. I proceeded to follow his advice and inserted the comics into the news. The pile of papers I ended up with was clearly not going to fit into my bag. I squeezed in all the papers that I could. I would have to put the leftover ones in the bottom of the basket and the bag on top of them.

All of the other boys had left when I was finally ready to lug my papers out to my bicycle. It was difficult putting the loose papers neatly into the basket, which had been dented and skewed by the horseplay, and I had first to pull the basket top back into a semblance of a rectangle before I could proceed. With the pile of loose papers in place, I was faced with the problem of getting the bag on top of them without the bike falling over.

Seeing me struggle with the situation, the stationmaster came out and held the bike steady for me, just as I had done for my predecessor a few days earlier. With the bag of papers put in place on the edge of the basket—the way I had seen it done on Thursday—I prepared to set off to begin my route, but I was unprepared for how recalcitrant the bicycle would be with a fifty-pound load well out over its front wheel. It was much harder to maintain balance and steer with the dead weight than it was with my brother sitting on the handlebars or sidesaddle on the crossbar. Letting the front wheel turn too far left or right threw it into an unstable condition that threatened to bring the whole bike down with the papers on it.

I could see that I would have to negotiate turns and curbs very carefully. When I rode off the first curb, in front of the office, the bag bounced on the rim of the basket, working some of the papers up and out of it. I stopped to reseat the papers and then proceeded toward Springfield Boulevard. The elevation of Cambria Heights above the surrounding area was no more apparent than on the roads and avenues leading up from Springfield. Through reconnoitering, I had decided that the gentlest grade was along 115th Avenue, and so I headed for it. About halfway up the hill I lost forward momentum and had to dismount my bike to keep it from falling over or rolling backward. I walked the bike the rest of the way up to the plateau that was Cambria Heights and then mounted it again for the relatively flat ride to my paper route. The sun was up, and I was riding directly into it.

I rode along 115th Avenue, one of the widest and most smoothly paved of the avenues. During a weekday afternoon, I would not use this route, for it was by far the busiest and the one along which cars traveled the fastest. It was the only street between Linden Boulevard and Hempstead Avenue that had an underpass at the Cross Island Parkway, and it continued into Nassau County as Old Dutch Broadway, a route that increasing numbers of cars took to beat the toll on the Southern State Parkway. Just two blocks short of the Cross Island, I turned right on 230th Street and rode the final three blocks to the beginning of Route 5812. A warm breeze had begun to blow up from the south.

When I reached the start of my route, I leaned my bike against a tree and took an armful of papers from the bag. I checked my memory against my list of subscribers and counted out the right number of papers for the block. With the armful, I walked across the lawns, leaving the papers before the appropriate front doors. Where there was no welcome mat to slip it under, I put the paper inside the screen door. Where the door was locked, I found something heavy, like a rock or a flower pot, to weigh the paper down. No one seemed to be awake, which was a relief to me, since I had not yet met any of my customers and I did not want to do so in this irregular way.

On the next block, I miscalculated somehow and ended up at the last house with one paper extra. Had I miscounted or missed a house? I retraced my steps, checking against my list. Where there was no paper or welcome mat in sight, I quietly opened the screen door to see if I had forgotten to leave one inside a house that needed one. I worried that I would be heard or would open a screen door just as a customer was opening the front door to retrieve his paper. I rushed from house to house, wondering if someone had already taken a paper inside. I became totally confused about who was and who was not a subscriber and had to recheck the series of houses. Finally, I found a subscriber house with a welcome mat but without a paper. I tried the screen door and found it locked. I concluded, rightly I hoped, that I had missed this house, and left the extra paper there.

On another block, I ended up one paper short. Again, I retraced my steps in fear of being found out as a green paperboy. Since I was a paper short, I wondered if I had left a paper in a house that did not subscribe. I tried the door of every house that was not a subscriber. Now I was really getting worried. What if I was caught opening a door where I had no reason to be? I imagined alarms going off and police cars converging on the scene.

As I neared the middle of the block, I heard a lock click and heard a door open. There was the sound of a dull thud, after which a screen door opened and a woman in a blue bathrobe looked out. I started to turn and walk back the other way, but the woman called after me, "Oh, paperboy!"

How did she know who I was, I wondered, as I turned back toward her.

"Why, you're not our paperboy," she gasped. I imagined her yelling "Robber," screaming for help, but she said nothing, apparently waiting for me to respond.

I told her I was the new paperboy, and this was my first day on the job.

"Well, I guess that explains why the paper isn't folded this morning, doesn't it?"

"Yes, ma'am," I answered.

"It also probably explains why you left two papers here," she responded. "We're only going to pay for one, you know," holding out a paper for me to come back and retrieve.

"Thank you, ma'am," I said, glad to have located the missing paper.

"I'm Mrs. Wright," she said. "I'm glad you're going to be our new paperboy."

I said, "I'm pleased to meet you, Mrs. Wright," forgetting to introduce myself as I rushed back to my bike to continue on to the next block.

On that block, where I left the bike against a tree, I came back to it just as it was falling to the ground. The papers, which had become loose in the emptying bag, were cascading over the curb and into the street. The unfolded papers fanned out like cold cuts on the platter of the road. I gathered up the papers and repacked them all into the bag, which now at least fit fully and neatly into the basket. The next time I left my bike against a tree, I made sure its handlebars and frame were angled around the tree trunk, as if they were hugging it.

The sun, rising over garage roofs, was beginning to warm the air to an uncomfortable degree. With all the walking I had been doing, I was running late on the route and getting hot in my flannel shirt, which I had put on at my mother's insistence against the predawn dampness. RECORD HEAT SCORCHES L.I., read the headline that I saw over and over as I dropped the paper inside a door or slid it under the corner of a welcome mat. I took off my shirt and tied it around my waist. When the shirttail got caught in the bicycle wheel—ELECTROCUTED INSTALLING FAN, ran another headline—I crumpled up the shirt and stuffed it into the basket, beside the twenty or so papers remaining to be delivered. By the end of the route, my body was ready to go back to bed, but my mind was thinking about how I would fold the papers tomorrow, throw them from my bike, and finish the route faster.

I arrived home about seven o'clock, with exactly one paper left in my basket. At least I had gotten the numbers to come out right, even if I could not swear that every paper had been delivered to a subscriber's house. I presented my mother with the family paper. She took it with a smile and asked me what I would like for my second breakfast. I opted for pancakes afloat in Log Cabin syrup, accompanied by a large glass of milk. I sat tight against the wall at the kitchen table and watched her test the griddle on the red Chambers with a sprinkle of water. As the drops danced on the hot surface, she scooped batter from the bowl and doled it out in large circles, delivering pancakes, as it were.

Speaking to the pancakes, she asked how my hands had gotten

so dirty. I had not realized that they had, but when I held them out in front of me I saw that my palms and fingers were black. At first I thought it might be grease from my bicycle, accumulated from the several times I'd had to pick it up off the ground. Once, I remembered, I had run and reached for it as it was falling around a tree and all my hands caught was the front tire and chain. But my hands did not feel dirty, and that must be why I hadn't noticed the dirt. I went to the kitchen sink and used Ajax cleanser, my soap of choice when removing grease from my hands, but the stains did not respond the way grease normally did. As I dried my chapped hands I realized that what had gotten on them was not dirt or grease but newspaper ink. I had had a second initiation that morning.

I returned to my place at the table and looked at my hands with renewed interest. They had done a lot that morning. As my mother brought the pancakes to the table, she asked how the first day had gone, and I told her everything had gone O.K. She said how glad she was that it had gone so perfectly for me. She was proud of her paperboy.

5

KIDS GET LESSON
IN PRESS TRICKS

BEFORE I BECAME A PAPERBOY, I thought little about how a paper looked or how it was delivered, let alone how it was folded and flipped onto a stoop. Because my father always brought so many papers home with him from work, we had never gotten the *Brooklyn Eagle* delivered to our old house.

The waterlogged papers we had found beside the stoop of our new house on the day we moved to Cambria Heights had been thrown into the corner of the garage unopened and unexamined. It was only after I sought a paper route that I fully realized that the papers represented almost a week's worth of the *Long Island Press*, and then whenever I went into the garage to get my bike, I looked at those papers with anticipation. But because they had remained folded for six months, they were permanently creased, like bronzed baby shoes, into the shape in which they were last touched. I could not unfold them to practice folding them.

To me, papers had always come in the disarray my father had put them in, their pages misaligned, their corners torn, their ink smudged, their stories stained, their random items circled with coffee-cup rings, their crossword puzzles done. To me, a newspaper had been like a much-used road map, which could never be returned to its original state. Now, after having seen virgin papers counted out at the circulation office, I realized that a newspaper read is a different thing: dirty rather than clean, soft rather than crisp, curled rather than flat.

A newspaper from the middle of a bundle just off the delivery truck is an object of perfection, as flat and clean as a slice of fresh white bread. A newspaper folded by the paperboy was a different thing again. It was a paradox, a puzzle rolled in an enigma wrapped in a riddle. What's black and white and red all over? An apple? A newspaper! What's made fresh, delivered daily, and consumed stale? A loaf of bread? The news? A loaf of news! The paper delivered by a paperboy was never opened before it was closed. It was, rather, transformed by some legerdemain from a spare Euclidean plane into an Einsteinian warp in multidimensional space-time. It was a Klein bottle, a Möbius strip, a trick. The paperboy-folded newspaper was a mystery of the universe.

On the previous Thursday, after my tour of my future paper route, I had brought home with me a single folded copy of the *Press*. It was the last paper in my predecessor's bag. On any other day he would have taken it home with him, but on Thursday he gave it to me for good luck. Perhaps it was by way of apology for his inability to explain to me how he had folded it.

In any case, I knew that once I unfolded the paper, I might not get it back together, so I put it down on the bed and studied it. I picked it up with care, turning it around and around in my hands. The folded paper was a curious thing, like a snake eating its tail, but it had no fangs to hold the one end in the other. I hefted the paper, looking for clues in its balance. There were none. I looked through the crushed tube of a paper, as if through a broken spyglass, trying to get the inside scoop. The inside revealed nothing that I could not see from the outside. The light at the end of the tunnel was just light. It was like looking through a black-and-white kaleidoscope that never changed.

A folded newspaper

With the folded paper not giving up any secrets, I finally tried to unfold it. I placed my two index fingers inside the flattened loop—as if it were my mouth being pulled out of shape to taunt my little sister—then pushed outward, creating a grotesque smile. Nothing happened. Since my first gentle tugs did not succeed, I pushed my fingers more forcefully outward, but the thing was surprisingly tenacious. It was like a Chinese finger prison; the more it was pulled and stretched, the tighter it got. Remembering the trick to releasing the finger prison's grip, I pushed on the outsides of the folded paper, reshaping the crushed tube into a looser, circular one. Now the caught tail came easily out of the gaping mouth, and the paper lay open on the bed.

My attempts to reverse-engineer the folded paper, to deconstruct it only to construct it again, to disassemble it only to reassemble it, were futile. I was trying to reinvent the pinwheel. My efforts took the form of my rolling the beast into a slit cylinder and then trying to fit the tail into the mouth. After I did that, I reasoned, I would flatten the tube so formed. It was easy curling the paper into a cylinder, but it was incredibly difficult getting the tail down into the throat of the snake. The end of the paper flared out like spitless thread pushed into a needle's eye, or a ferrule-less lace pushed into a shoe's eyelet. Even when the paper could be formed into a tube and flattened, it barely held itself together in my hand, and would certainly not have survived intact a toss at a stoop.

All day Friday and Saturday, I had tried to practice folding a bunch of stale newspapers that I took from the pile in the garage, using the *Journal-American* and *World-Telegram and Sun* because they were most like the *Press* in size. I hardly knew what I was doing, trying to mimic what I had watched the silent paperboys do with the speed of a party clown twisting long thin balloons into squeaky little animals and colorful, tubular, crownless helmets. Still, I knew that I had to learn by Sunday how to perform the act of transforming the paper at the altar of the *Press* office; I had to figure out how it worked. But since the papers that I had were not fresh from the bundle, they either did not fold neatly or fell stubbornly into the shapes into which my father had creased them during his coffee breaks. They were not the real thing, but I had to practice folding something, so that I could also practice throwing—flipping, as *Press* boys would say—papers onto stoops and porches. I did the best I could with what I had, using some old dry masking tape from my father's toolbox to hold down pages that sprang up like a cowlick as soon as my hand let go.

Since it was raining outside, I had to do my practice flipping inside. I cleared off the top of the bureau to serve as a stoop and opened up its drawers to represent steps. Across the room, I ran beside the bed to simulate being on a moving bicycle and threw the folded papers over the green-bedspread lawn. My accuracy was not bad, but mine was a small room and certainly not as wide as the distance from the sidewalk to the stoops on my paper route. Still, and in spite of the masking tape, too many of the papers came undone before they reached the bureau top or even the open steps leading up to it. And it was not even windy in my room. I hoped that the fresh, unread papers I would get at the *Press* office would take and hold a fold better. But how was I to learn the act that all the veteran paperboys seemed to perform so thoughtlessly and so effortlessly?

My efforts at folding were in imitation of the folded product. What I needed to understand was not its form but how it was formed. I tried to remember the *Press* boys folding their papers at the bench, but understanding how their hands manipulated the papers was as difficult as following the fingers of a prestidigitator. I had listened to my mentor begin to explain the process, but his instructions were of no help. "Take this part and slide it into here," he said, "like this," his hands moving faster than his tongue and covering up the very act that I wanted to see. "Then pull the sides out and flatten it," he continued, "like this," which concluded the trick. By the time he had said the presto words he had already picked up the next paper and formed it into a tube. He was soon lost in a rhythm of his own devising, in silent and thoughtless folding that excluded me. Being up the pole without my pants on Sunday morning, I had missed any significant chance to observe and practice folding then, and my next opportunity to watch how it was done would not come until Monday afternoon.

How could I have expected all of the tricks of the trade to be transmitted in one day from a practiced paperboy to a novice like me? Dan Healey, my predecessor on the route that was now mine, so emphasized the special delivery instructions and foibles of cranky and crotchety customers that I missed the fundamentals, which he took for granted. None of the boys on Sunday morning, for all their good intentions, could not tell me what I needed to know. They folded their papers mechanically, not able to think about what they were doing lest their hands lose their own train of thought. The boys' discussions focused on the exceptions to the rule, the paper that was too light or too thick, the man who wanted his paper flat, the woman who wanted hers rolled.

Newspaper customers were like bicycle parts: the squeaky wheels got greased. I had been shown by Dan how to put one paper into the milk box next to the side door, to lay a second flat and unfolded under the ceramic cat on the stoop, and to slide a third through the mail slot. What I wasn't taught was how to fold the bulk of the papers properly and toss the typical paper from my bicycle onto the stoop intact. Dan demonstrated these skills, but he only let me watch while he performed. He did not explain to me how he did what he did. I had been on my own to learn to ride a bike up a hill with fifty pounds of papers in the basket over its front wheel and to learn to balance my unbalanced bike against a tree while I walked from house to house. And on my first morning on the job I had only begun to learn how to be a paperboy, for I had not yet even attempted to fold and flip a single paper when it counted.

On Sunday afternoon, I again practiced folding papers, this time in my backyard, for delivery in my driveway. I looked through the pile of papers in the garage and selected the neatest and least creased broadsheets from among them, and piled them on the seat of a chair, pretending it was a bench in the *Press* office. Because the chair was low, I knelt before it, as if I were facing backward in a church pew. I moved my hands toward each other, as if to join them in prayer, but instead I picked up the top paper on the pile and tried to fold it. It ended up looking like a party hat. Others looked like a stalk of celery and a fallen cake. I blamed the used papers that I started with for these poor excuses for folded ones.

In the meantime, I conceived an alternate scheme for practicing my flipping. I abandoned the possibility of folding the papers on the chair. I merely rolled the old newspapers into a tight spiral and this one time placed rubber bands around them. I placed the rolled papers in my bicycle basket as if they were Monday's folded. I rode my bike up and down the driveway, flipping the papers from the far concrete track onto the side stoop. At first the bike shuddered every time I swung my arm across my chest, and once I fell over into the neighbor's fence. In time, I learned to anticipate and compensate for the changing momentum of my arm flinging the paper, and so I was able to maintain a steady course down the drive.

I had tried both forehand and backhand motions and decided

that the backhand was my choice. Without thinking, even though I always had thrown a ball with my left hand, I had flipped the papers with my right, perhaps in imitation of my mentor. It was possible to be a left-handed paperboy, I am sure, but it was not recommended. Newspapers were by tradition folded with the lead headlines inside, protected from the rough concrete and brick surfaces along which the flipped papers would slide. It was the natural way for a right-hander to fold a paper. A lefty could turn his papers upside down and fold the headlines out, but I never saw it done.

Soon I was pretty good at flipping the paper the ten feet or so to our side stoop, but I knew that a real stoop was twenty or thirty feet from a real sidewalk. But I was not prepared to practice out in front of my house, where my friends might see me flipping a paper with a rubber band on it. Even they must have known that no real paperboy in Cambria Heights would ever use a rubber band on a newspaper. Besides, flipping through the narrow gap between the spruce trees encroaching on the front walk might have provided an advanced challenge even for a veteran paperboy. I declared myself ready without that test.

On Monday afternoon, I entered the *Press* office resolved to master under real-world conditions the art of folding, packing, and flipping from a moving bicycle. I did not want to suffer, in broad daylight and in front of my customers, the embarrassment of walking my route with an armful of flat papers as I had on Sunday, placing them under the mats and inside the doors even of customers who would not tip me for it. I had been willing to do that more or less privately in the long shadows of Sunday morning, but I could not imagine doing it in the bright sunlight of Monday afternoon.

Every *Press* boy, I learned, had experienced on his own first days on the job some of the same failures that I had and would. Folding newspapers was an art, not a science, and there were only two ways to learn how to do it right. One was by practice and by trial and error, learning the hard way all by oneself what did and did not work. The other way was to listen to the voices of experience and preemptively exclude as much as possible their errors from the trials. In the end, though, this second way only shortened the first, it did not eliminate it. Those who knew what they were doing could tell you what not to do, but they generally did not. It was very difficult, if not impossible, for them to tell anyone exactly what to do and why and how. Failure was private; success was ineffable.

Nevertheless, generations of paperboys had tried to share their knowledge, honestly tried. The same boys who had tugged at my dungarees and abused my bicycle on Sunday morning now offered to pass on to me what had been passed on to them. They offered to show me how to fold a paper so it would not come apart in the air. But, as I already knew, showing a novice how to fold a paper was like showing a baby how to walk. Sure, it was done one step at a time, but what exactly was a step and how did it take place in time? Was there a first step, like a first cause? As carefully as the parent whispered the theory to the child and as steadily as the parent held out a finger or two for the child's hand to grasp, the child would not walk until it walked. Did it learn by watching its parents and siblings walk? Did it learn step by step? Was it an innate form of locomotion? Or was it done just by being done?

Fortunately, the Monday paper was the perfect one for a new paperboy—a mere 22 pages, as opposed to the 116 of the Sunday paper. I would learn quickly that, generally speaking, the paper's size grew from Monday to Thursday, the day for the supermarket and department store ads. Then it shrank back to Monday proportions on Friday and Saturday, as if to give the paperboy a break before he had to deal with the Sunday monster once again. The changes in size tested the paperboy's adaptability, forcing him to accommodate in the same bag, in the same delivery basket, on the same bike, papers ranging from 16 to 160 pages, or thereabouts, and requiring him to feel comfortable folding and flipping across that order of magnitude. The weekly cycle gave the newspaper the characteristics of a natural phenomenon, its effects expanding and contracting from day to day, repetitive but not susceptible to simple mathematics, like the wind in the trees and the waves on a pebble beach.

In addition, I would discover, the size of the *Long Island Press* over the course of a week was an epicycle of its size over the course of a year, the daily changes superimposed upon the seasonal ones, which reflected the mercantile and religious calendar by which Long Islanders lived. Predicting the exact number of pages in the *Press* on any given day was as difficult to do as predicting the exact high temperature. But, like the editor of the *Farmer's Almanac,* an experienced carrier could come incredibly close to convincing his peers that he had inside information.

The only inside information I had desired was how to fold my papers so they stayed folded from my hand to the customer's stoop. One thing I was sure about, after observing the boys in the office, was that once it was learned, it would not be forgotten. Once mastered, the process would be with me for life, like walking or tying my shoes or riding my bike, programmed into me. I would do it without thinking. Indeed, if I did think about it, I would not be able to do it. The trick was to begin to do it in the first place.

Instructors remained of little help. To be sure, they themselves had mastered the act, but they could hardly describe it. All they could do was say, over and over, "Take this end and put it into here, like this," and do it. But they did it so fast, lest their own hands freeze at the thought, that I could not follow the sequence of movements. It was only by trying as best I could to imitate their movements and imitate their product that I would do it myself.

On Monday, I drew my daily allotment of newspapers and took them to the bench where I had left my bag, snug against the wall. Following the example of the boys beside me, I put the pile of papers on the shelf below and took from the pile a handful of papers and placed them flat before me. The boy to my right slowed his hands down to where I could see what he was doing, and the boy to my left did the same thing. They were competing to teach me to fold, and the mirror-image twins gave me a good look at the process from two points of view. What the left hand hid on my right was revealed by the right on my left. Between the two boys, I had a complete picture of the process, and I began to follow these guides as if they were instructors for folding paper airplanes.

My papers were not nearly as neat as those piling up in the bags beside me, but I was getting the hang of it. Still, though my partners placed their papers as neatly as loaves of fresh bread into their softened old *Press* bags, I placed my papers in my stiff, if scuffed, new bag as if they were wood being chucked into an iron stove. Like split firewood, they were of uncertain size and uneven shape. Nevertheless, each successive paper resembled increasingly a properly folded one, and the more papers I folded the more uniform they became. My neighbors finished and, wishing me luck, left the folding bench before I was half through. But I had gotten the hang of it by then and was folding, if slowly, the last of my papers on my own. When I finished, I could see an improvement from the bottom to the top rows in the bag.

With the bag packed to a crested shape, I lifted it off the bench with ease, for even full of the slight Monday papers it weighed barely ten pounds. It was not difficult to straddle the bike, steadying it between my legs, and reach down to lift the bag of papers off the ground and into the basket. The load fit neatly into it, being neither too snug nor too loose, and it sat squarely on the bottom. I took off with a sense of purpose, steering the bike smoothly and riding up the hill effortlessly.

My confidence diminished shortly after the start of my route. I had been determined to deliver my load high in the saddle that afternoon, but from the very first flip of a paper I proceeded with all the tentativeness of my first ride on my two-wheeler, avoiding trees beside the sidewalk like the steel columns in our basement. Even though the load was light, the bike was far from stable under its front-end burden and my flailing arm. Forgetting all the confidence I had developed in my driveway, I became very unsure of myself. I was trying to steer with one hand, the same one in which I held the diminutive but blessed route list that I could not see well, while using the other hand to throw the papers onto the stoops.

I essentially stopped my bicycle before each house, braced it between my straddling legs, brought the route list close enough to my eyes to be able to read it and double-check my memory, took a paper out of the bag, and tossed it toward the stoop. More than a few of the first papers I threw caught the wind of their own creation and unfolded into a sprawling blanket on the lawn, or rather a party of blankets on a crowded beach. When this happened, I leaned my bike against the nearest tree, gathered the scattered newspaper, reassembled it so that it looked at least as good as the papers my father brought home, and placed it flat under the corner of the doormat on the porch.

I continued on with the route, but I began to check each folded paper for tightness before throwing it. Some, even though they looked fine in the basket, came apart in my hands. I tried to refold these, but I fumbled them in the openness between lawn and street. When it occurred to me that I could save the unfolded papers for the special deliveries, I proceeded faster but hardly more confidently along my route. On average, every other paper that I threw came apart in the air. As I gathered the scattered pages and reassembled them on the front lawn of someone I had yet to meet, I feared that I would be found out for what I was, a novice paperboy.

After a dozen or so errors, I stopped flipping from my bike altogether. I parked it midway between a series of subscribers' houses and walked across the lawns, just as on Sunday. But instead of laying the papers down flat, I tossed folded papers ever so softly the last five or ten feet onto the stoops. When I ran out of folded papers, I just carried the remaining flat ones and tucked them under the corner of the doormat or placed them inside the screen door. It took me almost an hour to finish the route, and I was not sure I was any better at it than I had been on Sunday.

In fact, I had come up two papers short at the end of my route. Because of my experiences on Sunday morning, I had taken extra care not to miss a house or to deliver two papers to one. Also, since I had followed my route list so carefully, I was sure I had not delivered to any nonsubscribers. I could not see where I could have made a mistake. Since my route ended at Linden Boulevard, I was right across the street from a candy store. I bought three copies of the *Press* there and left two of them at the last two houses on my route. The third one I took home. It would not occur to me until months later that I might have been tricked out of two papers by the boys who taught me to fold.

Among the things that slowed down my progress on the route were fences and hedges, like those around our house. Whenever I encountered a house with its lawn enclosed, I had to skirt the perimeter of the lawn and walk up and back down the path to deliver the paper, which just about tripled the transit time across a squarish lawn. I was grateful that there were not a lot of houses like that among my subscribers. In fact, most of the houses that did have hedges or fences belonged to nonsubscribers, and I considered then how curious it was that I had found the unopened papers beside our stoop on the day we moved in. Most people who lived behind hedges and fences seemed not to encourage visitors or paperboys. I liked to think that that was not the case for our family, but my father had canceled the prior owner's paper the same day we moved into our new house, and it would be a long time before we cut down the hedges. Good fences make good neighbors, my father seemed to feel. I wondered what the neighbors who did not have hedges thought of our hedges.

The Tuesday paper was exactly the same thickness as Monday's, and Wednesday's was only four pages thicker. This near-constancy in size gave me a chance to improve my folding technique, which in turn increased greatly the chance of my papers reaching the stoop without unfurling. That is not to say that all of my papers were landing as intended, but enough of them did to reduce my embarrassment and give me hope.

At forty-four pages, Thursday's paper was twice the size of Monday's, but my hands had already come to know their task and my fingers had developed some strength. Folding the heavier papers came surprisingly easy. They did not fit so easily in the *Press* bag, however, and I ordered another bag in anticipation of even heavier papers in the weeks ahead. By the time I would need to use two bags, I believed, I would be good enough on my bike to balance one bag atop another, as I had seen the older boys do on Sunday.

Friday's and Saturday's papers were again light like Wednesday's, and my folding and packing style was beginning to look to be almost as good as my neighbors' at the bench. The papers in the bag were nearly as uniform as cigarettes in a freshly opened pack. My flipping success rate had also improved since I had begun tossing the papers with the seam of the fold down. I had noticed that tossing them the other way led to a lot of failures, because they trapped the wind rather than cut through it. I had also learned to give the papers a slight rotation when folding them and to give them a good cross crease before packing them in the bag. This most important fillip kept the tail from pulling out of the mouth or sliding out the bottom of the paper.

After less than a week on the job, I began to feel like a veteran. I gained confidence after Thursday and picked up my pace on Friday, only to have a paper fly open right in front of a house with a woman standing at the screen door, curlers in her hair and a cigarette dangling from her mouth. As I stopped my bike and maneuvered it to lean against a tree, she opened the door and asked me if I was the new paperboy, ashes falling as she spoke. I told her yes, I had started just that week. She asked me my name and told me hers, which I did not catch. She said I should go on—she would pick up the paper. All the paperboys miss the first few days, she said, flicking her butt into the street, and I would get better in a week or so. I believed her, but I also wondered if the learning would ever fully end. I expect that she knew it would not, but she did not tell me that.

In spite of my imperfect record on my route, by my second Sunday on the job I had the confidence that I could fold with the best of the paperboys. After my initiation the previous Sunday, I had only half paid attention to how the boys were preparing that day's papers for delivery, especially after they had discouraged me from folding them. The older boy who became my mentor this second

Sunday morning—his name was John—showed me how to arrange the papers proper in one pile and the inserts in another. John arranged one pile in front of the other, on the bottom shelf, and explained to me that there were two main options for preparing the Sunday paper for delivery. The comics-clad section could first be inserted into the newspaper proper and the whole thing then folded as on a regular day. Since on most Sundays this made for a very thick paper that was difficult if not impossible to fold, as it did on this Sunday, most *Press* boys took the alternative approach. As I had seen the previous Sunday, but now understood, they ignored the inserts at first and folded each main paper as if it were complete. With the papers folded and packed into the *Press* bag, the insert was then folded like a letter several times over and onto itself, until it was of a size small enough to be stuffed into the center of the folded paper, like mail into a slot or jelly into a doughnut. The full bag of papers ended up looking like something at the bakery. It was what I had seen the other boys do the previous Sunday, but I had forgotten it in the course of the week. It was a nonintuitive solution to a problem that would likely have baffled me had I been left on my own to solve it.

Even with the benefit of the accumulated experience of the boys in the *Press* office, it took me quite a long time to fold the papers and stuff them with the inserts. I could fit only about sixty of the folded and stuffed papers into the bag, and the second bag I had ordered had not yet arrived. So I assembled the rest of the papers flat and put them loose on the bottom of my basket, with the packed bag on top. When I got to my route, I found that flipping the papers was not easy. The rolled and folded logs of news had a bulky feel that made the Sunday paper seem like a softball compared to a weekday's Spalding. The stuffed paper's unfamiliar shape meant that I could not control it the way I had learned to do with the lighter papers during the previous week, and my missiles fell far short of their mark. Most of the early papers I threw landed barely ten feet up the front walk, and most landed on their end, coming apart on impact. I had repeatedly to stop my bike and retrieve the papers, which I found myself again leaving unfolded under the doormats. As well as the last week had ended on Saturday, the new one had begun on Sunday with my feeling I was back at square one.

My second Monday restored my confidence that I had mastered folding a reasonable-size paper. But Tuesday's paper was only sixteen pages thick and felt like tissue paper in the hand. It was one of the thinnest papers in memory, the older *Press* boys asserted. If such slight papers were folded in the conventional way, they would not fill out the *Press* bag and would bounce right out, like cigarettes from an almost empty pack, on the ride to the route. Also, they would, like a playing card sailed at a hat across the room, twist errantly four times out of five. Here I was being confronted by still another variation on preparing the paper for delivery, and I had not yet been on the job ten days. Newspapers that once looked all the same to me now seemed to come in too many variations.

Since paperboys had had to deal with the complication of a too-thin paper in the past, an alternative way of folding had evolved and had become absorbed into the institutional memory of the *Press* office. In this case, instead of the standard long fold, a short or square fold was called for. The paper was first creased in half, with the headlines below the editorial fold brought upside-down to cover the major ones above. This half-paper, which now had the feel of a thirty-two-pager, perhaps the ideal thickness and weight for folding, packing, and flipping, could be prepared for delivery in the conventional way. Since the bag was designed to hold papers in their normal configuration, it had to be rolled down like a woman's stocking to accommodate the smaller half-folds.

If multiplying its thickness solved the problem of a too-slight paper, then dividing it addressed that of a too-hefty one. The idea of stuffing the comics, ads, and feature sections into a folded Sunday paper had evolved to respond to the oversize problem. When the Sunday paper got too thick to fold like a conventional one, some unsung *Press* boys had devised alternatives. One of the first solutions may have been to fold the paper proper and the inserts separately, and to flip one of each at each subscriber's stoop. This would have worked, of course, but only if the bike was going slowly enough to allow time to find and flip two different parts. In fact, paperboys may have ended up walking their bikes to deliver the two-part papers, and thus looked for a better way.

The technique of stuffing, like the invention of Teflon, may have been discovered by accident, perhaps even before the two-flip solution had been tried. Did some paperboy, not fully awake one Sunday morning, fold his papers and pack them into his bag, completely forgetting to insert the comics and feature sections beforehand? Facing the prospect of unfolding a bag full of papers to add the forgotten sections and then refolding them, and not wanting to flip two parts separately, did he leave the papers as they were in his bag and stuff the comics and features inside? How can we guess how this or any invention really goes from mind to matter?

Did noting such evolutionary developments in basically technological processes, done first when I was a paperboy, later contribute to my thinking about engineering, design, invention, and the evolution of artifacts generally? I expect that it probably did. Though perhaps not commonly thought of as a technological system, the news business in which I was engaged was in fact a tour de force of technology: from the reporting, writing, and editing of the news, to the translating of it into type and the daily printing in hundreds of thousands of copies on rotary presses fed with carloads of newsprint rolling down the highways from Canada, to the baling of the finished papers into standard counts, to the maintaining of a fleet of trucks capable of delivering the bundles to the corner cigar store, and, yes, to their being unloaded at the local circulation office, from which we paperboys re-formed them and reloaded them onto our bicycles and delivered them to the subscribers. It was as much a technological system as the electrical network, in which power generated from water impounded behind a dam is transmitted through an international grid of high-voltage lines to transformers that step it down to a voltage suitable for the wall outlets in a suburban home.

Delivering papers was full of frustrations, as is all technology, as

is life. But frustration and disappointment with things as they are is
the essence of invention and of progress. I would someday understand this well enough to articulate it. I suspect that my introduction to a host of frustrations as a paperboy helped me to better
understand invention and design, and the technology within which
they work, and thus become the engineer that I did. As a paperboy,
I was part of a technology larger than myself. In time, technology
became a part of me.

Like any technological system, the process of delivering papers
was subject to the laws and whims of Nature. Gravity was both
friend and foe to the paperboy—without it, the whole process of
flipping a paper on a ballistic trajectory to the target of a stoop
would not be possible, for the paper would float away like a balloon.
But gravity also pulled the bicycle ever downward, and the papers
with it. Paperboys also usually learned early on that their papers
and bicycles were not the only things attracted to the earth. Gravity also pulled rain out of the sky.

Press boys knew there was no sense in folding papers at all on a
day that began windy and wet and showed no signs of clearing up.
On those days we arrived at the *Press* office with our clothes dampened, some of us with our backs sporting a stripe of water thrown
up by a fenderless back bike wheel. Though we usually ignored the
content of the paper, on bad-weather days we, like everybody else,
looked for something to delay our departure into the elements. On
this afternoon, the lead headline was hardly news: HURRICANE
WALLOPS LONG ISLAND: QUEENS STREETS FLOODED. On days like
this, the papers were counted and placed unfolded flat in the bag,
giving the paperboy, who was in no hurry to go out on his route,
plenty of opportunity to ponder the headlines, the paradoxical
(HOT FISH TURN UP IN FREEZER), the enigmatic (BABY BUFFALO
FLIES TO GERMANY), and the puzzling (THEY DEFY LAW OF GRAV-
ITY). Who was in a rush to go out into the wind and rain? Wouldn't
it be nice if there were no paper today? NO GNUS IS GOOD GNUS.

The *Press* bag's canvas flap, which was usually kept inside the
bag and layered over with folded newspapers, was used on rainy

days to cover the papers to try to keep them dry. Mothers may have ordered raincoats and rubber overshoes to be worn, but we boys usually delivered in flannel shirts and sneakers, using our raincoats to cover the bag and the rubbers to wedge the raincoat tightly around the papers in the basket. By the beginning of the route, the shirt was heavy with the smell of wet cotton, and each step in the Keds sloshed water inside and out, pumping it over the high canvas sides that continued to stand up only because the long laces had been wrapped around the ankles.

Like a postman making his rounds in the elements, a paperboy in the rain had to walk up to each stoop, climb the steps, and open the screen door. But unlike the mailman, who had a mail slot to receive the daily charge, the paperboy was faced with the open void between the outer and inner front door. Only the thinnest of papers could fit through a standard mail slot without a third of the front page being ripped off. The normal-sized paper had to be held up between the inner and outer doors and dropped from a sufficient height so that the screen or storm door could be closed quickly before the paper fell into its path on the threshold. This was easier said than done in a driving rain, and the task of delivering a household's paper dry was often made all the more difficult, if not impossible, by those residents who locked their outside doors. Worse, some locked their screen doors but left the house door teasingly open, so that a paperboy could only look forlornly into the still and silent house, and the warm, dry rug onto which the paper might have been dropped.

On rare occasions, a paperboy seeking relief from the rain would ring the bell and wait under an awning until someone might come to unlock the door and receive the paper, but mostly we boys wanted to get back to our precarious bikes as soon as possible. In these cases the paper was truly, literally doorknobbed: It was folded over upon itself as many times as was necessary to achieve the right thickness to be squeezed snugly between the round doorknob and the square doorjamb, or the leverlike door handle and the door itself, there to be held out of the rain, until someone from the house came to retrieve it. The trick remained, of course, for the sub-scriber to turn the handle to open the door without dropping the paper into the puddle on the stoop. The fortunate man of the house would return home after work and see his paper held high and dry in the front door and, detouring from his usual side-door entrance, go up to the front stoop and retrieve the paper before going inside.

All sorts of dilemmas and scenarios were discussed in the *Press* office, but that was there and then. Delivering in the rain was here and now. Save for folding and stuffing, which could be immediately put to the test, what was discussed in the office was theory. When we paperboys were alone on our routes, theory was as useless as folding and flipping a tabloid. The *Press* office was where we told war stories; the paper route itself was the front line.

6

TV MAGAZINE ADDED TO SUNDAY PRESS

THE *LONG ISLAND PRESS* TRACED its journalistic roots to 1821, when the weekly *Long Island Farmer* began publication in Jamaica. At the end of the nineteenth century, at about the same time that Nassau County seceded from Queens, the *Farmer* incorporated the *Queens County Advertiser* and began daily publication. Within a decade, the name of the paper was changed to the *Daily Long Island Farmer*. Farming, however, was then becoming less and less common in developing Queens, or even in Nassau County, and it was ultimately to be associated primarily with Suffolk, "where they grow potatoes." In the meantime, a short-lived independent Queens paper, the German-language *Long Island Freie Presse*, ceased publication, leaving the name *Press* unattached. In the early 1920s the *Farmer* changed its name to the *Long Island Daily Press and Daily Long Island Farmer*. The awkwardly incorporated *Farmer* retained its minor billing only until the middle of the decade, when all reference to the *Press*'s agrarian past was dropped from the paper's masthead. Queens had become urbanized, and as Brooklyn had its *Eagle*, so Queens had its *Press*.

In 1967, the paper would once again change its name, to the *Long Island Press*. Daily newspapers were dropping like the flies they once swatted, even in New York City, where most commuters read one paper on the bus in the morning, another on the subway in the afternoon, and still another on the sofa in the evening. But, whereas readers once flipped back and forth between news, documentary, drama, and comedy in the newspaper in their hands, they would increasingly do so on the television in their living room. A press operator in a square hat made of blank newsprint posed with the last issue of the *Long Island Press* in 1977, when the paper joined a host of dead afternoon dailies.

But that was in the future. Throughout my tenure as a paperboy the Monday through Saturday editions of the paper were identified as the *Long Island Daily Press*. Every seventh day the masthead read *Long Island Sunday Press*, a title of as uncertain legitimacy as the middle name I used. To those of us who delivered it, the paper was always simply the *Long Island Press*. Whatever its name, the paper carried a capricious mixture of international, national, and state news, but its readers came to it mainly for its local news and advertising. Though comparable to the *New York Times* in size and shape, it was certainly no *New York Times*. Very few front-page stories bore a byline, and few were continued on the inside of the *Press*. But it was also more than a tabloid like the *Daily News* or the *Daily Mirror*, both of which my father pored over at lunchtime and brought home, limp and studied, from work each night. In fact, the *Press* was an amalgam of New York newspapers, and it was many things to many people in the competitive afternoon news market of the time, which included the *Post*, the *Journal-American*, and the *World-Telegram and Sun*.

To us paperboys, the *Long Island Press* was just the paper we delivered. In fact, according to the *Press* itself, it had been purchased by "the one-time $2-a-week office boy" S. I. Newhouse back in 1932, and it was one of his earliest acquisitions in the newspaper and broadcasting empire that by the 1950s controlled more circulation in the New York City area than the *Times*. The *Press* itself accounted for over a quarter million each day. It was during my service as a paperboy that the *Press* reported the mogul's latest acquisition: NEWHOUSE BUYS 2 ALABAMA PAPERS IN $18 MILLION DEAL. The headline announcing the purchase—then the largest in American newspaper history—was folded over by the *Press* boys as if it were no big deal.

But that is not to say that paperboys did not see headlines at all or were not drawn to a bold or offbeat one, especially on a rainy day. How a given headline might catch our eye is hard to say, for the layout of the newspaper's front page seemed to me then as now to be a jumble of stories competing for attention. Naturally, the biggest, boldest headline was always over the lead story in the upper-right-hand corner of the front page, but it was not necessarily the one that a paperboy's eyes first saw. I certainly would not read it first. The headlines that I and my fellow *Press* boys really saw were the ones that struck close to home, the ones that reflected us, the ones that titillated us, the ones that promised more. And whenever one of us did notice a promising headline and announced it, the whole *Press* office stopped to read the story. It was this kind of headline that would pop into my mind spontaneously, that would interrupt my train of thought, that would ruin my concentration. SHOWGIRL ADDRESSES NUDISTS.

Though the text type of the *Press* was not very much different from that of the *New York Times*, the display types could not have been more distinguishing, even to a myopic kid at twenty feet. Whereas the *Times* carried its familiar conservative typeface into its headlines, the *Press* used a modern sans serif to announce its stories, a look in sharp contrast to the ornate display typeface in which the paper's name was set. Collectively, the different headlines on any given day's front page presented a gallery of typography, with italic, condensed, bold, medium, and light versions of the *Press*'s stock headline typeface varied over the page, as if it were torn from a specimen book. Though banner headlines were only rarely

printed in all capital letters, in my reminiscing all the old headlines
have come back to me at my word processor in capital letters.

Like the working-class neighborhoods in which the *Press* found
its largest readership, the front page of the paper was a patchwork
quilt. It was designed anew each day, I imagine, by grandfatherly
editors sitting around the news desk, and then stitched together by
Linotype operators in the basement sitting before their Rube
Goldberg machines. The resulting front page was a hodgepodge of
a dozen or so stories and pictures about Queens, the nation, and the
world, as the editors saw them and communicated them to the
readers.

For all the uniqueness of a day's news, each issue of the *Long
Island Press* did have a sameness to it. This, I realize now, is in the
nature of newspapers, for it is in the nature of life and of the events
of it that are mirrored on the page. Understanding this helped me
understand why the *Daily Mirror* was named as it was. In fact, when
I grew up and began to travel beyond New York City, I became fascinated by the names of newspapers generally. They fell into categories, I noted. Like the *Mirror*, some connoted a passive
record-keeping function: *Camera, Observer, Recorder, Register, Tran-
script.* Some suggested a more aggressive approach to news gathering and interpreting: *Argus, Enquirer, Examiner, Intelligencer, Monitor,
Review, Sentinel.* Others connoted being out in front with the story:
Advance, Banner, Leader, Pilot, Pioneer. Some emphasized announcing
the news: *Call, Herald, Tribune, Voice.* Others were merely the carriers
of the news: *Courier, Dispatch, Mail, Mercury, Post, Telegram.* Still others simply declared their daily vigilance: *Chronicle, Gazette, Journal,
Record.* Some emphasized an ideology: *Democrat, Independent, Republican, Statesman, Union.* Some alluded to an ambitious beat, the earth
and beyond: *Globe, Planet, Star, Sun, World.* Still others seemed to suggest that all news was local: Bakersfield's *Californian*, Portland's
Oregonian, Santa Fe's *New Mexican*. Or self-referent: Missoula's *Mis-
soulian*, Oak Ridge's *Oak Ridger*, Saratoga's *Saratogian*. Some clever
towns named their newspapers after their heritage, albeit sometimes a distant heritage: Oil City's *Derrick*, Pueblo's *Chieftain*,

Toledo's *Blade*. There was also a miscellany of names that included some of my favorites: *Bee, Breeze, Nonpareil, Pantagraph, Picayune*, and *Plain Dealer*.

The name *Press* could be put in any of several categories, depending on whether Gutenberg's device was interpreted as a piece of neutral technology, which people used for good or ill, or as a metaphor for the freedom of expression guaranteed in the Bill of Rights. Whatever its name connoted, it was not something I reflected on when I delivered the paper. As far as I was concerned at the time, I was simply a *Press* boy, one who delivered the *Press*—a cog in the gears of commerce.

The overall appearance of the *Press*, its sameness, was fixed by the size of the page (eleven by seventeen inches), by the number of columns the front page carried (eight), and by the characteristics of its typography. As precise as such specifications were in the newsroom, at the composition desk, and on the rotary-press floor, there is probably not one paperboy or reader in ten thousand who noticed them. I know I did not at the time. Yet the *Press* was the *Press*, and its readers, its subscribers, its delivery boys knew it when they saw it. They each knew immediately what they were picking up off the newsstand, the folding bench, or the front stoop. They did not have to measure its size, count its columns, or analyze its typography. All they had to do was look at it. It was instantly recognizable as the *Press*; it was not the *News*, or the *Times*, or the *Herald Tribune*. It was the *Press* not by its size or its heft or its texture but by the warp and weft of the stories on its front page. Most of us recognized the *Press* the way we recognize a familiar face.

For all of its apparent qualitative sameness and for all of its quantitative specificity, the *Press*, like all newspapers, was in essence a diurnal phenomenon. It had a circadian rhythm to its content that was as sure as the sun. Today it might be a plane crash and tomorrow a train accident, but it was all the same. Whether China was fighting with Taiwan or Egypt with Israel, it was all the same. Whether a teenager was shot or stabbed, it was all the same. The

THE WEATHER
FAIR TONIGHT,
MILDER TOMORROW

Long Island Daily Press

FINAL

155th YEAR   NO. 59   WEDNESDAY, FEBRUARY 9, 1955   28 PAGES   5 CENTS

Soviets Step Up Blasts at U.S.

Watchman Averts LIRR Wreck...Again

Delbert Montgomery and piece of steel he found on tracks

Whoever set out to wreck a Long Island Railroad train last night succeeded in (scheme) Delbert Montgomery in his (vigil)...

Ave and GOP Square Off on Rent Control

GOP Urges $$ Fund to Create Jobs

ALBANY (AP)—Republican legislative leaders today pushed a plan to create a $150,000,000 trust fund to fight growing unemployment in the state.

Malenkov Saved by His Wife, She's Khrushchev's Sister

By ERNIE HILL

LONDON — The London Daily Sketch claims that Georgi M. Malenkov was saved from imprisonment by his wife, Elena.

The Sketch claims that Elena, a former actress, is the sister of Russia's new tough boss, Nikita S. Khrushchev, first party secretary.

Exports Relieve Malenkov Doomed

By WARREN ROGERS JR.

WASHINGTON, (AP)—Some American officials view with alarm the ways of the Kremlin bullies...

Truck Pins Couple In Car

Reds Shoot Down U.S. Navy Plane

By ERNEST HOBRECHT

TAIPEI, Formosa (AP)—Communist anti-aircraft shot down a U. S. Navy plane today and the mighty Seventh Fleet began closing in for increased firepower and anti-aircraft sighting to protect the evacuation of the Tachen Islands.

Will Stand With China, Konev Says

By KENNETH BROONEY

MOSCOW (UP)—Soviet Marshal Ivan Konev warned today that a Red Army mass powerful than in World War II will even war Western attack on Russia with "all types of modern weapons."

New A-Reactor Coming Here

Morty Gold Robbed Of Birthday Jewels

Maritime (Marty) Gold, favorite chairman, was robbed last night of $2,500 in jewelry in...

Boys' Best Duds Make Girls Blush

DOVER, N.J. (P)—All the stylish goods hats at McFarland Street Grammar School were their "Sunday best" to class yesterday—and wore a big impression on the girls.

L.I. Still Has Him

Manhattan Dentists Don't Want Peress

The 1st District Dental Society has rejected the application on...

In Today's Press

Today's Chuckle

A chrysanthemum by any other name would be as costly to spell.

stories were ostensibly different, but they were all the same. Whether or not adults admitted this, all of them—editors and readers alike—knew it, and they looked for any little distinguishing thing to play up, to conceal the fact that all news was old news. There was nothing new under the headlines of the *Sun,* the *News,* the *Times,* or the *Press.*

If any pubescent paperboys knew any of this, they probably could not have articulated it then. After delivering the paper for a while, *Press* boys might have been able to recognize a folded copy of the *Press* lying on a stoop at thirty feet, but they could not say what was in it. To the youngest of them, the front page was a jumble of different-sized headlines with words at different slants. To the oldest of them, the front page was a portent of more of the same. They delivered it; they did not think about or interpret it.

Publishers, editors, and avid readers alike made believe the news was fresh. They called newspapers the most perishable product in the world. Newspapermen reveled in this thought, knowing their work was never done; the nature of the news provided job security for those who crafted it. To them, yesterday's news was an oxymoron, the paper it was printed on good only for keeping rain off a new haircut, sheltering a hobo on a park bench, or wrapping the fish bones for the garbage. The obsession with the freshness of the news put pressure on paperboys to deliver it hot off the presses with the ink still wet. Though readers cursed when the black stuff came off on their hands, they got what they wished for. The wet ink was the sign of authenticity, and I have pondered the fact that the disappearance of afternoon dailies accelerated with the development of fast-drying inks. Once the ink was dry, the news was stale and the newspaper was late—it might as well have been a history book. It was easy to blame the paperboy. It was his fault and not the fault of the system, the technology, or the human condition that today's news looked like yesterday's. No one in power would admit that one day's news was much the same as any other's, but the headlines did not lie.

The news repeated like a radar scan, but since the *Press* was

above all a family paper, not all blips got reported. Wholesome
sweater girls and models in one-piece swimsuits were about as racy
as the photos got, and unless the women were famous, like Jane
Mansfield or Marilyn Monroe, they were usually found inside,
clothed in the news. The front-page stories below the fold (as newspapermen called the news that was hidden when the paper was face
up on the newsstand) were as likely to be about Korea as about
Cambria Heights. No matter what the dateline, front-page headlines would pass under the eyes and between the fingers of the *Press*
boys for the most part unread. My own most careful reading of the
paper would come only decades later, after it had been committed
to microfilm.

The same microfilm confirmed my recollection that in the mid-
fifties the paper was growing in size, not from Monday to Thursday
but, on average, from week to week. Friday, September 10, 1954,
marked the approach of the end of my sixth week as a *Press* boy,
and it was the day of a perfectly sized thirty-two-page paper, one
light enough to fold easily and yet heavy enough to defy the wind.
Well into my sixth weekly cycle of drawing, folding, packing, and
flipping, the *Press* had become to me an object of familiarity. Even
the pages of headlines, which passed under my paperboy's hands,
now moving with a motion as fluid as if I were conjuring a better
world out of the bad news, had the ring of familiarity of something
looked at but not seen:

Hurricane Due to Hit Tomorrow: Edna May Be Worse Than Carol
Night Club Manager Slain in Feud over Hat Check Girl
McCarthy 'Jury' Will Read FBI Letter
City Transit Service to Be Cut to the Bone
Cop Saves Old Woman from Thug
Reds Deny They Downed U.S. Plane
DeSapio Ignores Queens in Boom for Harriman
Chiang's Guns Blast Reds for 5th Day
Thaler Ordered to Lick Roe Tuesday
TV Magazine Added to Sunday Press

This day's headlines competed with a trio of pictures of busty Marilyn Monroe, tying up traffic at Idlewild the day before as she was caught vamping the photographers. But the *Press* boys were torn between curvaceous Marilyn's sexy mouth and her well-filled blouse on the right top of the front page and the straight sans-serif headline in the lower left. Each fresh paper that presented itself atop the pile on the bench put Marilyn squarely into view, but she was robed in newsprint each time the *Press* boy folded the left side of the paper over to receive the right, and she was forgotten as he glimpsed the upside-down words TV ... ADDED ... SUNDAY.

By the end of the afternoon, the whole office had read the story, which announced that "the new magazine will be the eighth section of the Sunday Press. It joins the four news sections, the big color comic section, Parade magazine and the full-length novel-of-the-week." As much as a television program guide might have been welcome, for the *Press* boy *TV Time of the Week* meant another insert to thicken the week's thickest paper still further. Though it would be but an incremental variation that would take little adjustment by paperboys who dealt with papers whose size could vary tenfold over the course of a week, it was the principle of the thing.

All of us paperboys continued to watch television, of course, but it certainly was not the focus of our waking attention. My paper route gave me another purpose in the afternoons, and I spent more and more time hanging out at the *Press* office and meeting up with other paperboys after we delivered our routes. We no longer watched *Howdy Doody*, save on rainy summer afternoons when we waited at home with our younger siblings for the storm to pass, after which we would ride to the *Press* office on the steamy wet pavement. Increasingly, when I did sit down on the floor with my brother and sister, it was less to see Howdy or Buffalo Bob or Clarabelle than to see Princess SummerFallWinterSpring and hear her voice.

Real girls, as opposed to Marilyn Monroe, were a growing topic of conversation among the younger boys at the *Press* office, and I had begun noticing their chests and legs, though without fully understanding why. The older *Press* boys spoke of girls in coarser terms than I had been used to among my schoolmates, and much of what was said seemed to be in a code I did not fully comprehend. My first quasi-discussion of sex with anyone was with Frank O'Connor, who knew that a French postcard meant more than "Wish you were here in Paris."

Frank was not fat, but neither was he thin. He had a round face and a round head, which was topped with fine, thin flaxen hair that was never in place. He had fair skin, with a hint of freckles, and blue eyes. He was shorter than I, by a foot or so, but he walked with an authority that I admired. Frank's full name was Francis Xavier O'Connor, but he never told anybody his middle name. The X in Francis X. was officially the unknown, but nobody who was Catholic could imagine it being anything but Xavier. St. Francis Xavier, who was known for being crucified upside down, was the only saint any of us had ever heard of whose name began with an X. Since no Catholic was supposed to be baptized or confirmed with a name that wasn't a saint's, the conclusion followed. Nine out of ten Catholics could guess correctly just from his initials, F. X. O'C., exactly what Frank's full name was. But his mysteriousness went beyond his middle name, and I never felt that I fully knew him.

Frank was the *Press* boy I spent the most time with away from the office. We watched movies on the television set in his basement and, after delivering our papers and rendezvousing, smoked cigarettes behind the handball wall in the public-school yard. For a long time, I thought we shared the same level of naïveté about girls, but he began increasingly to talk about them as we watched television. He declared that he was a "leg man," and that he was attracted to older girls with more developed figures. He commented on calves the most, getting especially excited at the sight of a thin-but-muscular-legged woman in high heels.

When we met after delivering our routes one afternoon, riding our bikes aimlessly somewhere between his street and mine, I became aware that Frank was riding in a curiously agitated manner, circling my bike with his and alternately leading and trailing me. On a quiet street, overhung with trees that made the way dark and tunnel-like, he sprinted ahead and in passing me asked if I knew where babies came from. I was not prepared for the question and so said, "Sure." He wasn't looking for an answer, however, but for an opportunity to show off some recently acquired knowledge. He began to ride his bike no-handed and, holding his arms over his head, formed his left hand in a loose fist and stuck his right middle finger into the hole thus formed. "Just like plumbing," he shouted, and rode farther ahead, his back to me so I could not tell if he was grinning or blushing, pleased or somewhat embarrassed at the thought. Neither could he, continuing to look straight ahead, see the expression of discovery on my face.

I did not know for sure what I knew as a twelve-year-old. I had seen pictures of the male and female anatomy in some health books and encyclopedias that were stored in our attic at home, but I had never put one and one together to make a new one. I had not asked how a dog got puppies or what made a mother's belly swell. Those things just happened, like the news. The graphical explanation provided by Frank made it all come together in a flash, and the finger in the fist was my image of coitus well into my teenage years, but it never intruded on my concentration as a paperboy, at least not consciously.

When the summer was drawing to a close, I had begun to show up at the *Press* office no sooner than four o'clock each weekday afternoon, the earliest I figured that I could count on getting there after school, which was scheduled to start in a week. There seemed to be no reason to give up my paper route just because I had to go back to school. If the papers were on time and I did not ride bikes with Frank before or afterward, I could fold, pack, and flip my route in an hour, leaving plenty of time to get home and do any homework before supper. I had become comfortable with being a paperboy, accustomed to the routine and competent in the process. But as good as I got at folding and flipping papers, I cannot say that at the time I ever reflected upon exactly what those actions entailed. As with a lot of what we reflect upon years later in the abstract, the act of folding a paper became charged with symbolism.

The folding process began by taking the flat paper in the two hands, as if I were offering it as a gift to a Chinese delegation, with the thumbs marking the third points just above the fold. The thumbs served as fulcrums around which the paper was turned and creased by the pressure of the fingers spread across the back, collecting ink from the headlines and stories below the newsstand fold. As the right-hand third of the paper was brought up and over the middle third, the whole paper was given a twist, with the left hand pulling the paper in its grasp back toward the paperboy and the right hand pushing the paper in its grasp away from him. At the same time, the lower-right-hand corner of the paper was manipulated into the opening in the left side, and, with a reciprocating motion, the fore edge, stiffened by the paperboy's one hand, was slid into the crevice opened by the other. The fore edge was worked deep into the paper's warm insides by a thrust of the right hand deep into the dark back page of the paper. The paper was now in the form of a twisted and skewed tube, and the male part was given a final seating in the female with a firm thrust, with what was beneath the fold now enveloping what was above. Finally, the fingers of the hands caressed the haunches of the paper and the whole process was climaxed by a back arching motion that left a sidewise crease that marked the act as done.

For all of its suggestive potential, the folding of newspapers was never talked about in sexual terms among the paperboys I knew. In fact, there was seldom any extended discussion of sex at all in the groups that tended to congregate around the *Press* office. There would be smart remarks about a woman or girl walking across the street, or an allusion to some picture in the paper, but these comments dissipated like puffs of clandestine smoke. There were girlie calendars from garages and gas stations hung now and then behind the drawing counter, where the stationmaster worked counting out papers and keeping books, but I never saw full frontal nudity. Even my initiators had let me keep my underpants on.

To talk openly about the folding of papers in sexual terms might have been considered sacrilegious by many newspaper boys, for folding papers was serious business in the *Press* office. We clearly had to fold our papers tightly and pack them in our bags snugly if they were to be delivered with a minimum of malfunction. The additional sexual imagery of placing folded papers into bags and stuffing inserts into Sunday papers seemed to escape our notice. We worked silently and diligently at our tasks, as if part of a guerrilla attack force checking and double-checking our parachutes and waiting for the signal to strike out on a raid.

After all the papers had been folded and the bags packed, many of the boys sat on the edge of the bench with their backs to their packed *Press* bags and, if the circulation manager was not around, smoked a cigarette in silence before heading out on their assignments. The moment of truth would soon be upon them, as they reached the first house on the route and took the first paper from the bag and flipped it toward the stoop. With each paper that held, the paperboy gained confidence that the day's paper had bite and tenacity and that his folding that day had been done right. With that confidence, he began to ride his bike more quickly down the sidewalk and flip his papers with more vigor, confidence, and élan.

It was the rare day, one almost of myth and legend, that a paperboy could finish his route without a single paper unfolding in the wind or missing a stoop. But the more good luck a boy experienced delivering his route on a sunny day, the more he began to feel the hubris of success, to accelerate his pace, to flip his papers with a flair. With the wind in his hair and the sun at his back, he might even begin to dream of the pretty girl who lived in the third house on the odd-numbered side of the 116 block of 231st Street. Invariably, the bubble of success would burst, and a paperboy could only hope that a paper didn't explode in front of the house where any young girl lived, let alone the girl in the third house from the corner.

Even as we paperboys were thinking about folding our papers and beginning to think about girls, our parents were occupied with other things. Senator Joseph McCarthy and his hearings dominated daytime television. For a time, my mother had positioned her ironing board in front of the console set in our living room. Just as his photo in the paper had passed through my hands so many times, so I passed in front of the senator's television image many times, but seldom stopped to watch. He had become as familiar a face in the *Press* as the paper had become familiar with him, taking the liberty of calling him "McC" when space was needed to fit a headline into a column. The long and short of the senator's name also passed before my eyes in countless headlines, which in the closing months of 1954 chronicled the story of his free fall from power.

McCarthy Wants to Question Accusers
McCarthy Probe May Take 3 Months
No TV for McCarthy Hearings
McCarthy Says Foes Lack Guts to Fight Reds
May Lift TV Ban on McCarthy Hearing
M'Carthy's 'Trial' Opens
McC May Testify in Own Defense
McC Denies He Asked for Top Secrets
McC Censure Asked on 2 Counts
McC Expects Only 33 Votes
Censured on First Vote, McC Faces 2 More Today
Censure Won't Stop McCarthy
Legion Honors McCarthy: Voted Queens Americanism Award

If Senator McCarthy occupied the afternoon press and daytime TV, evening television was ruled by the *Milton Berle Show*, starring Uncle Miltie, often in burlesque drag, scuffing his overturned high heels all the way downstage toward the camera. When the show was known as the *Texaco Star Theatre*, after its oil-company sponsor, we watched the commercials as closely as the show proper, enthralled with the service station attendants wearing their hats and uniforms as proudly and smartly as policemen, firemen, soldiers, sailors, or marines. Their singing of "We are the men of Texaco" seemed to spring from as much emotion as "The Battle Hymn of the Republic." The men who wore the Texaco star were heroes and role models for Jim Wall, certainly, and for me also. What could be a more honorable calling than taking care of a car that drives up to the gas pump, for was not in every boy's mind a car the successor to his bike?

But even a learner's permit was years off for most of us, and so cars were fantasies rather than dreams. We assembled plastic models of automobiles to set on our bureaus, to be sure, but they went nowhere, consumed no gas, never had to have their oil or water checked. All they needed was a dusting now and then. For the time being, it was the bike that had to be serviced and its engine, the boy himself, fueled. It was the bike that was the reality.

But Sam the Bicycle Man did not wear a uniform like the men of Texaco, and paperboys serviced their own bikes not as conscious prelude to adulthood but as necessity. No bike that provided the mechanical advantage that enabled a paperboy to deliver as many as fifty pounds of papers, more or less, could be kept as clean as a new convertible in a Texaco commercial, especially on this side of the television tube. The *Press* boy's bike, his most essential possession, was tested to the limit by thick papers and weather. If the *Press* wanted to add a TV magazine to the package, so be it. If rain in September, like snow in December, was pulled by gravity and blown by wind into the interstices of the bike's chain, axles, and brakes, it was also hurled into the boy's hair, eyes, and clothes, and he, like his bike, would have to take it all in stride.

7

QUEENS PARENTS DEMAND MORE SCHOOLS NOW

MY PAPER ROUTE had kept me from thinking about starting eighth grade at Sacred Heart, but going to school was to make it impossible not to think about the paper route. In PS 147 we had a homeroom and moved from classroom to classroom to study different subjects throughout the day, but in Sacred Heart we had one room in which we spent the entire day, except for lunch and recess. My classroom was in the northeast corner on the third floor of a brick box of a building. Uncharacteristically, the school building towered over the church, which was an unpretentious structure that looked to me like a gigantic breakfront lying on its back.

Instead of the arrangement of forty-eight desks that I remembered from St. Thomas Aquinas, Sacred Heart's Room 305 had sixty-four desks, arranged in eight distinct rows of eight. The sixty-four pupils that filled the desks were presided over single-handedly by Sister John Michael, whose desk sat in the front of the room, off to the window side. Dressed in her long full habit, black except for a starched white headband covering her forehead, a cinch of white masking her cheeks and neck, and a stiff, broad white bib—her

120

wimple—shielding her bosom, Sister showed her humanity only in her face and hands. Pinched beneath the headband and above and between the bandagelike apparatus that comics like Red Skelton used to signal anything from a toothache to a fractured skull, Sister's face looked to be of indeterminate age and of indeterminate gender. (It was endlessly perplexing to me why nuns took masculine names, like Sister John Michael, and priests wore dresses called cassocks.) The mechanics of the nun's habit, how it was pieced together and fastened to the various parts of her shape-denying and invisible body, were beyond comprehension. Sister wore a large crucifix suspended from a cord encircling but not cinching too tightly her waist. She used no makeup, and the only jewelry she wore was a plain silver band that, we had heard, symbolized her marriage to Jesus Christ.

We eighth-graders were assigned seats in alphabetical order, which put me in the next-to-last seat in the sixth row. I was lucky, one of the boys told me, because in the other eighth-grade class, the one in Room 303, the newest kid had to sit in a folding chair beside the back door and had to move every time someone wanted to leave or enter through it. That location would have made little difference to me, for I was already too far from the blackboard to read what was written upon it. From the earliest grades, I had had difficulty seeing from a distance, and I could not read from twenty feet the eye chart on the back of the classroom door. But with my name placing me well within the alphabet, I had always had plenty of time to memorize the chart by the time I was called to the front of the room to read it. My position in the alphabet saved me even when the class was tested in reverse alphabetical order. Rather than call them as I saw them—or didn't see them—I called out the letters row by row as I had heard them called out by my sharp-eyed classmates.

My poor eyesight had hampered my participation in the classroom, since I could not readily see the topic of discussion outlined on the blackboard or the map that had been pulled down like a window shade in front of it. Instead of owning up to my problem, I gave smart or stupid answers when called upon, and so I acquired a reputation as a troublesome student of ambiguous abilities. My poor eyesight did not hamper close work at my desk, however, and I excelled at tasks for which I did not have to see the board, so that my examination grades were generally quite good. On those occasions when the exam questions were written on the board, Sister usually also read them out loud. When I needed to, I asked permission to go to the pencil sharpener, which was usually fastened to a windowsill closer to the front of the classroom, if not to the blackboard frame itself. This got me close enough to read what was written on the board.

Though I needed eyeglasses badly, as long as I masked my myopia I was not identified as someone to be sent to the school nurse or an eye doctor. As I did in the classroom, I got by on my *Press* route by compensating for my nearsightedness with inference. From the first day, I knew that from the sidewalk I could not see the house numbers clearly enough to match them with the numbers on my route list, which I could read only by holding it up to my face, which I could not do easily when steering my bike. I delivered the papers by memorizing the list and keeping track of the position of the houses on the block. I knew, for example, that a house on any southwest corner of 118th Avenue was always designated 118-02 and that the house numbers increased in increments of 4. (This was apparently done to allow for a new house that might be built between two existing ones, but I could not see where such a new house would go, unless it displaced a garage or was a garage.) As long as I did not lose track of where I was on a block, I usually knew a house's number. On those occasions when I ended up at the end of a block calculating the house number to be 118-54 when I knew it was 118-58, I had to retrace my steps. I walked across the lawns, close enough to the front doors to see the numbers, until I discovered where I had gone wrong. Those few houses in Cambria Heights that had oversized house numbers or numbers on gates at the sidewalk saved me time and embarrassment the way a teacher's reading the test questions off the blackboard did.

Not surprisingly, among the things we were asked to do on the first day of eighth grade was to explain what we did over the summer. Unsuspecting that it was anything to conceal in the classroom, I announced proudly that I had gotten a *Press* route and that I delivered papers every day after school. Having become self-confident about my entrepreneurship, I expected Sister to be approving, but before commenting on my accomplishment, she corrected my pronunciation of "rout," explaining to the class that what I meant was that I had a paper "root." A "rout" was a mob, not something a paperboy delivered. Then she proceeded into a lecture—a tirade, really—on how eighth-grade boys should not have jobs after school because they should be playing and studying then and preparing for high school and maybe, if they were lucky enough and smart enough to go, for college. It should be possible to earn plenty of money by working only during the summer, she of the vow of poverty opined, and she declared that I should tell my parents that they should not be making me work during the school year. This was my introduction to my new teacher and my new school.

None of Sister's assumptions and presumptions made sense to me. My parents had not forced me to take a *Press* route, no matter how it was pronounced. It was something I had identified, wanted, and pursued pretty much all on my own. It did not take me away from my studies, for it occupied only an hour of my time each afternoon during the week. The real time commitment associated with collecting money and Sunday delivery took place over the weekends, when there usually was no school homework. Besides, I really had gotten reasonably good grades in school and had no intention of not studying or not doing whatever homework was assigned. For all of Sister's deflating my sense of self-satisfaction for being an independent paper carrier, I had no intention of quitting my route, which I continued to pronounce "rout."

Sister had labeled me an interloper and a rebel, a student not to be truly integrated into the classroom, and her prophecy became self-fulfilling. When I raised my hand, she ignored me. When I sat on my hands, she asked why I didn't participate. Whenever I tried to become a full member of the class, it seemed that I was thwarted, and I began to feel the way that I imagined Lenny had felt in PS 147.

On the rare occasions on which I was given a responsibility, I was provided no preparation for it. The first time I was sent out into the schoolyard to clean blackboard erasers, I got in trouble for talking in the stairwell and for beating the erasers against the building instead of clapping them against each other. Coming into Sacred Heart at the eleventh hour, I was left to my own devices to learn its rules by inadvertently failing to observe them. The rules seemed much fairer at the *Press* office, where the initiation was decisive and swift, and when it was over, the rules were freely shared.

Once, when I was assigned crossing-guard duty as a reward for good performance in the classroom, I was scolded for not raising my open palm sufficiently high to an approaching car. It was as if that would have increased the repulsive force emanating from my hand or from the exposed crossing-guard belt and shoulder strap that I was issued to wear. The reaction of Sister was not to give me another chance to show that I had learned to raise my hand correctly, but to ban me from the force. I was given no chance to learn from my mistakes.

Not all of my disappointments were during class or recess. Young boys of twelve and thirteen were given to believe that it was an honor, if not an obligation, to serve mass. When it was announced in class that the parish was in need of altar boys, I reported for the after-school meeting to express my interest. Father Herlihy, who was in charge of the altar boy corps, gave us a short lecture on how important it was to serve God and issued us small mass books with the script for the priest and the responses of the altar boys printed in different colors. We were to return to church the next week with the responses memorized.

I had heard plenty of Latin in my years of attending mass every Sunday, but I had never followed it very carefully in written form in a missal. Now the words I had heard for years of Sundays seemed to bear no relationship to the words I read without comprehension. Though some priests spoke distinctly, many mumbled and ran the words together into strings of sounds. Most altar boys spoke their responses so quietly that I doubt that the priest, let alone the churchgoers in the pews, heard them. Everything seemed to be done by cadence and timing, not by communication. I had no idea how to pronounce most of the words I encountered in the mass book, and so when I reported to the altar boy meeting the next week, I was sure I would be cut from the squad.

To my surprise, no other boy could recite the Latin responses any better than I, and so I was admitted to the next level of altar boy school—serving at an early-morning weekday mass, which was to be said by a still-sleeping priest and attended by only the most devout and presumably the most forgiving. On the appointed morning, I reported to the room beside the altar where the priest donned his vestments and the altar boys their white surplices. The mood in the sacristy was somber, otherworldly, somnambulant. I was to serve the mass with another boy, who was several years older than I and, I was assured, an experienced server. I was to follow him out to the altar steps and do everything he did. I served the whole mass with my head pointed straight ahead but my eyes on the altar boy to my left. I mumbled the responses in close proximity to what to him must have become second nature, and I tripped on my surplice only once, upon leaving the altar after the benediction.

I could have become an altar boy who showed younger ones how to walk to the altar and mumble in step, but I was not satisfied with my performance on my first try, nor was I satisfied with the performance of the veteran altar boy or the ordained priest. If they did not take what they were doing more seriously than they appeared to, then I didn't want to have anything to do with it. I resigned from the altar boy training program, giving as an excuse the fact that I had to deliver papers early on Sunday mornings and so could not work my way up through the early masses to the late. In fact, I often attended the 6:00 a.m. mass right after I delivered my route, though I usually went without changing into clean clothes and so tended to sit well in the back of the church, where I could hear little and see less.

If I could not be a good altar boy, I could be a good acolyte to my classmates. When the boys in the back row of the classroom began to shoot broken paper clips with rubber bands, something I had not seen done before attending Sacred Heart, I imitated them the way I did the model altar boy. But unlike learning Latin, learning how to break a paper clip in two and shoot the resulting U's was easy for me. This was a thing to do, not a response to be memorized, and I was in my element. I quickly got very good at hitting what I aimed for, but, as in flipping papers, 100 percent accuracy was always a goal and never an accomplishment. I almost got caught one day when my missile, intended for the hanging folds of habit falling down Sister's back, something the whole class would see but she would never feel, shot past her ear and struck the blackboard just to the right of her hand. The hushed class was interrogated about who shot the paper clip, but no girl had seen me and no boy who had would rat on me. They evidently realized that there but for the grace of God went they, and my bond with the back-row boys was cemented for the rest of the year. Rather than punish the whole class, Sister gave us the lecture on how someone could lose an eye to a paper clip, and she told the familiar story of the boy in Brooklyn who was blinded, the only one we ever heard about it happening to.

There was one aspect of classroom activity that did not extend across the back of the room, and this was the official and ongoing class competition. For this we students were teamed up by rows, which meant confusingly not the seats equidistant from the front blackboard but the lines of seats that went straight from the front to the rear of the room. Whenever any student gave a right answer to a question asked of the whole class, that student's row would get a star on the chart made out of construction paper and fixed permanently on the far right panel of the blackboard, which was made not of slate but of cork. When called upon, I was especially good at getting correct answers to arithmetic questions, at least when Sister read the numbers off the board so that I did not confuse a 1 and a 7 when trying to read them myself from the back of the classroom. My arithmetic prowess gained me some respect even among the girls in my row, and for all of my putative badness, I became Sister's pet when it came to what she called mathematics, which I know now was really nothing more complicated than simple linear equations with a single unknown. Near the end of the year she signed me up as one of two class representatives to take a special admissions test at St. Francis High School for mathematically gifted students.

As good as I was at mathematics, school generally held no special attraction for me, and I approached the placement and scholarship test at St. Francis with no preparation or anticipation. For me, the most exciting aspect of taking the test was riding the bus on my own to a new destination. I found the test difficult and unfamiliar and did not do well enough to be awarded one of the scholarships Sister had hoped I would capture for Sacred Heart. But apparently I did not do as badly as I thought, because at a pregraduation communion breakfast attended by my parents, Sister came up behind my chair and put her hands approvingly on my shoulders. Looking over my head, she told my mother and father that in spite of her disappointment in the St. Francis competition, they should be proud of me for having the mathematical talent that I did. This was the same nun who had ridiculed my pronunciation of "route" and who had deducted stars from our row when she caught me with a broken paper clip in my pocket. Those things were not reported to my parents, and I was grateful to Sister for her discretion.

If I was not to go to high school on a mathematics scholarship, how and where would I go? I did not want to go to the local public high school, Andrew Jackson, even though it was free and just a few blocks from the *Press* office, because the school and its environs had a questionable reputation. Jackson was very near to where the north-by-northwest streets of St. Albans, the east-west streets of Queens Village, and the north-by-northeast streets of Cambria Heights clashed like the massed armies of three warring nations, leaving the triangular shards of blocks that accommodated only oddly shaped stores, like the *Press* office.

Andrew Jackson occupied a double block near the intersection of Francis Lewis Boulevard and Linden Boulevard. It would have been very convenient for me to walk to the school or even to ride my bike and then go directly to the *Press* office after school. According to my mother, however, Jackson was a school where there were a lot of gangs and where a lot of gang fighting went on. I had heard about and on occasion seen at the *Press* office brass knuckles, chains, zip guns, and switch-blade knives, but I had never seen any of them used in a fight. I could imagine what it felt like to be on the receiving end of one of these weapons. It was not something I wanted to experience. Jackson was also attended by many black kids from St. Albans, and we were not used to going to school with them. Just as they did not deliver the *Press* out of our circulation office, so blacks did not attend Sacred Heart with us. Though we cheered for Jackie Robinson and other blacks who followed him into baseball, dark-skinned people were virtually unknown to us on a personal level.

The nuns, who seldom spoke of race outside their appeals for contributions for the missionaries who fed the poor starving children in Africa, promoted Catholic high schools for us soon-to-be graduates of a Catholic grade school. Whether inadvertently or not, the insularity and self-satisfaction of the parochial school system, which had fewer desks than students seeking seats, did little to ameliorate racial prejudice or religious smugness. Persuading students to continue in the Catholic educational system ensured not only that they would receive a solid Catholic education but also that the upper levels of the Catholic educational system would have a steady enough stream of students to remain viable without themselves having to reach out to non-Catholics. (They would have to do just that, of course, when enrollments dropped in later years.) With Andrew Jackson dismissed as an option, my parents and I began to look to Catholic high schools, none of which was conveniently located for a resident of Cambria Heights. Among the closest was Chaminade High School, located in Mineola, about six miles into Nassau County. Prospective students were taken there by the busload to marvel at its facilities.

A new public high school, Martin Van Buren, was scheduled to open in the fall much closer to home than Chaminade, but it was not considered an option because of the stigma that the gang fights at Jackson gave to all public high schools. Instead, the sisters brought to our attention a new Catholic high school, located about six miles up Francis Lewis Boulevard, in the awkwardly named community of Flushing, at the mention of which we boys snickered and pulled the chain of an imaginary toilet tank. If we had known any regional history, we would have known then that Flushing was the first permanent settlement in Queens, dating from 1643. It would become, because of its excellent location on bus and subway lines, a place of choice for new immigrants to live.

Although Holy Cross High School was still under construction, it was accepting applications for its first class, which would enter in the fall of 1955 and graduate in the spring of 1959. The school would be brand-new, promising new classrooms, new laboratories, a new gymnasium, a new library, a new auditorium, and a new cafeteria. Students in the first class would be "seniors" for their entire four years in high school. Such were the attractions of Holy Cross, and my parents agreed that I should attend it, if I could get admitted. In retrospect, there wasn't much chance of being rejected by a school that had no reputation, no alumni base, and no apparent predetermined class size.

What was not pointed out by the sisters at Sacred Heart or by the brothers at Holy Cross was that with the exception of some completed classrooms, construction would lag ambition. In fact, few of the amenities would be completed when the school "opened" in September. During the first few months, while the cafeteria floor was being cleared of a large pile of sand, we students would have to bring sandwiches from home and eat them in what would become the library, which in turn would not have any books until it stopped serving as a cafeteria and was fitted with shelves. And the faculty would be as much under construction as the physical plant.

Moreover, there would be the logistical problem of getting to and from a school six miles away and getting back to Cambria Heights in time to deliver my *Press* route every afternoon. But high school was still more than a summer away as graduation from Sacred Heart approached. The last few weeks of eighth grade had been occupied with preparing for the New York State Regents Examinations, which we had to take to prove that we had mastered English, mathematics, and social studies. Day after day we were drilled in sample Regents questions from thick yellow paperbacks. Just before graduation, we received certificates attesting to the fact that we had been cleared to go on to high school.

Graduation ceremonies were on a Sunday afternoon in late June. My diploma was issued by the Diocese of Brooklyn, which oversaw Queens churches and schools. "The Salvation of Souls is the Supreme Law," the diploma declared, and it attested that I had been awarded the honors of graduation not only because I had satisfactorily completed the eight-year elementary school course but also because I had "given evidence of a good Catholic character and of true citizenship." The printed program included "The Graduates' Pledge":

I promise:

To worship God and serve Him faithfully all my life by obeying all His Commandments.

To love our Lord and Savior, Jesus Christ, by striving to follow His divine Counsels.

To honor Mary, His Blessed Mother, by reciting her Rosary frequently.

To be a faithful member of His Church by observing all its laws, especially those concerning the Sacrament of Matrimony.

To shun all companions who are a danger to my Faith and Morals.

To abstain from all intoxicating drinks until I have graduated from High School.

To recite my prayers every morning and night.

To assist at Mass every Sunday and Holy Day of Obligation.

To receive the Sacraments of Penance and Holy Eucharist regularly, at least once a month.

To be a loyal and faithful citizen of our beloved country by obeying its laws and cherishing the noble ideals of the Constitution.

I took the pledge and had every intention of abiding by it, even the parts about shunning bad companions and abstaining from drink. I had no bad companions, I thought, and no one in my family drank, except at weddings, wakes, and reunions. For the moment, I had forgotten that I was a paperboy. The official pieces of paper that I was being handed captured my attention, and I was careful to not fold them, even as I read and reread them, taking them to heart. The graduates' pledge was distinctly different from the "Code for Citizenship" that I had been handed the previous year at PS 147. I was struck by their divergent emphases. Did the code still apply, or was it superseded? Did the Catholic students graduating from public school promise to be good Catholics? The questions did not linger beyond the time I looked at the diploma I was handed by our pastor.

Whereas my name was given as Henry R. Petroski on the Regents certificate, the diploma identified me simply as Henry Petroski. This suggested to me strongly what I had long suspected, that my confirmation name had never made it into the record books. It was as if the Church itself was as confused as I about what my real middle name was, and so it hedged and left out all middle names. Or perhaps it didn't care. Still, I had applied to Holy Cross High School as Henry Joseph Petroski, and that would be the way I would be known for years to come.

With my grammar school diploma I also received a picture of the class that called Room 305 home, all sixty-four of us. Weeks before, we had had our portraits taken one at a time, dressed in the robe that the student before us in line had just taken off, and the

The girls and boys of Room 305; with author in bottom row, second from right

thumbnail-sized photos were arranged like pennies pressed into the cardboard holes in the page of a coin collector's album. (We also had individual portraits taken, complete with mortarboard. Mine showed the chipped tooth I had suffered years earlier in a sledding accident.) In the composite photo, the girls, dressed in white gowns, were arrayed around our pastor and at the top, as if closer to heaven. The boys, dressed in black, were crowded to the bottom, closer to a netherworld. Everyone was identified by first initial and surname, and so I am simply H. Petroski. What is striking is the overwhelming number of Irish surnames. Even Italians, whom I remembered to be larger in numbers, are a distinct minority. Cambria Heights may have been a saucepan, but it was hardly a melting pot.

Eighth-grade graduation portrait

If I noticed them at all, such details were as unimportant to me then as the name of the family that lived in a particular house on my paper route. I was more interested in numbers than names, in things than ideas, in newspapers than books. What mattered most to me were the day-to-day practicalities of delivering the *Long Island Press.* I was an engineer long before I understood all the connotations of the word.

8

24 PAGES ... 5 CENTS

ONE OF MY MOST DREADFULLY anticipated activities in eighth grade became one of my warmest memories of it. Sister John Michael had informed us on a Friday afternoon that on Monday morning we were going to visit a newspaper and learn how the news was made. The paper was in Jamaica, she told us, just a short bus ride from Sacred Heart, and we should bring our lunch in a brown bag with our name written on it in crayon. She didn't mention what paper we were going to visit, but I knew of only one in Jamaica, the *Long Island Press*. I also knew how much Sister had detested my having a paper route, and as much as I wanted to see up close how the newspapers that I delivered were made, I resolved to stay in the background that Monday.

We rode in two buses, with all the girls in the first one accompanied by Joyce Kelly's mother, who helped Sister John on field trips. I had tried to ride in that bus too, because I figured I would be less likely to get into trouble, but Sister said all the boys had to ride in the second bus. By the time I got onto that bus, all the seats in the back were taken, and so I had to sit all alone behind the driver, just across from Sister John. For the first time, she talked softly to me, asking me if I still had my paper route. I said I did, expecting her to berate me for it, but all she did was smile across the aisle.

The fifteen-minute ride to Jamaica was uneventful, and our buses stopped in front of a large building on 168th Street. It was a perfect location for a newspaper, being right next to the last stop of the BMT subway line, which was here elevated above Jamaica Avenue, and within a block or two of the Long Island Rail Road and the bus terminal. As we assembled two by two on the sidewalk, I saw inscribed above the door "Press Building." I knew it was the *Long Island Press* that we were visiting.

When everyone was off the bus and lined up properly, we were led through the front door, where a receptionist met us and took us upstairs. We were going to the newsroom, she told us, where we would meet our guide. As we entered the room, an older man wearing suspenders greeted Sister, and they spoke quietly for a few moments.

The room looked like a giant classroom, except that the desks were larger and arranged not behind but next to each other in long rows. Every desk had a typewriter, a telephone, and a pile of papers on it, and there were a constant clatter of typing and chatter of conversation going on, punctuated frequently by the ringing of phones and end-of-the-line typewriter bells. All the people working in the newsroom were men, and they were all dressed in shirt-sleeves and ties, though most of the ties were pulled down below an open collar, something the sisters would not let us do at school. Some of the men wore hats, something else we could not do in the classroom.

Sister John called us to order and began a little speech. She thanked the man in the suspenders for inviting us, and she introduced the class as the Room 305 eighth grade from Sacred Heart School in Cambria Heights. We were there because we were studying how newspapers were made, in preparation for the citizenship part of the Regents Examination, she said, which was news to us. She said the class was very interested in learning all about the man's paper. One of the students in the class even had a *Long Island Press* paper route, she said proudly, pronouncing the word correctly, of course, and for the first time before the class without disdain.

I was taken totally aback. After all the agony Sister had caused me early in the school year over my *Press* route, here she was bragging about me in the place where the paper originated. All I could figure was that my connection with the *Press* distinguished our group, in Sister's mind at least, from all the other school groups that must visit the paper. She expected us to get the deluxe tour. After a moment of embarrassment, I moved up closer to the front of the crowd, closer to the girls. When Sister saw me, she introduced me as the class's paperboy. The man held out his hand and introduced himself as Mr. Brown. We shook hands, and I felt like the class president.

Mr. Brown explained to the class that he was the assistant managing editor, and that while waiting for us today he had been sitting at the copy desk, which he waved his hand over. It was here that all the stories in the day's paper were checked and edited and given headlines, he told us. To me, the copy desk looked like a bunch of tables sitting up on a platform. It reminded me of the stage in a school auditorium, from which standardized tests like the Regents were proctored. All the men at the copy desk were older and most of them had a pipe or cigarette in one hand and a pencil in the other.

Mr. Brown told us that an editor was responsible for assigning reporters to cover stories that were breaking. He used words like "cover" and "breaking" a lot, and they didn't help me understand what he was talking about. It sounded as if he gave out assignments like teachers at school. Like a teacher showing visitors a class at work, he walked beside the desks, slapping a rolled-up sheet of paper in his hand the way sisters slapped rulers in theirs. Our class followed, uncomfortable watching adults at work.

I was most taken by the typewriters and noticed that the reporters were typing with their first two fingers, just the way my father said they did. And they typed even faster than he. Mr. Brown stopped at one desk and showed us what a reporter was typing. It looked like a neat letter, but with the lines very far apart. Then Mr. Brown unrolled the piece of paper he was carrying in his hand and held it up. It had typed words crossed out and new words written in all over the page. There were arrows going from the bottom to the top and circles around words that were underlined. There seemed to be more pencil marks than typewritten words, and he called the page edited copy. He told us that the editors helped the reporters learn to write news stories this way. It seemed to me to be like a teacher correcting a student's essay.

In the back of the room were rows of machines, some of which were typing all by themselves onto rolls of paper that spilled out onto the floor like toilet paper that had spun out of control. These were the teletypes, Mr. Brown told us, that brought in news stories from around the country and around the world. As we were passing out the door, a bell on one of the machines rang and it began typing by itself. That was breaking news, the editor said, and he leaned over to read it before continuing on.

Next, Mr. Brown led us to a brightly lit room in which men were working at high desks with tilted tops. This was the layout room, he said, and it was where the different stories and photographs were fitted into the newspaper. Men with long strips of paper were cutting them with scissors and, on a table with light coming up through it, fitting them around photos. It was a light table, he said, and it helped the men lay out the newspaper pages. He picked up a large sheet with eight columns and lots of pencil lines and numbers. This was the dummy of Page One, Mr. Brown said, pronouncing the words as if they were capitalized. I could see that it looked like what we *Press* boys called the front page, but without the words and pictures filled in. He said that when the dummy was done, it was sent down to the composing room, where the typeset stories were arranged according to the plan.

Now, he said, we were going to see where the type was set. We walked down several flights of stairs, more than we had walked up. Mr. Brown told us we were going into the subbasement, where the

Linotype machines were. There were lots of them, and they were
lined up all along one wall. The Linotypes were tall, seeming to go
right into the ceiling of the room, like a furnace. They also had lots
of arms and pipes coming out of them, making them look even
more like a furnace. The men seated before the Linotypes looked
like they were typing, but the only paper in sight was hanging from
a hook in front of them, and they were looking at it and not at their
fingers, all of which were moving more like a piano player's than a
typist's. They were creating the lines of hot type that would quickly
cool and go to the composing room, we were told, and we were
taken next to the press room.

The press room didn't look like a room at all. It was impossible
to get a sense of how large it was, because it was totally filled with
the presses themselves, as if a bunch of locomotives had been
squeezed and piled into too small a space. Only a dozen of us were
allowed in at a time, and we stood on a small platform of perforated
steel like the entrance to the Ferris wheel at an amusement park.
We looked directly into a maze of rollers over, under, and around
which the paper was moving so fast that it was impossible to read
even the largest headlines. The principle of the thing reminded me
of my Kodak, in which the film traveled around rollers, but there
was nothing else I could compare it to. Mr. Brown told us that the
machine was called a rotary press and was descended from one
invented by a Richard Hoe over a hundred years before. Mr. Hoe's
press could print something like ten thousand pages an hour. The
machine in the Press Building could print and assemble 100-page
newspapers by the tens of thousands per hour. It did seem fast and
hopelessly complicated, but the men working on the floor and
climbing ladders around the enormous machinery seemed to be as
familiar with it as I had become with my bicycle. They all wore
square paper hats held on with the straps of green eye shades. Mr.
Brown told us that each man made his own hat fresh every day, and
I thought of the hats and boats my father used to make us out of
newspapers. Crowded around the presses, some of the men were
using oil cans, others held screwdrivers, and still others were read-

ing the paper that was coming off the press, to check if the ink was taking right, we were told. I looked down at my hands, which were clean.

Our last stop on our tour of the Press Building was a room near the loading dock, where the finished papers were coming down a conveyor belt, overlapped like a deck of cards spread out for inspection by a dealer. Our guide explained that at the bottom of the belt, the papers were gathered up into piles of fifty and wrapped with a single piece of wire that was automatically twisted closed by a special machine. It was only after that that the bundles of papers were touched by human hands and loaded onto the trucks that had been backed into the loading dock. Here, finally, was the *Press* I knew, wrapped in the familiar bundles we unloaded at the circulation office. Would one of these bundles be mine? I imagined using the crayon in my pocket to mark my initials on the wrapper, the way men marked dollar bills to see if they ever got the same one twice. What were the odds of that happening, I wondered.

Mr. Brown said goodbye to us on the loading dock and told us to watch our step when climbing down the stairs. Our bus was waiting just around the corner, on Archer Avenue, and we were told to take the same seats we had that morning. After Sister counted us all present, she told us to sit still and eat our brown-bag lunches while riding back to Sacred Heart. I ate in silence across the aisle from Sister John, who was grading papers. In my mind, I went over the steps in making a newspaper, thinking what would make a good Regents question. I felt good, knowing that I was a part of the great enterprise of getting the paper to the people who read it. That afternoon, I delivered my papers with no inconsiderable pride. The next day, as I was still wondering who made the machines that made the papers, a couple of boys asked me what it was like to have a paper route.

The distribution system was the weakest link in the chain of getting the news from an editor's desk to a reader's stoop. It depended upon Teamsters driving trucks, from the open backs of which young thugs in tight white T-shirts threw a bundle or two of papers against the door of a mom-and-pop candy store as the truck careened around the corner to a cigar store up the block.

The trucks that brought the papers to the *Press* office, a more pedestrian task, seemed to be poorly maintained and slow, and they often broke down. When that happened, a working one would have to be summoned and hundreds of bundles of papers transferred from one truck to another backed up to it somewhere between Jamaica and St. Albans. In the meantime, dozens of *Press* boys milled around the district office, waiting to draw their daily dough and fold it into loaves of news.

Some of the waiting boys straddled their bikes out front, cradling their heads in their arms on the *Press* bags crumpled into pillows on the handlebars, rolling back and forth on their wheels, some of them chewing on the bag strap like horses chafing at the bit at Belmont. Other groups of boys hung out behind the office, where the truck would eventually pull up and back into the doorway, without bells or horns to warn any boys behind it to move out of the way or be crushed against the wall. We relied on each other for protection from that, and no one ever got hurt.

If it was late in the week, the stationmaster and a few *Press* boys would work inside, taking advantage of the dead time to prepare the inserts for the Sunday paper. The comics, rotogravure, television guide, and other Sunday feature sections came with the regular delivery run in separate bales over the course of a couple of days at the beginning of each week, when the regular paper was thin. It was the responsibility of the *Press* office to figure out how to assemble the supplements and insert them into the Sunday paper. The individual bales could have been left until Sunday to be dealt with, and each boy's draw could have been given to him in several separate piles. That would take a long time to do, however, and anyway there was not enough bench space for all the *Press* boys to consolidate the inserts at the same time on Sunday morning. And so it was not done that way.

As soon as all of the feature sections were in the *Press* office, the stationmaster looked for slow times to assemble them into a single insert. Each of the half-dozen or so separate sections was arranged in a separate pile, along a clear stretch of bench. For a right-hander, the smaller *TV Time of the Week* and *Parade,* which opened like tabloids, were in the rightmost piles, because they had only a single fold. The feature sections, which were folded and then folded again to produce the familiar newspaper configuration that resulted in a pocketlike opening along their shorter side, were in the next piles. The leftmost pile contained the comics section, which was to form the cover of the completed insert.

The act of inserting in this context consisted of grabbing with the right hand a *TV Time* off the first pile and with the index and middle fingers pulling it across the pile of *Parades,* picking up one of them with the thumb and index finger of the same hand, while at the same time opening up the feature section next in line with the left hand. The sections coming from the right were thrown with an audible "thuck" into the partially opened section, while at the same time the left and right hands moved down the line into position to take the already assembled sections and insert them into the next feature section in line. The last motion was to insert the package that had been assembled from the piles stretching to the right into the comics section on the extreme left, and to put it on another pile farther to the left. For a left-hander, the inserting process would naturally have had to be reversed, with the upside-down sections being pulled from left to right, for insertion into the upside-down comics, but I never saw it done that way. Whatever naturally left-handed *Press* boys there may have been seemed to have adapted to the right-handed system.

When the spacing between the piles was just right, and when the boy doing the inserting had developed a rhythm, he could assemble a dozen or so sets of inserts per minute, a whole route's worth in less than ten minutes. The time went fast, and there was a pile of colorful products to show for it. The assembled inserts were stacked in the back corner of the *Press* office, awaiting Sunday morning, when they would be drawn with the papers proper.

Mr. Vitalis argued that each boy was responsible for his own inserting, and so the stationmaster was performing a service for which he should be compensated. Those of us who wanted to do our own inserting were reminded that there was not enough bench space in the office for all the boys to be inserting on Sunday morning. And any staggered schedule presented impossible logistics and record keeping. With the stationmaster taking over the responsibility, Sunday mornings would not present a bottleneck for bench space. The question remained open as to whether a *Press* boy should be charged an insertion fee if he helped insert during slack times, such as waiting for the delivery truck to arrive.

Regardless of the policy on inserting, when the delivery truck was late there was always a large group of boys engaged in games on the sidewalk behind the *Press* office, where I had seen so many cigarette butts on my initial visit. Baseball card collecting occupied the youngest of the paperboys. Every young boy accumulated boxes of the cards, and he usually carried a stack of the more common ones around with him, even though they had little if any trading value. The cards were the currency of a game known as simply as flipping. Flipping baseball cards took several forms, none of which had anything to do with flipping papers. In the one-on-one version, one boy held a card by its longer edges between his thumb and fingers and with a flick of the wrist sent the card turning side over side to the ground. How many fingers were used to grasp the card was a matter of style, as was whether the card was held face up or face down, whether it was held parallel or perpendicular to the ground, whether it was buckled in the hand or held flat, and whether it was flipped with the wrist cocked backward or forward. A second boy would next flip a card, according to his own style, hoping to match the heads or tails of the card already on the ground, and thus win it. Boys swore they could produce a heads or a tails at will, but the outcome of the contests belied that belief.

Older boys, those aged fourteen and up, who had long put their baseball cards away in shoe boxes under their beds or in grocery bags in their closets, gambled in more direct ways. Rather than converting their pennies to baseball cards, they pitted the coins head to head directly. Pitching pennies could be played by more than two boys at once, and it tended to attract crowds. The game was especially popular on Saturdays, when the fruits of collecting weighed heavily in the boys' pockets.

The only equipment needed, besides a pocketful of change, was something toward which to toss the coins. Preferably, that something was the riser of a stoop's bottom step or some other vertical surface, such as a building's wall. The ideal penny-pitching court was a concrete sidewalk, with its scored lines defining the bounds. A contestant stood at the curb and tossed a penny toward the wall, trying to get the coin as close as possible. The toss was more than a drop, but less than a throw; it was a pitch. Like flipping baseball cards, pitching pennies was done with a personal style and flair, different boys grasping the coin with different fingers in different configurations. Most held the coin lightly between the thumb and index finger. Some always held the coin heads up, others always tails up. Some boys swung their arms in great arcs from well behind the back; others used just an upward flick of the wrist to launch the coin. The most common release technique involved a low, flat, almost arcless trajectory toward the wall. When every contestant had pitched, the coin closest to the wall was the winner and its owner claimed all the other coins that had been pitched short.

The hardness and coarseness of concrete and brick surfaces were unforgiving, and a penny whose edge did not strike either the sidewalk or the wall quite right was likely to roll out of bounds or bounce back toward the curb. The ideal pitch was one that made the penny skid or skip, like a flat stone on a still pond, up to the wall and snuggle against it. Just about the only thing that could beat a kisser like that would be a leaner, when the coin somehow, usually by rolling forward slowly, ended up leaning against the wall. A leaner made it obvious whose coin had won. Even without a leaner, the result was usually obvious. But every now and then two or more coins would lie almost equidistant from the wall, if far from each other, and an impartial spectator, of which several were always on the sidelines, was enlisted to decide the winner. The most common way of doing so was to find something like a broom straw, candy wrapper, matchbook, or cigarette pack in the gutter and measure the distance of the coins from the wall. The task of measuring was not always performed without contention. When the delivery truck was especially late, pitching pennies could escalate to pitching nickels, dimes, and even quarters against the brick wall, and some paperboys could be in danger of not having enough change left in their pockets to pay for the week's papers.

Though there likely were some boys who were introduced to a life of gambling by these dalliances with baseball cards and coins, most *Press* boys either lost interest in these activities or soon realized that the odds of winning big were not worth the risk of even a modest monetary loss. These same boys were willing to sacrifice their bodies to their competitive urges, however, and the game in which to do that was the handball game called Kings in a version known as Moons Up.

Like pitching pennies, handball required a court defined by a wall, a sidewalk, and a curb. The number of sections in the concrete sidewalk between the delivery door of the *Press* office and the rear entrance to the drugstore on the corner defined how many boys could play at one time. Unlike in the other games, in handball the spotlight was more on losers than on winners.

In Kings, each competitor had his space defined by the section of concrete in which he stood. The players lined up according to how close to the curb they had gotten the ball to rebound from the wall, and they lined up in the descending order of a card suit: Ace, King, Queen, and so forth. The boy occupying the first section of sidewalk, the Ace spot, was the server. He stood perpendicular to the wall, looking down the line of players, who usually began the game facing him. When the ball was put into play, the positions of the boys in the middle was constantly changing, as they turned to face whoever had a play on the ball.

Because of the limited space between the curb and the wall, the ball always had to be bounced on the ground before hitting the wall, and it was kept in play by being returned directly off the wall or after at most one bounce on the sidewalk. The ball had to be kept in play by the boy in whose sidewalk section it landed. A player who did not keep the ball in play added a letter of the word K-I-N-G-S to his score and had to go to the end of the line. As players completed the word, they were eliminated, and the last player remaining was the winner.

Moons Up was a variation of Kings in which the first boy eliminated had to stand around for the game to end, at which time his moon became the target of the ball. The loser had to crouch down on the sidewalk, with his head held between his arms and facing the wall, and his rear end up in the air and facing the curb. The other players took turns throwing the ball at the loser's behind. The idea was to throw the ball as hard as possible and try to get the loser to say "Uncle," or better yet to get him to cry. The winner of the game got to throw the ball first, and so had the first chance to bring the loser, who had already been brought to his knees, to admit that he had had enough. The other boys lined up for their throws in the order in which they were eliminated from the game.

Getting the mooner to cry or drop out of the next game was better than winning for the collective victors. The game lent itself to picking on one boy, with everyone trying to return killer shots to his square, and it was much crueler and more unfair than any game involving baseball cards or pennies. When the delivery truck was especially late on a Sunday morning, but still before the sun came up, the loser at handball often had to produce a real moon for the boys to throw at, one that was unprotected by dungarees or even underpants. The game taught some of us humility; it gave others glee.

All games stopped as soon as the *Press* truck rounded the corner. Some boys ran to the front of the store to get in line for drawing their papers. These were seldom the boys who had been humiliated on the handball court. Another group ran into the back door to form a brigade to unload the truck, realizing that the more help back there the faster everyone would get out on his route. Thus there formed two distinct lines of boys, parallel in space but divergent in purpose.

Each day's newspaper was itself distinguished by two parallel lines, two long straight rules that ran across the entire width of the top of the front page. It was here that the declarations could be found that marked each day's paper as a new edition in a long tradition. But I had been delivering the *Press* for over a year before I read what had fallen between the lines: This day's paper was appearing in the 135th Year of publication of the paper; it was issue No. 247 in that year; it was the news for Tuesday, September 6, 1955; it was "Entered as Second Class Matter at Postoffice, Jamaica, N.Y."; it was twenty-four pages thick; and it cost five cents. Below all this were the day's headlines:

Chinese Reds Free 9 Yank Civilians
Mom 'Can't Wait to See' Freed GI
Pressure Mounts on Ike to Say He'll Run Again
Denies She Robbed Nude Suitor
DiMag Says Bums Can't Win Series
Hurricane Flora No Threat to U.S.
UN Says Egypt Violated Truce
Nationalist Flag Flies on Red Isle
Fire Threatens Sequoia Forest
Sammy Davis Jr. Nabbed as Speeder
2 Killed in Holiday's Last Hour

What did Joe DiMaggio know about the Brooklyn Dodgers? His sarcasm about their not being able even to say the word "Yankees" without calling them lucky was lost on a thirteen-year-old. Some of us didn't even remember seeing him play baseball. We knew him more for his marriage to Marilyn Monroe, whose picture often appeared in the *Press*. Where did DiMaggio get off saying that the Dodgers suffered from "deep psychological problems"?

All the headlines and stories—regardless of whether they were weird, world, national, or local news—were folded together into a twenty-four-page omelet by *Press* boys like me, usually oblivious to the content and focused on the size of the edition. For myself, I had especially liked the size of the previous day's paper. It was zero pages, for Labor Day was one of the few days off for *Press* boys. The paper also skipped publication on the Fourth of July, Thanksgiving, Christmas, and New Year's Day. For the other 360 days of the year, it was never the news but the number of pages, the most inconspicuous little piece of information, always located in the upper-right-hand corner of the front page, that first caught the eye of the paperboy. Few subscribers noticed it, let alone paid attention to it. But to the paperboy, even one with a year's experience, it signaled whether he would fold the day's papers single or double, whether he would fold the paper entire or stuff that day, whether the day's papers would fill one bag or two, and whether he would struggle that day riding his bike up the hill from Springfield Boulevard to the plateau of Cambria Heights.

After the number of pages in the paper, it was the weather forecast that most interested the paperboy. The ride to the *Press* office was sufficient to tell him whether it was raining or threatening to, but forecasts were also important in letting him know the conditions expected after he delivered his papers, which was the more critical time as far as his subscribers, and therefore his circulation manager, were concerned. If the papers were delivered at five o'clock in the afternoon and it began raining at five-thirty, chances were a lot of papers were still going to be lying out on stoops and walks and so were going to get wet. Once I had gambled that it would not rain and delivered my papers accordingly. No sooner had I gotten home than it began to pour. A half hour later I got a call from Mr. V telling me how many angry calls he had gotten from my customers and that I had better get back to the office and get some dry papers to doorknob.

"The Weather," when I first began to deliver papers, was in a box so labeled in the upper-left-hand corner of the front page, giving the forecast for that night and the next day. Watching this box daily gave me reason to be skeptical about weather forecasts generally. Since the *Press* forecast was the only one we had, we still read it, but increasingly we studied the sky as we rode our bikes to the office. Before beginning to fold our papers on a cloudy day, we walked outside the *Press* office and made a judgment about what to expect. In time, the paper itself stopped giving top billing to the weather. In its place were advertisements for feature stories and for ads themselves: BEST FOOD BUYS OF THE WEEK! SEE PAGES 21 TO 33.

In the upper-right-hand corner of the front page was a box identifying the edition of the newspaper, and different "final" editions were signaled by different numbers of stars. Breaking news stories often drove older news off the front page. On one Thursday, for example, the three-star final edition of the *Press* carried the banner headline COPS ROUND UP 'BEACH BANDITS.' A gang of six boys, pretending to be playing ball, had snatched a purse from the sand at Rockaway Beach, continuing a spree of similar incidents. Below the fold, in the bottom left of the front page, was another headline, announcing BOY SCOUT DIES AT CAMP, SPINAL MENINGITIS FEARED. The five-star edition of the same day's paper had a new banner headline, MENINGITIS SCARE HITS SCOUT CAMP, and the story about the beach bandits, while still above the fold, had been downgraded to a single column headed TEENSTERS PREY ON BATHERS.

Knowing the edition that we *Press* boys delivered, the commuter going home to his wife and two sons, who were scheduled to go to camp that summer, might have snatched up another edition from the newsstand to read on the subway. Whether the *Press* hoped to sell more newspapers by updating the headlines throughout the afternoon I cannot say, but the microfilmed archives suggest that the *Press* went through as many as seven editions each afternoon. The evolving headlines emphasized the urgency of the news, especially the local stories, in a time when an afternoon paper was still an essential thing to most people.

The Sunday paper, coming out on the morning that people sleep late, had fewer pretensions of being serious about breaking news. It devoted one of the boxes on the top of the front page to announcing that the paper cost ten cents that day, rather than the daily nickel, and the weather forecast was relegated to being a filler at the bottom of a story that did not fill the column. The inconspicuousness of the weather forecast put it in its place for the day of rest.

Another feature of the front page had a similar role as filler most days of the week. Nevertheless, other than the paper's size and the weather in which it was to be delivered, "Today's Chuckle" was often a topic of discussion in the *Press* office. The name always reminded me of the colorful gumdrop candies in a cardboard tray. Everyone had a favorite order in which to eat the licorice, lemon, orange, lime, and cherry jellies, and that was mine. As a small child I had prized the empty tray as a coal chute to play with at the beach. As a paperboy, I threw it away.

I was introduced to "Today's Chuckle" my very first week delivering papers. The first few offerings provided not only a fair representation of the genre but also an insightful quality that seemed to have an uncanny relevance to life: "A boy becomes a man when he stops asking his father for money and requests a loan." "Everyone is of some use in the world, even if only to serve as a horrible example."

The relevance to my life was uncanny. I had asked my father for a loan to put up the bond that I needed to become a *Press* boy, a *Press* man. I had also provided in my first days a horrible example of a paperboy. But after only a few days of disastrous failures, I had learned to fold papers and flip them with precision. And after only a few weeks I had come to be fully comfortable among my fellow entrepreneurs. I had helped unload the truck several times, and I had learned how to insert. My first Sunday's initiation was a thing of the distant past, and it was never mentioned, even when initiating another new boy. And I had been both the recipient and the deliverer of a hard Spalding to the ass. Progress came fast to a serious *Press* boy.

On those rare occasions when the daily chuckle was pushed off the front page, the *Press* office took on the pall of a bus stop, with everyone standing at the folding benches paging through the paper searching for the daily joke. The competition to find it was as intense as a game of Moons Up, but uncharacteristically urbane for the office. Reading "Today's Chuckle" in the *Press* office was as much a communal event as reading a fortune cookie at a Chinese restaurant.

"Today's Chuckle" was alternately wry and racy, at least for boys in their early teens, and even those chuckles that we did not fully understand had the ring of truth to them because of the voice of authority in which they were couched. "Self-made men usually have a lot of working parts." I was immediately hooked on the chuckle, and have never lost my passion for reading one-liners. When I discovered "Daffynitions" on the editorial page, I had a new respect for the inside of the paper. "BEER: A beverage that's used to improve the taste of salt." I didn't always understand their meaning, but I knew that daffynitions contained information I should know.

After more than a year at it, I knew that being a paperboy agreed with me. I had started my route on a hot August day, when Long Island was experiencing soaring temperatures, but I had survived. I had plowed my bike through the snow when cars were being abandoned in the street. I had survived the downpours that forced me to doorknob all of my papers on three occasions during my second week on the route. I had grown accustomed to going to bed early on Saturday evening and waking up before 4:00 a.m. on Sunday mornings. I reveled in the distinction of being awake while almost everyone else was asleep.

Like a seasoned milkman, an experienced paperboy progressed through his route at a sure and predictable rate, and so in time I could tell within a couple of houses where I would be at a given time on Sunday morning. Some paperboys were instructed to put a customer's paper into the milk box, which made for another affinity between the deliveryman and -boy. A thick Sunday paper—whether folded, stuffed, or flat—would not fit easily into the box, and the lid was left ajar, like a milk-bottle cap pushed up by a plug of frozen cream.

Early on, I had come to like riding my bicycle through the dark and deserted streets on Sunday mornings, taking an alternate route when I wanted to be free of the milkman's rigid ways. I had quieted the mysterious noise from my front wheel by removing the odometer. The only sound the bike made was the click of the pedal crank on the kickstand, but I could control that at will, by using the heel of my sneaker to reset the stand every few revolutions of the crank. To this day I seek to replicate the quiet and solitude of a Sunday-morning ride to the *Press* office whenever I am working. I have even let an old mantel clock run down because its ticking reached my ears in my study, three rooms away. I also came to eschew wrist-watches because their ticking, like a dripping faucet, is too much like a water torture to me.

The odometer was no longer necessary, because I knew from many a clocking that it was exactly 0.8 mile from my home to the *Press* office. I also knew that it was 1.2 miles from the office to the start of my route, 1.5 miles to cover my route from start to finish, and about 0.5 mile to get back home and deliver my last paper, to my mother. I thus put about four miles on my bike each day, just delivering papers, and the signs of wear accumulated like distance and time.

Even when I took a totally new detour, I didn't need an odometer to know how far I had ridden. I had come to be able to tell how far I had come by the feel of my feet on the pedals and my seat on the saddle. My sense of distance had become calibrated through my body, and I unconsciously knew how far I was going and how far I had to go, not only to deliver my papers but to ride into regions unknown. Time was calibrated to biking distance, and so neither did I need a watch. I knew how long it took me to get to the *Press* office and to deliver the route. All other sense of time followed from these fundamentals.

Similarly, drawing papers every day, folding them, packing them, and delivering them had developed in me a sense of quantity. Just as Henry David Thoreau, working in his father's pencil factory, could tell by feel when he had exactly one dozen pencils in his hand, so I could look at a pile of papers and have a good idea whether I had drawn the right amount. Likewise I could tell by looking at the aggregate whether a customer had given me ten pennies or nine on collection day. Developing senses of quantity would serve me well as an engineering student and later as an engineer.

For all these heightened senses of distance, time, and number, beyond the *Press* office banter I did not develop a strong sense of how to interact with people. My communications with customers and adults generally were clipped and quick. I could have engaged them in conversation about "The Weather" or "Today's Chuckle," but I could not tell them from what state Senator Joseph McCarthy came or what was the significance of the Chinese island of Quemoy. As bold as the headlines might be and as often as the stories about national politics and international affairs were repeated, what I saw in the papers that I folded every day did not register. After seeing the number of pages in the paper, if my eye wandered from "The Weather" and "Today's Chuckle," it was because of headlines like MOTHER ABANDONS LITTLE BOY and BOY KILLS HIS MOTHER IN ACCIDENTAL SHOOTING. I couldn't imagine such actions, and so I had to read about them.

It could not have been that I didn't see headlines about McCarthy and Chiang Kai-shek, for had I not seen them I would also not have seen the stories about boys being arrested and sent to reform school. Rather, I had no personal interest in hard news. I and most of my fellow paperboys were embryonic technocrats, focused on the mechanics of folding and packing and flipping and collecting. The *Long Island Press* was a thing to be delivered, not a thing to be read, at least for the moment.

If a rare story did become a matter of discussion among the paperboys, it was because of its potential impact on us. One such story was headlined 18-YEAR-OLDS ARE TOO YOUNG TO DRINK! LAWMAKER WANTS AGE RAISED TO 21. Those boys who were already seventeen and had been looking forward to being of legal age in a matter of months became deeply engaged in the story, and they interrupted their folding and packing to read and discuss it in the *Press* office. Those of us who were still thirteen and fourteen did not see what there was to get excited about and so went on folding and packing. As we did not appreciate what the implications of stories about Joe McCarthy and Chiang Kai-shek might be for us as adults, so we did not appreciate how passionately we too might feel about the issue of drinking age as we approached it. "Today's Chuckle" was about as much reading and thinking as any of us younger boys wanted to do out of school. School was the place where we had to pay attention to civics and geography. A *Press* route was where we gained experience and made money.

9

GYP BUREAU URGED FOR
LONG ISLAND

THE ECONOMICS OF A PAPER ROUTE were simple. A *Press* boy bought his papers wholesale and sold them retail. He was charged four cents for each daily and eight cents for each Sunday paper that he received, and he sold them at a 25 percent markup, meaning the customer paid forty cents per week to have the daily and Sunday paper delivered. In other words, the paperboy made a base profit of eight cents per customer per week.

The weekly bill from the newspaper company for a route of one hundred papers came to thirty-two dollars. If the paperboy collected the forty cents due from each of the subscribers, he netted a profit of eight dollars for the week. Assuming the time spent delivering and collecting was eight hours a week, this amounted to a dollar an hour, which was well above the minimum wage of seventy-five cents that prevailed in the mid-1950s. In a typical week the paperboy made about twice the base amount, because most customers tipped, with the most common tip being a dime on a forty-cent subscription. The paperboy took home about fifteen dollars a week, and taxes were never mentioned.

Tipping was an integral part of life in New York City. Just about everyone who performed some kind of service was tipped, if not at the time of service then annually in the form of a Christmas gift, most often of cash, sometimes in an envelope but more frequently just from a closed fist to an opened fist. Like a lot of their fellow New Yorkers, *Press* boys expected and counted on their tips year-round.

In spite of its benefits, collecting for the paper was an aspect of the job that was unappealing to many of the *Press* boys, for it took a lot of time, required precise record-keeping, and involved interacting directly with the customers. I did not mind the time or record-keeping so much as talking to the customers. I was, at least at first, rather shy and quiet around adults, and would have preferred to carry out the process of collecting on some less personal level, but that was not the way monetary transactions took place in New York and its environs. Money was most commonly exchanged face-to-face. In time, I became more comfortable ringing doorbells and asking for money, but it did take a while.

Usually I began my weekly collecting late on Friday afternoon. I would deliver my route first, for we paperboys were reminded frequently that the customers wanted their paper delivered as early as possible. If I was seen standing on a stoop collecting for the paper I was holding in my hand when the subscriber next door came out looking for her paper, which was still in my *Press* bag in my bike basket leaning against a tree, my circulation manager might hear about it. If he did, I would certainly hear about it from him. Even if he did not hear a complaint, I would not likely get a very good tip that week.

My not atypical style of collecting was to go up to the front door, ring the bell, and wait for someone to open the door or shout from inside the house, "Who is it?" My response was usually "*Press* boy." Sometimes I said only "*Press.*" Most customers put two and two together and nothing more needed to be said, which suited me fine. When I was asked what I wanted, which seemed to be a silly question, since just about the only time the *Press* boy rang the doorbell was to collect, I would respond, "Collecting." If I felt especially loquacious, I would answer, "Collecting for the *Press.*"

The woman of the house, and it was almost invariably a woman who answered the bell, would go back to get the money or bring her purse to the door and fish around in it for the right amount of coins. There was a story told among the older *Press* boys of a woman coming to the door wearing a bathrobe that was not tied in the front, so that as she turned to get the money or reached to open the door the boy caught a glimpse of her underwear or, in one version, her naked breasts. Such was an opportunity that all paperboys looked out for, but few if any really experienced. Every Friday evening, after a few houses of anticipation, most *Press* boys forgot about sex and concentrated on money.

Every customer should have known what she owed, and so the question "How much?" was seldom asked. When the door opened and the money was dropped into my hand, I always said, "Thank you," and usually nothing else. On those rare occasions when a man answered the door, he frequently asked, "What's the damage?" I would tell him, but it seemed like a dumb expression, for there was no damage. The paper cost the same from week to week, and even when the new section, *TV Time of the Week,* was added, the *Press* reassured its subscribers, "The price of the Sunday Press will continue to be ten cents."

Most customers counted out the exact amount they wanted to give me, which often included a nickel or dime tip. If they gave me two quarters, I fished around for change in the handful of coins I pulled out of my pocket. If the customer hadn't by then said, "Keep the change," or "Just give me a nickel back," she was unlikely to give me a tip. Nevertheless, when I did have to give ten cents in change, I gave two nickels, because that not only lightened my load of coins more than a dime would have, but also held out the slim possibility that I would get at least one of the nickels back. To this day, I am surprised whenever a waiter or waitress brings me change in bills larger than should reasonably be expected as a tip.

For the first few weeks of collecting, I had entered in my *Press* book the exact amount paid, including tip, so that by summing the entries in a week's column I could tell the total amount of money I had collected. This usually agreed within a dollar or two with the money in my pockets, and I attributed any discrepancy to the change I had started with but had not remembered to count beforehand. After several weeks, it became very clear that 90 to 95 percent of the customers gave the exact same amount each week, and so I began just to check off whether someone paid the usual amount.

Most customers were as honest with the paperboy as they were with the corner candy store, which left the morning papers, which were generally not delivered in Queens by boys, unattended on the sidewalk out front. The *Times,* the *News,* the *Mirror,* and the *Wall Street Journal* were arranged in separate piles on a makeshift low counter consisting of a plank of wood resting across two soda cases. The piles were kept in place in windy weather by lead weights with the logos of the newspapers cast into them, but more often than not a particular paperweight was upside down or on the pile of a competing paper. Regardless, the practiced newspaper buyer could, like a jokester yanking a tablecloth out from under everything, on the run pull a copy of the *Times* from atop the pile, leaving the paperweight undisturbed. On windless days, the unnecessary weights were set aside, but the papers were occasionally topped by a scattering of coins that had missed the cigar box at the end of the plank. In these cases, commuters rushing for the bus deftly slid the next-lower paper in the pile out from beneath the coin-topped one. The pile was otherwise left undisturbed, as was the cigar box full of cash, which was dipped into only to make change for a dime or a quarter. It was mostly a time of trust and good citizenship. Even if we were tough, the vast majority of us were honest.

Curiously, in a city with so many morning and afternoon newspapers, there were in the 1950s few newsboys standing on New York street corners hawking the day's latest final edition or the evening's "Extra!" The ubiquitous candy store, cigar store, and streetside newsstand had obviated them. Nevertheless, the image of the young boy holding a sheaf of loose papers under one arm and waving an example in the face of passersby remained the prevalent dramatic image of the news disseminator. The statue of Thomas Edison on the bank of the St. Clair River in Port Huron depicts him as a news butch, and celebrates his selling fruit and the *Detroit Free Press* for as much as he could get in railroad coaches and on the platforms where they stopped.

The newspaper boy in Manhattan or Brooklyn, I imagined, had a route entirely contained in just one or two large apartment buildings, and could be, like young Edison, a pedestrian. With a bag slung like a sash over his shoulder, the city kid walked up stairs and down hallways dropping the daily paper flat before doors that no wind reached. He did not need to learn how to fold or flip a paper or even how to ride a bike. But he did have to collect and then protect his earnings from the bullies in the stairwells. Ironically, in his mode of transportation, the boy delivering to apartment dwellers may have been closer to the carrier boy in a small company town than to his counterpart in Cambria Heights. If the town and the subscription list were small or compact enough, there was no need to ride a bicycle to cover the territory or to bear the burden of the Thursday papers. But no matter where a newspaper boy found himself, he often had the same two chief responsibilities: delivering daily and collecting weekly.

On foot or on the seat of a bicycle, the young newspaper boy, often in shirt and tie and knickers with his canvas bag slung lightly over his shoulder, remains a most enduring icon of the early to mid twentieth century. It is at heart a solidly wholesome Midwestern image. We New York City paperboys wore black leather jackets and motorcycle boots and combed our hair into DAs as soon as school was out. The closest we got to the Midwestern ethos was through the route books used by the *Long Island Press,* which were manufactured and distributed by a firm in Lafayette, Indiana.

Route Book Size No. 1, which we used, had a title page, if it could be called that, announcing, "This Carrier's Route Book is the

Property of _____ Newspaper." Maybe in the Midwest, where authority might have been taken seriously, the newspaper owned the book and maybe just loaned it to the carrier. No *Press* boy in Queens believed for a second that his belonged to the paper. A *Press* book, like a *Press* bag, was bought from the circulation manager, who kept a supply in the trunk of his 1947 Cadillac sedan. The paperboy had to pay for each item, and that made it his to use and abuse as he saw fit. The route book was merely a convenient place to keep track of who paid and who didn't pay and who was generous at Christmas, though no one needed a book to remember that.

Below the false declaration of ownership, the title page had a blank to be filled in after "Route No." There was also a space for the "Carriers' name and home address," as if more than one boy were needed to deliver a route covering just two compact, if long, suburban streets spanning three suburban avenues. Even if he had to crowd it onto and below one line, a *Press* boy did find space on the page to write his address. He certainly did not subscribe to the printed note stating, "If this book is lost, finder will kindly notify this newspaper." The title page had it all wrong. The newspaper boy in the Midwest might have been a "little merchant" working for a paper, but the *Press* boy, even at the outer edges of New York City, was a tough entrepreneur who dealt in cash.

If the front matter of the route book was ridiculed, the back matter was completely ignored. One page was headed "This Book Issued to Carrier _____(date)_____ with _____ Total Subscribers." Beneath were spaces for the carrier to keep a weekly tally of "Starts" and "Stops" and "Total Subscribers," with spaces at the bottom to summarize the "Gain" and "Loss." These columns made little sense to a *Press* boy, since he had to deal with some distinct daily-only and Sunday-only subscribers.

Even if they didn't keep the numbers in their books, all *Press* boys knew exactly how many papers they had to draw each day, and many of them tried to get an extra or two. Each boy was entitled to a carrier's own copy—a COC—but that, if it was not taken home, was often delivered and collected for off the books. The station-

master kept the official count, adding a paper for every new subscriber we brought in and subtracting one for every stop or vacation
reported on the appropriate form. All the paperboy ultimately
cared about was the financial bottom line, the difference between
how much he collected each week and how much he owed to the
heavy man in the black suit.

Newspapers ultimately cared about the same thing, of course,
and they in turn collected from two sources: advertisers and readers. Adult employees may have brought in revenue from the former, but it was the network of small corner stores, newsstands, and
the army of paperboys that provided links with the latter. Paperboys were a mainstay of the enterprise, and so they were cultivated.

A group of newspaper publishers had formed an organization
known as the Newspaper Boys of America, "to promote the general
welfare and business training" of their delivery force. In a handbook issued in 1932 from its national headquarters in Indianapolis,
the NBA was compared to the Boy Scouts, and in a foreword to parents the benefits of letting their children deliver newspapers was
spelled out:

> As a member of the "N.B.A." your boy plays an important part
> in one of the greatest businesses of modern times—the distri-
> bution of the daily news to home, office, street and factory. It
> gives him a chance to render a real service to his community,
> and to earn a regular and substantial sum of money for his work.
> It keeps him busy in the spare hours of the day, when idle boys
> might be in mischief. It helps to develop good habits, by teach-
> ing him the value of time, money, honesty and courtesy. It
> instructs him how to meet, talk to and deal with people. It
> teaches him business methods by training him to make regular
> collections and reports to his team captain, coach or station
> manager.

If we *Long Island Press* carriers were members of the NBA, neither we nor our families ever knew it. We were never asked to take

the pledge to "play the game fairly and squarely," nor did we receive Junior Pledge Cards whereby we agreed to work toward earning, in our first six months on the job, the four seals designated Punctuality, Junior Carrier, Junior Collector, and Junior Salesman. *Press* boys no more knew the meaning of "junior" in this context than I did the suffix I casually appended to my name. Once we were initiated by being stripped of our pants and splintered by a utility pole, we didn't need anyone to tell us we were full members of the *Press* office. After that, who could tell us to report for work "every day for the first month, with clean hands and face, hair combed, shoes shined, clothes brushed and teeth cleaned" just to earn a Punctuality Seal? Our circulation manager was a thug, not a coach, and all you could get for a seal and a nickel was five pennies, if you were lucky.

No one tested a *Press* boy, as NBA captains did a junior member, for his "ability to properly fold twelve papers in the required time, and properly fold papers while walking his route." That may have earned a Junior Carrier Seal for a kid in Peoria, say, but no one walked a route in Cambria Heights, except maybe his first few days. We tested ourselves. Nor would we have earned a Junior Collector Seal, as a St. Louis carrier-in-training might, for keeping "a neat, clean and accurate record of collection, with all of his subscribers' names and addresses properly entered." If we knew the names of half a dozen people on our route, we were lucky. And no one but ourselves got to look at our route books. To us, the Midwest was where the weather came from, not the model for how to be a paperboy.

To earn the Junior Salesman Seal in Kansas City, a boy might have had to have perfect attendance at the weekly Night School meetings, know all the editorial features in the paper, make an acceptable sales talk at Night School, and prove himself a salesman by signing up a new subscriber a week. Since our circulation manager moonlighted as a chauffeur, he could not lead a night school. We learned what we learned about folding, delivering, and collecting from the boys beside us at the bench. The introduction to our obligations came through our inheritance of a nameless route list penciled on a piece of loose-leaf paper or on a ragged sheet torn from a spiral-bound school notebook or on the back of a newspaper subscription card. Some departing carriers would not even hand this over until the last day of their last week, after they had collected the route for the last time. If a departing carrier did otherwise, the new carrier might collect the route before he was entitled to. On some occasions, it was rumored, the old carrier continued to collect the week after the new boy had taken over the route. But these remained unsubstantiated rumors.

Any meeting that we had as a group was held early on a Saturday afternoon, before the delivery truck arrived. At such a meeting we might be told that we would get two extra papers free each day of the coming week for use in canvassing for new subscribers. For some boys, this meant that they would have to steal two fewer papers to cover their unreported customers over the next week. For other boys, it meant that they would not have to buy a couple of papers at the corner candy store when they came up short at the end of their route. Even though they would count and recount their draw in front of the stationmaster, as I did my first week, some of the newer boys would now and then find themselves "losing" papers between the draw at the *Press* office and the end of their route. The thieves must have worked in pairs at the folding bench, one distracting and the other snatching the papers.

Presumably, such things did not happen in the Midwest. When Junior Newspaper Boys in Iowa City filled their pledge cards with the four seals, they became Senior Newspaper Boys, at which time they were awarded the organization's official belt buckle. The only belt buckles some *Long Island Press* boys cared about were the heavy brass ones that could be swung at the end of a wide black leather belt, preferably covered with metal bosses and studs. This was the weapon of choice in tough high schools, to fend off knife attacks, or so I was told. Some of my fellow *Press* boys sharpened the edges of their belt buckles on the curb as they waited for the delivery truck. 3 BOYS HELD IN 'BELT HOLDUP.'

Membership cards, certificates, medals, contests, prizes, and scholarships meant little to boys who kept a cigarette behind their ear, a pack in their sleeve, and matches in their pocket, possibly along with a switchblade knife. Their career plans were to drop out of school as soon as they were sixteen years old. These were the boys who admired the circulation manager's black Caddy and who talked with him in whispers behind the *Press* office. If a circulation manager in the Midwest kept his eye out for gung-ho delivery boys who might move into training positions with the newspaper after high school, some circulation managers in Queens were looking for thugs-in-waiting who could become gofers and flunkies and drivers of black cars.

Not even the most forceful of adults was going to get a storefront full of streetwise tough guys to sit around a *Press* office and sing songs while waiting for the papers to come. The Night School games and activities that the NBA encouraged to develop camaraderie and loyalty to the newspaper enterprise were distinctly Midwestern. Who can imagine New Yorkers with Irish and Italian names, with red or black hair, wearing sleeveless white T-shirts and greasy duck's-ass haircuts, singing:

> *My name is Yon Yonson,*
> *Aye come from Visconsin,*
> *Aye verk in de lumber mills dere.*
> *Ven aye valk down de street,*
> *All de people aye meet,*
> *Dey say, "Hello, vat's your name?"*
> *And aye say,*
> (Repeat)

The inside back cover of the Midwestern route book had a table headed "Savings Deposits," which was also seldom filled in by *Press* boys. There was a space at the top to record the "Cash Bond" deposited with the circulation manager, and long columns for savings deposits. But if a *Press* boy saved, he did so in a Christmas Club at a nearby bank. What did not get put away for Christmas was deposited in the candy store or the record store or the bicycle shop. It certainly did not get deposited with our circulation manager, for we all had heard stories of what happened to cash bonds. The bond, which went up with the number of papers we delivered, returned no interest, and the principal itself might never be returned at all.

The Newspaper Boys of America culture did not travel well from the Midwest to the East Coast, in its songs or in its discipline, and so it would have been little surprise if the *Long Island Press* was not a member. The paper merely passed on to its carriers, for a price, the necessary route books that just happened to be printed in Indiana and happened to reflect the Midwestern values of the NBA. These books were used grudgingly and selectively by the *Press* boys, who only wanted to collect enough on Friday evening to pay for the week's papers, so that everything collected on Saturday would be gravy. Most of the features of the book were ignored, but the book itself was not.

The *Press* book was, like an engineer's field book, made for rough use under rugged conditions. The pages were composed of good rag-content paper stock that would long outlast the newsprint of the *Press* itself. The design of the route book was also not unlike that of a teacher's grade book, containing as it did alternating full and half pages, the latter leaving exposed names next to which numbers were to be entered. In the *Press* book, instead of space for the names of pupils, the two wide columns on each left-hand full page of the route book were headed, without regard for agreement, "Names" and "Residence." All the other columns on that page and the three that followed it were headed "Week Ending" and sub-headed, with similar disregard for number and for tense, "Owe" and "Paid." When the half page was turned over, it covered all but the "Names" column on the first page. As a result, *Press* boys did not enter names in the "Names" column, but put addresses there, for it was by their house numbers and not their names that our subscribers were known.

Most *Press* boys used the first "Week Ending" pair of columns to indicate whether the customer subscribed to the daily, Sunday, or daily and Sunday paper, thus effectively recording the amount due each week. There were nineteen additional "Week Ending" columns, and so in theory a route book could last for about four and a half months, meaning that a *Press* boy would go through about three books a year. In practice, few books lasted more than about three months. But they did look handsome when new.

The first entry in my first *Press* book was that of my own house, after which a name—Petroski—did appear in the "Residence" column. But though our address was listed first, I usually delivered our paper last, just in case I had been shorted a paper by the stationmaster or lost one when my back was turned. There were no entries in the Petroski "Paid" columns, and in later books our address was moved to the back to reflect my true order of delivery.

The second customer listed in my route book was 229-14 Linden, followed by the notation "Sam's." His store was not in my territory, and so I should not have been delivering to him, but the circumstances allowed it. When I had told Sam that I was going to deliver papers, he offered to take a subscription from me. My route book showed a notation next to his address that the paper was to be delivered "in store," and I gladly walked in each day and put the paper on the counter, usually exchanging a few words with Sam, but never when he was busy with a customer. I don't believe he read the *Press* very regularly, because I often found the previous day's paper still folded where I had left it on his counter. His subscription, like his store hours, was daily only, and he gave me a hefty fifteen-cent tip each time I collected the thirty cents due.

Customers living in adjacent houses naturally got adjacent lines in the *Press* book, but a blank line was left for each house skipped, just in case it decided to subscribe someday, or in case someone new moved into the house. New residents of Cambria Heights almost always subscribed to the *Press*, at least for the standard new-subscriber agreement period of thirteen weeks. I was fairly typical of *Press* boys in that the only houses I ever canvassed were those with a moving truck out front.

I believe I was also typical in the way I handled my *Press* book. As I walked back to my bicycle from each house, I took the book out of my left rear pocket and recorded the payment. I seldom used a ballpoint pen. The vast majority of my accounting was done with a black-lead pencil, over which the book was closed to hold the place like a bookmark. The book was then returned to my pocket and sat on as I rode my bike to the next house on the route. As good as the book's paper was and as well sewn as its binding was, no *Press* book could continue to look good for long the way it was used. My book acquired a characteristic dog-earing of the lower right corner, which was due to the way it was inserted into my pocket; a distinctive wear mark beside its spine, where the pencil increased its thickness; and a series of more-or-less parallel horizontal creases where it conformed to the shape of my left buttock. These signs of use grew progressively exaggerated as the book was opened and closed upwards of a thousand times and was not infrequently dampened by rain or snow. It was the rare book that lasted until all its columns were filled.

Though each new route book was a handsome thing—flat and straight and clean—as it quickly aged, the book's once light-blue cover became dark blue with newspaper ink and a paperboy's perspiration. Then it became progressively abraded, crazed, and creased from the bulging, folding, and bending to which it was subjected. In time, the blue covering became worn off in spots. The final stage of deterioration occurred when the blue laminate separated from the base entirely and so was torn off, leaving a thin buff-colored cover with the texture of old flannel pajamas. By the time this happened, the inside pages were as soft and pliable as a much-used dollar bill that had been left in a pants pocket and gone through the washing machine. Like such a bill, the book had eventually to be taken out of circulation.

If a route book looked bad after three or so months, the pencil that accompanied it looked worse. Most pencils started whole, but after being sat on repeatedly, few ended up more than an inch or so long. The point naturally broke first, and out on the route a pencil had to be repointed with a penknife or, in a pinch, with a piece of broken glass. In the beginning, I sharpened my pencils further by scraping the exposed lead on the sidewalk, as if it were a gigantic sandpaper pad. But no route-book pencil could hold a sharp point, and paperboys soon learned that the duller the point the less likely it was to break with use. With a short point as blunt as a piece of spaghetti, a long pencil body tended to break in half, leaving an eraserless stub that had to be held in the fingers like a bit in a brace. It was not comfortable, but it had only to be used to write two digits at a time.

Some customers made collecting and accounting very easy, like the lady who each week left me fifty cents under a basket behind her house. Only the odd customer seemed to think the paper was free. An especially awkward situation arose infrequently, when my records showed that the paper had not been paid for the week before. This meant that I had to tell the customer, "You owe for last week, too," which could amount to a bill of as much as eighty cents. On rare occasions, the customer would swear that she had paid the previous week. It didn't happen too often, but when it did I would write the week off as a loss and subsequently make a point of entering that customer's payments in my collection book before I left the stoop.

For all of the citizenship pledges that mothers must have signed, there still seemed to be gypping going on on Long Island, if *Press* headlines were any indication. But then again, maybe it was headline news because it actually happened so seldom. Once, the *Press* ran a "Press Spotlight" series on "Fly-by-Night Gyp Artists." It was ironic that some of the paper's subscribers themselves were "Stay-by-Night Gyp Artists," taking advantage of thirteen-year-old merchants who were never asked for or gave out any receipts. The *Press* book was the document of record, and only the gyppiest customers took advantage of the situation. Queens customers were supposed to be protected by the New York Better Business Bureau, the *Press* reminded its readers, but Nassau and Suffolk residents had no such champion. "Long Islanders are bilked out of thousands of dollars every year by fast-buck operators who prey on unwary home owners," according to the *Press,* but the paper never seemed to go to bat for the naive paperboy who was taken for forty cents, either by a cheap customer or by a shady circulation manager.

Since collecting on a Friday evening could take hours, I often went home about midway through my route to have supper. (I knew that it was not good for tips, not to mention not being polite, to collect during mealtime.) After supper, I returned to the route again to try to collect from the rest of the customers, often starting again at the beginning of the route to see if those who had not been home before dinner were there after. Collecting went on into the dark during the winter months, and it was always necessary to return on Saturday morning to catch those who had not been home on Friday evening.

After an evening of collecting, my pockets were full of money. I kept dollar bills in my left-front pocket and coins in my right-front, so that I could scoop them out with my right hand and count out change with my left. It felt natural for me to hand the change back with my left hand, though I learned that it was good manners to use the right to hand things to people. When asked whether I was right- or left-handed, I said right-, because that is the hand with which I write. But I was ambidextrous when it came to hitting a ball—I discovered a natural ability for switch-hitting at the plate—and to counting change. In fact, I was confused about my handedness, for I used a fork and flipped papers with my right hand, but I bowled and threw a ball with my left. To confuse myself further, I kicked tin cans with my left foot and footballs with my right. Regardless, I still had to keep the bills from the coins when collecting on my *Press* route, and I used my right- and left-front pockets to help me keep things separate.

The bills were kept folded over once, and I made sure each new one was added to the pile with George Washington facing the same way. On those rare occasions when I had to change a five- or ten-dollar bill, I put it on the bottom of the pile as I walked back to my bike, so that when I folded the bills over it looked like I had a pile of singles. When I pulled the roll of bills out of my pocket, I could peel off singles for change without revealing that I had larger ones inside. Some paperboys believed this was a way to make it appear that you had less money than you did, and so to be less likely to attract robbers. The competing philosophy present in the *Press* office was to fold the bills over with the largest bill facing out. This made you look like a big shot, seeming to have more money than you really did.

Coins were different, of course, and too many of them in the pocket were a distinct burden. If I was lucky, the candy store needed change and gave me paper for my silver. That was not always the case, however, and I often had to go home with my pockets heavy. I was happy to get home so I could take the coins out of my pocket and spread them out on the kitchen table to pile up and count and then wrap into colored paper tubes to take to the bank and exchange for bills. Mr. Vitalis would never let us pay our bill in coins, and so converting the change was a necessity.

Before rolling up any of them, I always went through the coins carefully, because I collected pennies and was on the lookout for dates and mint marks that I did not have. I kept all of the 1943 white pennies—we called them "lead pennies"; others called them zinc—that were actually made of zinc-coated steel to conserve copper during the war. I also kept all of the Indian-heads and a lot of Liberty coins. Though smooth as a greased washer between my fingers, with their ridges and knurled edges worn away, and dating from years now almost impossible to read, a lot of Liberty coins were still in circulation in the mid-1950s, at least on my paper route. Either my customers didn't care about the nature of these coins or they were dipping into their collections to pay for the paper. I would certainly dip into my own collection of Liberty-heads to buy the candy and soda I had more time for after I quit my *Press* route. I also kept silver certificates, because the word was that they were the only true dollars, redeemable on demand by a silver dollar coin. But they too were spent when necessary.

No one on my route ever gave me a check to pay for a subscription, and credit cards were unknown to us paperboys. People growing up in New York at mid-century became so accustomed to paying their bills in cash that they continued to do so even when long out of that milieu. One New Yorker I know, who after graduating from college went to work in the Midwest, would drive his car from phone company to power company to water company every month to pay his bills in cash. He got a receipt, but he promptly crumpled it up and discarded it among the spent tissues that piled up on the floor of his car's backseat during allergy season.

Though no one asked for or got a receipt from the paperboy, that is not to say that the same casualness existed between the paperboy and the *Press*. In fact, transactions between billing and collecting in the *Press* office were very serious and formal matters indeed. Each week each *Press* boy was presented with a carrier statement for the week ending on Saturday. The cumulative numbers of papers drawn daily and Sunday were listed, and the total amount due was stated. If collecting had gone especially well on Friday, if the bills were ready, and if we had been able to convert our silver to paper, the bill would be paid, in cash, on Saturday. Otherwise the bill would be paid on Monday.

One week, without warning, the statement carried an additional charge of forty-five cents for "insurance." The stationmaster explained that it was to cover doctor and hospital bills if we were hurt while on the job. We griped, but we paid the new charge. After a few months, in conjunction with the introduction of computer-printed bills by the *Press,* the insurance charge disappeared as suddenly as it had appeared. Then, after another few months, the charge reappeared, added by hand to each week's computerized bill. The extra amount wasn't written in the "insurance" column of the bill, however, and so we paperboys began to speculate that it was for something "off the books." When asked, Mr. Vitalis gave

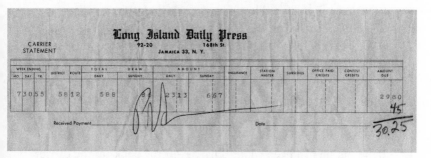

CARRIER STATEMENT

Long Island Daily Press
92-20 168th St.
JAMAICA 33, N. Y.

WEEK ENDING			DISTRICT	ROUTE	TOTAL		DRAW		AMOUNT		INSURANCE	STATION MASTER	SUBSIDIES	OFFICE PAID CREDITS	CONTEST CREDITS	AMOUNT DUE
MO.	DAY	YR.			DAILY	SUNDAY	DAILY	SUNDAY	DAILY	SUNDAY						
7	30	55	58	12	58	8			23 13	6 67						29 80

45
30.25

Received Payment _____   Date _____

A weekly bill

inconsistent answers. At first he said that it was for inserting, but
when some of the boys complained that they had helped the stationmaster insert and so shouldn't be charged, he said the money
was for a kind of insurance. Some of the older boys interpreted this
to mean it was for protection, so that our papers would not be
stolen and our bicycles not damaged. We younger paperboys felt
this was not something to challenge. We paid our bills promptly
and quietly.

After another few months, the extra charge again disappeared,
and shortly thereafter so did Mr. V. A new circulation manager
took over, and he spent a lot more time at the *Press* office, which was
soon repainted. Extra charges did not reappear on our carrier
statements, and fewer papers and inserts were unaccounted for.
The word around the *Press* office was that Vitalis was wanted by the
police, who had been going to some of the homes of former paperboys and asking them questions. It was only years later, long after I
had given up Route 5812, that I saw him again.

My father was atop a ladder painting the back of the house, and
I was working on my bike in the shade of the garage door. Mr. V
came into the backyard and, without any preface or small talk, told
us that he was there to return some bond money that was due us. I
had forgotten about the bond, since I had not myself paid it, but I
had the distinct impression that my father had not forgotten. He

came down from the ladder and approached Mr. Vitalis, but the two men did not shake hands. My father said nothing. In silence, Mr. V took a roll of bills from his pocket, with hundreds on top, opened it up to the fives and tens inside, and counted off the bond money due, gave it to my father, and left. My father muttered something about "the lousy show-off crook," but never did tell me the details of what had happened. My inference was that Vitalis had absconded with the bond money when the newspaper company found out he had been adding charges off the books to the carrier statements. Now, after being released, he was distributing the long-overdue bond money as part of his restitution.

In spite of the experience with Mr. Vitalis, most of my own transactions at the *Press* office were honest and straightforward. The stationmaster, the older, experienced boy who counted out the papers each day and kept the record of what each carrier drew, was central to the operation and integrity of the delivery system. It was he who made sure that the right number of bundles of papers was received from the delivery truck, and it was he who made sure that each bundle was stacked in the rear corner of the office and not diverted. (What happened after the younger boys left the counting bench was beyond his jurisdiction.)

When the bundles were all off the truck and accounted for, the stationmaster began to distribute the papers to the carriers, who lined up in front of the counter. The bundles were bound in wire so tightly that the top paper or two were usually cut through their edges. (Those papers went to customers who didn't tip.) The bundles were opened by wire-cutting tools that looked like squat pliers and were the prized possession of the stationmaster and a few of the older boys. When a pair of wire cutters could not be located, the whole process was slowed down. Bundles had to be undone by pulling a bunch of papers from the center of the bale to loosen the considerable grip of the wire on the rest. This was naturally much more time-consuming and difficult than just snipping the wire.

The same wire cutters that were used to open the bundles of papers were also on occasion used for mischief. The spokes on my bike's front wheel were cut one afternoon, but I didn't discover the vandalism until I was riding toward Springfield Boulevard and heard a curious tinkling sound. The half-dozen or so cut spokes were located at different places around the wheel and so did not render it totally useless. The missing spokes did, however, distort the wheel to the point where it began to rub against the fork tines, and as soon as I had finished my route I stopped by Sam's to buy replacement spokes and a spoke wrench. I spent the evening replacing spokes and truing the tireless wheel on my upside-down bike in the driveway. Who cut the spokes and why were questions I didn't ask, and since the incident was not repeated I took it as a random practical joke by someone who had gotten a new pair of wire cutters. It happened to other *Press* boys all the time, even when we all believed we were paying insurance against it happening.

I paid small heed to such little annoyances. A few clipped spokes, easily replaced, or an extra forty-five cents added to the weekly bill, seemed like a small price to pay for what my *Press* route was teaching me.

10

CAUGHT BY A SLEEPLESS CONSCIENCE

DELIVERING AND EVEN COLLECTING on my paper route had become routine, and I had come to count on the money I was making. Some of it was to be saved, to be sure, "for high school," but I did have a lot more pocket money than when I relied on a weekly allowance from my parents, even with a supplement from Aunt Jean. I had been able to buy packs of baseball cards, stacks of 45-rpm records, boxes of model car and plane kits, piles of *Hot Rod* and *Motor Trend* magazines, and numerous electric-train accessories with what I made from the paper route. Now and then I even bought a pack of cigarettes, nursing an egg cream until there was no other customer in the candy store to witness the purchase. I kept the pack hidden in the garage, away from my mother's eyes or hands, but where I could easily stow and retrieve it under the pretense of putting my bicycle away or getting it out.

Because I delivered papers each afternoon, I had developed few strong after-school relationships with my one-year Sacred Heart classmates, and I had pretty much lost touch with them after graduation. My summer was spent mostly with Jim Wall, whose house was in shouting distance of mine but who always called on the phone when he wanted to talk with me. When the weather was dreary, we hung out in his basement, going through baseball cards and listening to records. When the sun was out, we rode our bikes everywhere.

Jim's grandmother, who lived with his family, called his bike a "wheel," and so we began jokingly to call every bicycle a wheel, not appreciating that the name was really apt only for the high-wheeled "penny-farthing" she probably remembered from her girl-hood days in Ireland. The machine's nickname derived from two English coins of the time. The penny-farthing's profile was domi-nated by a single large wheel (the penny), atop which the cyclist rode and pedaled. Because it had such a large wheel, the bicycle went a good distance on each turn of the rigidly connected pedal cranks, which was desirable. The smaller trailing wheel (the far-thing) was, rather than an integral part of the machine, more like a training wheel, placed to prevent the rider from falling backward off the main wheel. Unfortunately, when the penny part struck a rock, hole, or curb, the farthing was of little help, and the rider was thrown over the handlebars. A new, safer "farthing-penny," as it might have been called, with the smaller wheel in the front, thus evolved, remembered today mainly through a dramatic publicity photo of the contraption being ridden down the steps of the U.S. Capitol. Though penny-farthings of both orders were used for decades, the five-foot-high wheel, whose size was limited only by the reach of the rider's legs, was clearly awkward to mount and dis-mount safely.

The "safety bicycle" was developed in the mid-1870s. With its two medium-sized wheels of the same diameter, its seat located above pedals placed between the wheels, and its chain drive, it very soon became popular. The chain allowed for gears of different sizes to be attached to the pedals and the driving wheel, thus achieving with a smaller diameter the same effect as the larger wheel of the penny-farthing. Though solid rubber tires improved the perfor-mance of the old high-wheeler, also known as an "ordinary," the introduction of pneumatic tires and other improvements in the safety bicycle in time made it the wheel of choice. Early models of the safety bicycle had straight inclined forks, but the capacity of curved forks to absorb more shock and their tendency to keep the front wheel moving in a straight line soon made them standard. By the turn of the twentieth century, the bicycle was more or less fixed in the form I would use a half century later to deliver the *Press* and ride around with Jim. That is not to say that it was always safe.

When Jim and I rode our wheels, we couldn't have cared less about the history of the bicycle or the future of school. Jim, though older than I, was now two grades behind me and so was not even thinking about high school. That suited me fine, because I did not want to. September would come soon enough, and we rode our wheels from place to place and from activity to activity, talking little but conversing much, albeit laconically.

Jim's ambition seemed modest, but it impressed me, for it never wavered. And it certainly seemed achievable. He wanted to work as an auto mechanic in a local gas station and, ultimately, in a Ford dealership. Since he was only fifteen years old, he had yet to drive a car legally, though his mother had on occasion let him drive her faded red-and-white Oldsmobile into the garage and back out of it. Because the Walls lived on a corner, their garage was turned ninety degrees to the house and their driveway came out of a curb cut on 115th Road, making for a very short stretch of concrete between the garage door and the street. Jim wished he could drive in our much-longer driveway, but he never had the nerve to take the Olds onto the street for the fifty or so yards between our houses. Nevertheless, he was confident that he could do what he needed to do when given a learner's permit and the opportunity. He also had never worked in a garage or a bicycle shop or anywhere else, even over summer vacation, but he was sure he could work effectively when the time came. In the meantime, he appeared to have at least as much buying power in his pocket as I did in mine, and he and I would often shop for our purchases together.

Early on, baseball cards commanded most of our capital. The cards came in penny packs of a single card with a single thin piece of powder-covered, tasteless bubble gum that was often just discarded. Nickel packs had six cards and a couple of pieces of gum, which were also discarded. When we wanted to chew bubble gum, we bought Bazooka and threw away the minuscule comic strip printed on waxed paper.

Jim and I were both avid Brooklyn Dodger fans, and it was Duke Snider and Pee Wee Reese baseball cards that we most coveted. A Snider was a special rarity, but Jim had several examples, the result of buying many, many packs of cards. He always took the Duke's position, center field, whether we played stickball in the street or softball in the schoolyard, and he was good at it, chasing down fly balls as effectively in his oxfords as I did in my Keds. When not playing ball, we spent hours in Jim's basement comparing and trading baseball cards, studying and reciting the hitting, fielding, and pitching statistics on their reverse. I liked also to look at the players' signatures, which seemed to correlate with nothing else on the card.

My most solitary play came when I was putting together plastic models of airplanes and automobiles. I used Testors plastic cement, which filled my nostrils with a not unpleasant odor, but one that I never connected with getting high. Since the stuff caked up and hardened around the tube's neck so quickly, I kept it closed, as I did the little jars of enamel paint, which evaporated. Each airplane was, when finished, held in a perpetual climb by a plastic stand that irritated me in its intrusiveness, but the planes could not stand on their own. Model cars did stand on their own four wheels, and this pleased me.

Not satisfied with just assembling models from kits, I began to customize my cars. I left off chrome bumpers and hood ornaments, filling in each unused hole with a slug of cement and covering it with a heavy coat of paint. I left hoods off sedans to make them into hot rods, and I cut off roofs to turn them into convertibles. In time I collected enough spare parts to switch body panels and rear decks, turning family cars into hot rods. My paint jobs incorporated flames issuing from wheel wells, and I fashioned fender skirts out of scrap plastic. My car models displaced the plane models on my half of the bureau.

Billy did not share my enthusiasm for plastic models, baseball cards, or custom cars, but we did come together in one activity. We each had a set of electric trains, which had been given to us by our parents a couple of Christmases before we left Brooklyn. In order to keep the sets distinct—to avoid any fighting over whose boxcar or caboose was whose, I guess—our parents had given Billy a set of Lionel trains and me a set of American Flyer. This made sense as long as we wished to keep the train sets separate. In fact, our father assumed we would want to do just that, and so he had made two identical wooden platforms out of four-by-eight sheets of ply-wood, stiffened around the edges and across the middle by two-by-fours. To simulate the grass of the fields through which the trains would run, the platforms were painted a deep green with some paint left over from touching up the old house's trim. In the long narrow Brooklyn basement, Billy and I set up our separate layouts on our separate platforms and played back-to-back in our separate ways. We may have been in the same basement, but we were in worlds as distinct as the brands of our trains. Whether it was the fact of our having the different trains that encouraged our different ways or whether our parents' purchases merely reflected aspects of our personalities that were already apparent to them, I cannot say.

American Flyer trains were advertised as not just toys but scale models—¾₆ inch to the foot—of the real thing, as each year's catalog was quick to point out. Other makes, such as Lionel, had engines and rolling stock that were proportionally higher and wider but at the same time shorter than the corresponding prototype. Billy and I were aware of this difference, but it was not a big deal to us as boys, since we had not been around real trains enough to know their exact proportions. We were used to playing with blocks, Erector sets, and other construction toys in which scale was unimportant. As far as we were concerned, each set of electric trains was right for its own platform, entire of itself. We each accepted and built on what we were given by our parents.

To us, the most important difference in our train sets was in the track each used. American Flyer track was designated S-gauge and, in keeping with the verisimilitude of the brand, had two rails. The Lionel track on which Bill's trains ran was called O-gauge, and it had an unrealistic three rails. More important to us, however, was the number of track sections needed to create a standard layout. With Lionel, a complete circle of track could be made with only eight curved sections; with American Flyer, it took twelve. The smaller inventory of track and the smaller turning radius gave Lionel the clear advantage for making more creative track plans on a single four-by-eight foot platform. American Flyer trains had the look of authenticity, but Lionel had the potential for greater variety in a limited space.

In spite of the differences in our basic platforms, each Christmas and birthday Bill and I asked mostly for the same but separate things: additions to our train sets in the form of action cars, working crossing gates, talking stations, and the like. The accessories were no more interchangeable than were our personalities or our clothes, which made the gifts also as unlikely to be confused with one another. His trains could not run on my tracks, nor mine on his. More important, perhaps, neither of us wished to run in the same circles. We each had school and play friends as distinct and incompatible as American Flyer and Lionel. At home, however, we were brothers with separate but equal sets of trains.

The much brighter and more open basement in Cambria Heights had offered us a new prospect. We set up our train boards next to each other, elevated on fruit and vegetable crates to allow us to crawl beneath the platforms, pull wires through holes in the plywood, and string them to the control buttons and transformers, which sat on separate wooden boxes. There was just enough space between our platforms and the walls for us to sidle down to a derailment and set it straight, and to reach into the rural areas of our setups to right a fallen cow. Such operations were fraught with danger, for a single misstep could hurtle us down onto one or the other platform, setting it to vibrating like a drumhead and knocking over every plastic figure and sign in the four-by-eight-foot world.

We had painted light gray roads over the dark green fields, and the gap between the two incompatible railroads was spanned by makeshift bridges that carried car and truck traffic from one platform to the other (though, at first, our separate railroads did not invade each other's territory). While distinct in our minds, each of the towns was a Plasticville, the brand name of the inexpensive plastic buildings that were bought with much deliberation in the hobby shop and assembled without cement in a flash. Billy and I had an implicit agreement that we would not buy any two identical Plasticville pieces, and so each town had its own distinct character. His had a church; mine had a school. His had a ranch house; mine had a Cape Cod. His had a supermarket; mine had a post office. Had we been born a generation later, we could have been *Sesame Street* models of cooperation.

We future engineers played at being engineers of two kinds: those who wore gray-striped soft caps, and those who wore solid-colored hard hats. In the former role we had driven our engines with a transformer throttle and a whistle button. We imagined ourselves at the controls in the cab of my coal-black New York Central 4-6-2 steam engine and his red-and-silver streamlined Santa Fe diesel. We saw the right-of-way ahead of us and slowed down for curves and stopped at stations. We shuttled coupled and uncoupled freight cars back and forth in the yard and hauled them up inclines with a steady determination. Sometimes, however, we tested our engines, our tracks, and ourselves. We accelerated through curves and braked suddenly on straightaways, trying to tip over an engine or separate sections of track, either event precipitating a derailment. Our sense of drama overcame our sense of responsibility. Bill's engines usually held tighter to the track than did mine, Lionel being more stable on curves than American Flyer. As much as I once pampered my trains, as I had my bike when new, I had come to accept the fact that things, like people, accumulate scars as they age. Sometimes, however, I inexplicably accelerated the process.

In my more mischievous moments, I placed obstacles on the track. Plastic telephone poles and cars were easily pushed aside by the cowcatcher. Seeking further excitement, I placed boxcars across the tracks, which produced unpredictable results. On one occasion I dropped a finishing nail across the rails, thinking the engine would run over it and derail. As I should have known, the nail conducted electricity and shorted the circuit. The nail began to heat up and glow orange from the current passing through it. Where the tracks made contact, smoke began to rise and an acrid smell permeated the basement. With a piece of plastic fence, I flicked the nail off the tracks, which were left permanently scorched and pitted. BOYS ADMIT ATTEMPT TO WRECK LIRR.

Whenever we played so recklessly with our model trains, I was reminded of years earlier in Brooklyn when I went with a friend to see if we could get into Ebbets Field through the hole he told me was in the outfield fence. We could not find the section of fence he described, let alone the break, and so we wandered around outside the park, turning toward the outfield wall whenever we heard the crowd cheer. During lulls in the game, we wandered across the street.

Tracks for trolley cars were set in the streets around the ball park, and a pair of tracks for trains was located in a cut through the area. We watched the trains from the street above, and after a while became restless with the regularity of their transit. The banks of the cut were overgrown with weeds and bushes and were strewn with litter. We made forays down the slope to find small items to drop off the overpass and onto the tracks, hoping they would land on a rail and be crushed by the next passing train. Most objects either didn't land on the tracks or were blown away by a train passing the other way. To thwart that we looked for something heavy to drop on the tracks, and we hauled up a large roll of tar paper that we found in the bushes beside the overpass. We lifted it with great effort onto the rail of the balustrade and then pushed it off the edge and onto the tracks below. As the tar-paper roll landed directly across one of the rails, we heard a shout from behind and saw a man coming toward us with his fist clenched. We ran toward Prospect Park, where we knew we could elude anyone, and made our way home through the park.

Once I was safely home, the thought of the tar-paper roll across the tracks haunted me. I imagined that a train had struck it and become derailed, harming its passengers. TRAIN DERAILED, 5 INJURED. I knew a train must have passed over the track with the tar-paper barricade since the time we established it, and we would have heard if there had been a fatal derailment, but I continued to be haunted by the thought throughout the night and for days afterward. Years later I read in the *Press* a story that gave me some relief that I was not the only person haunted by my actions. It related a conversation that took place around midnight, when the Glendale station house telephone was answered by Sergeant Jim Wright:

Caught by a Sleepless Conscience

"Listen, officer, my conscience is killing me. I can't sleep."

"How come?" asked the sergeant.

"Well, back on October 24th I held up this woman over at the Loft candy store on Myrtle Avenue. I don't know why I did it, but it's driving me crazy."

"Go ahead," said Wright.

"I want to give myself up. I'll be at the corner of Greene Avenue and Woodward Street in Ridgewood."

The victim of his own crime was where he said he would be when the squad car arrived, and the man stepped into it. "I don't know why I did it," he said. "I never did anything like that before."

I don't know why I did what I did with the tar-paper roll, but I didn't call the police. I went to confession and told my sin to a priest, who didn't understand what I'd done. BOYS, 14, TAKE BACK CONFESSION TO SLAYING.

I had always felt that I should go back and see for myself that no damage had been done, but I was afraid to return to the scene of the crime and to the angry man who I was sure was still looking for us. Even years afterward, when I knew there had been no fatal consequences, I worried about what might have been caused by our carelessness, and what it might have done to the course of my life. I never again dropped anything on a railroad track, and I even kicked pebbles off trolley tracks when I came across them. The idea of placing a penny on a track to have a train flatten it filled me with horror.

So putting an object on the electric-train tracks was not something I did without trepidation, but I did it anyway because I did not imagine it hurting anyone. Besides, after a while there was so little else to do with the trains. On occasion I would put my head down on the track to watch the train come around the curve and head straight for me. It was the most realistic way to see the train, the perspective giving it a lifelike appearance and scale. I never had the nerve to let the train slam into my face, so I always jerked it away at the last moment. What flashed through my mind on those occasions was the roll of tar paper on the track near Ebbets Field. I was that roll of paper, immobilized by my tarriness. BOY TIED UP, LEFT ON TRACK AS 'PRANK.'

The second kind of engineer that Bill and I played at being was the kind that, we imagined, sat in shirtsleeves at a drafting table in a large room full of drafting tables and wore a hard hat in the field, where he carried a roll of plans under his arm and a pipe in his hand. He wore horn-rimmed glasses and looked smart. We did not know any such engineers, but we saw them in magazine advertisements, in *Life* and *Look*. In retrospect, what we did with our model-train layouts was not unlike what such engineers did in designing buildings and bridges, and so our play helped prepare us for our profession.

In our first major redesign of our train layouts, we kept them separate. But each of us would help the other think through the possibilities. We began by assessing what could be done with the budget of tracks at our disposal, how tight a circle they could form, and how much of a straightaway we could construct. We measured and counted and then began to draw possible layouts, relying on model-train catalogs and brochures for suggestions, but in the end coming up with our own novel schemes. When we had on paper two plans that satisfied us, we laid out the track, loosely at first but then screwed down firmly into the wooden platform. The track schemes looked exactly as they did on paper, but we had neglected to think in the third dimension. My coal-black New York Central locomotive and tender could not pull any sizable train of freight cars up the incline we had constructed high enough to allow it to loop around and carry the same train underneath itself. As handsome as the engine was, it seemed to lumber under its own weight, puffing smoke in place. I had to use only the lightest of boxcars or use the workhorse Union Pacific diesel switcher, which could negotiate the grade easily, if slowly. The boxy gray-and-yellow modern machine was our Little Engine That Could.

The trouble with electric trains and their towns is that they are static, even when the trains run around the tracks, blow their horns, and spew smoke from their stacks. After a circuit, they just repeat, and the motion becomes frozen in time. Perhaps anything O- or S-gauge set up within the confines of a four-by-eight-foot wooden platform is bound to lose its enchantment after a while, and about halfway through the summer I at least reached the limits of my enthusiasm for train layouts. To expand and reinvigorate our lines, and ourselves, we merged. We ignored totally the fact that we had incompatible track gauges and rolling-stock scales and laid out our track indiscriminately across the side-by-side platforms so that instead of being segregated on separate platforms, this time American Flyer and Lionel engines ran alongside each other on parallel tracks and freight cars resided door-to-door on juxtaposed sidings. One set of tracks climbed over another, and the gap between the platforms was spanned by railroad trestles and trusses as well as by highway bridges. The two Plasticvilles annexed each other and the school was dismantled and then rebuilt next to the church. The supermarket was relocated between the post office and the five-and-ten, making a small shopping center. Planning put the town on one platform and the farm on the other. It took a lot of work to remake two railroads and the town and fields they ran through, and Billy and I were pleased with what we had done. It was the apex of our cooperation. We took bird's-eye pictures of the layout with my Kodak Brownie camera.

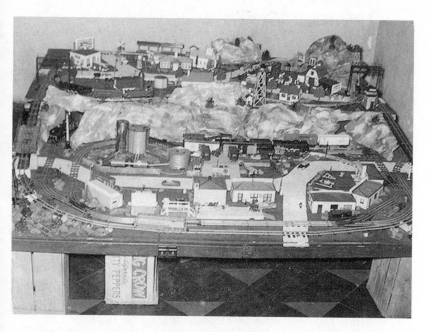

Electric trains in the basement

In time, the new train setups also became static. Even head-on collisions and full-throttle derailments were no longer exciting, and besides, they scratched and dented the rolling stock, something

Billy may have been more sensitive to than I. Increasingly, though, I became saddened by the beaten-up trains and the collapsing plastic village.

Perhaps I was also getting tired of my paper route. Like the trains going in their predictable circuit, I was delivering my route without getting anywhere. The only thing that relieved the tedium was unpredictable weather and the occasional gypping I got from a customer. Folding and flipping papers had by now become second nature. I could do it in my sleep. I could practically deliver my route with my eyes closed, my legs knowing the distance between the houses and my arms the distance to the stoops. But I always kept my eyes open to see where the papers landed.

The only part of my paper route that I really wanted to close my eyes to was at the end of 231st Street, where the sidewalk pointed straight into the northeastern corner of Montefiore Cemetery, across Francis Lewis Boulevard where it curved south again to cut through Laurelton. Just before reaching the graveyard, I veered off my course at the last driveway and sprinted across the street to begin flipping papers on the other side. I delivered that part of the route the fastest, putting as much distance as possible between my back and the cemetery as quickly as possible. As much as I enjoyed riding to the *Press* office in the pitch dark on Sunday mornings, I dreaded the cemetery even in twilight.

In the long days of summer, Montefiore looked just like a park, and the vine-draped fence around it gave me a feeling of security. As winter approached, it became increasingly likely that I would have to approach and retreat from the area in twilight or, when the papers were especially late, in darkness. The days before Christmas were the worst, and on many an occasion then I found myself racing through the first part of my route to get to the cemetery before the sun set.

It occurred to me that if I delivered to the houses near the cemetery first, I would be doing so in the maximum available light, but riding the route in any but the usual order was disorienting. By the end of my first summer delivering papers, my whole body and mind had become accustomed to beginning at Linden Boulevard and turning at the cemetery. The houses were recognizable only when approached from the usual direction. To alter the familiar course was to invite confusion. Whenever I deviated from the routine, instead of delivering my papers by instinct I had to think, perhaps even to refer to the route list, which I had ceased to carry.

Whenever I made my evasive maneuver across from Montefiore, I had to grit my teeth and arch my back against something catching me from behind. What I expected that to be, I cannot say. I had been taught that there were no ghosts, but I feared there were ghouls. I had glimpsed them in the movies, but having covered my eyes then, I had not gotten a very good look at what they did. I had also some vague notion that vampires came out of graveyards and all sorts of otherworldly things lurked there, and this little knowledge made Montefiore to me a dangerous place.

Because I had developed so rigid a pattern of delivering my route, I had willy-nilly followed the same pattern in collecting. As a result, as the days got shorter I increasingly found myself not thirty yards from the cemetery, standing on a stoop in the dark while some woman looked for her purse before coming to the door and turning on the light. When there were no cars passing, I could hear the wind blow through the brittle leaves, tearing them from the trees and rustling them along the ground. What was the sound of a body falling? What was the sound of a soul rising? I thought of the death of a young friend of my brother's, and it scared and saddened me. My heart beat fast and I wondered if it was wise to be so far from my bike, which was leaning against a tree that in the shadows looked like it was in the saddle.

In fact, I had become somewhat distant from my bicycle. It was not at all any more the wheel that I had mastered in the basement and that for the first few weeks I had polished in the driveway before putting it away in the garage. The initiation it had suffered at the *Press* office and the abuse it was being subjected to by the daily delivery schedule, in all sorts of weather, under front-heavy loads of papers, had given it a tired look. The basket had already been replaced twice, and the tires would be in need of replacement soon. I had fixed many flat tires, each time diminishing the appearance of the wheel rim with the too-small screwdriver I used as a tire iron. The fenders had been taken off, first the front and soon afterward the rear, because they had become so dented and damaged that, lest they rub on the tires, they had to be readjusted on several occasions each time I delivered papers. The chain guard was also bent and out of alignment, the chain scraping against it whenever I made a tight left turn.

In time, the guard came off and the cuff of my pants would get caught between the chain and the sprocket. When that happened, I had to become a contortionist and dismount the bike on the right side, then walk alongside it while bending down to advance the pedal with my left hand while the right held the handlebars in line. The pants cuff, being mangled between the teeth and chain, followed an epicycloidal motion of sorts until it fell free at the bottom of the sprocket. The operation of freeing the chewed-up and greasy cuff was especially difficult when the bike was loaded down with a basketful of papers. Keeping it balanced took such an enormous effort that most paperboys took to tucking their right pants leg into their sock or to wearing a metal trouser clip. Some boys did both, even if they still had a chain guard. Such measures were not considered fashionable or cool, however, and so they were seldom displayed in the vicinity of the *Press* office. Only old men who wore belts and suspenders would wear trouser clips on bikes with chain guards.

Paperboys were not old men, and for some time they did not believe they ever would be. They were growing into the prime of their life, a stage that they did not look beyond, but they were never making progress fast enough to suit them.

My bike aged faster than I did. It could not heal its own scratches, and so they accumulated and developed rust that did not drop off like scabs from a healing scraped knee. It could not pick itself up when it fell down. It could not learn from its mistakes and improve its behavior. My bike could not grow. It fell over whenever its kickstand was not properly deployed. It could not locomote. It could not deliver papers without a rider. It could not lay itself across a train track. It could not turn itself in. It could not sin. It could not retract its confession. It could not be afraid of the dark. It could not be more than it was.

But I fled from such thoughts as quickly as I pedaled away from the cemetery. For a boy of thirteen it was a great time to be alive, and I didn't want to think about the alternative. Even if I was losing interest in bicycles and electric trains, because I thought I had exhausted their possibilities, there was always something new on the horizon. Just as chemistry sets had made some boys into mad scientists and Erector sets other boys into structural engineers, so high school problem sets would make still other boys into mathematicians. It was the middle of the fifties, a time of rapid change in technology, and ever better things were believed to be possible in dreams and in life. This was especially true in New York, where the state motto is "Excelsior!"

11

CATHOLIC HIGH TO COST
2 MILLION

HOLY CROSS WAS THE FIRST Catholic high school for boys in Queens, and its plan was to phase in full enrollment over four years. This meant that from the very first day, my classmates and I were free of upperclassmen and their harassment, initiation rites, and restraints. Without traditions, our school was a *tabula rasa* on which we, the first class, could scratch the graffiti of what it meant to go to the Cross, to be a Holy Cross man, to be a Knight.

Yet even though almost six hundred inaugural freshmen were attracted to the school, it could not be expected to field a competitive sports team right away, and for a couple of years we had no varsity to cheer on, no trophies to display. We had constantly to explain to people where Holy Cross was and why we went there. (Our parents may also have had to explain to themselves and their friends why they paid three hundred dollars a year tuition to an unfinished and unproven school.)

The location itself was not hard to describe: at 29th Avenue and 170th Street, near the intersection of Francis Lewis Boulevard and

Utopia Parkway, midway between the Whitestone and Cross Island parkways, not far from where they came together to feed onto the Bronx-Whitestone Bridge. It was in easy reach of anyone with a car, which was of no help, since none of the students had one. The quick answer to why we went there was that it was a good Catholic high school, though who could say how good a school was that had not taught a single pupil when we agreed to attend it sight unseen.

Catholic schools were known by who ran them. Everyone knew the Jesuit schools were academically rigorous and strict. But no one in Queens knew exactly what to expect of the Brothers of Holy Cross, who were breaking into a new market. The order might have established a reputation in the Midwest with Notre Dame, but it had yet to do so in New York. It was not a familiar brand. The brothers had to prove their style of teaching just as the first of a new supermarket chain coming to the region had to prove itself against the long-established A&P.

Like shopkeepers living above their store, the brothers occupied

Holy Cross High School

the top floor of the school building, which was said to be five stories tall, counting the cafeteria level that was half belowground. The brothers' quarters, variously referred to as the "faculty residence" and "cloister," were accessible by some nondescript doors, a few located at irregular intervals between the banks of lockers set into the walls along the fourth-floor classroom corridors. It was only on rare occasions that I saw a brother enter or exit one of these doors. I never knew a single student who saw the brothers' off-limits penthouse, for which the sides of the building were set back, providing balconies on which the brothers could enjoy the sun and watch the traffic on the surrounding streets. We were under the vague impression that the brothers lived spartan lives in their cells, but we had to take that on faith. How many brothers there were upstairs could have been classified information; none of us thought to ask. No matter how many there were, there evidently were not enough of them to teach us all our high school subjects, for we had roughly equal numbers of brothers and laymen instructing us.

Each of the brothers wore an ankle-length cassock, long black pants, and several hats. Our Latin teacher was Brother Etienne, who was also responsible for stocking the library with books. He had the same short hair and rimless eyeglasses as most of the other brothers, but he was distinctly shorter and pudgier than average, and he seemed to me to be more distant, more ascetic. He loved Latin, he let us know, and he expected us to love it too. None of us, however, shared his enthusiasm. We memorized declensions and conjugations only for the tests. When, in the second year, it came time to translate Caesar's *Gallic Wars*, we got our mothers to buy interlinear translations for us. My mother found my copy of a trot at the Gertz Department Store in Jamaica. Under the opening sentence, "*Gallia est omnis divisa in partes tres*," was the translation "All Gaul is divided in three parts," the English words irregularly spaced to fit roughly under the Latin to which they corresponded. The only thing we mastered was how to modify the translation enough in what we turned in to mask the trot's familiar rendition.

Class recitations were dismal experiences, and one afternoon, after futilely going around the room looking for a student who might demonstrate a modicum of emotion for and mastery of the dead language, Brother Etienne broke down at his desk. After one too many dumb or smart answers from the class about the declension of *puer* and the conjugation of *lavare,* he threw up his arms, as if supplicating his Lord, and then dropped them to the desk, buried his head in them, and sobbed. What was he to do? TEACHERS TOLD THEY MUST NOT MAKE BOYS EAT SOAP ANYMORE.

After Brother Etienne's breakdown, Latin class was depressing. After telling us to copy down what he was going to write on the board, he turned to it and announced a noun or verb and its meaning and then wrote its complete declension or full conjugation, which was already in the textbook. "*Amo,* I love," he might say, and write in a slow, deliberate hand, "*amo,* I love; *amas,* you love; *amat,* he, she, or it loves." When he finished with that, without turning back to the class, he would announce another Latin word and repeat the exercise. As he faced the board, the students behind him read novels for English and did problems for math. We had all caught on that when he filled the last panel of the blackboard, he would turn to the class and ask if everyone had had enough time to copy the first panel. When he did turn around, all of us were bent over our notebooks, looking as if we were copying, and we all said in unison, "Yes, Brother Etienne." He smiled and proceeded to erase the first panel of the board and then write more declensions and conjugations. No one copied anything that he wrote, but we all did well on the exams, which were as simple as the words. We had learned all the Latin we wanted to in the early weeks, and we just couldn't get excited over a dead language.

Since he hardly had to prepare for class, Brother Etienne spent more time selecting books for the bare library shelves, which were to be stocked as soon as we stopped eating lunch at the library tables. Even before that happened, the Latin requirement would be relaxed, and most of us would register for Spanish—also to be taught by Brother Etienne, who knew nothing but languages and books—as soon as it was possible to do so. The school, rather than shaping its pupils, was being shaped by them. Cocky freshmen, who would be without role models or oppressive upperclassmen for four years, would be even more difficult to tame, but some teachers tried to rise to the challenge, if in what appeared to be an arbitrary way.

If Latin was taught by a patsy, algebra was taught by a tyrant. Lambert Duncan was a retired army drill sergeant whose stature was short and whose countenance was as hard as his heart. He may once have worn a uniform smartly, but he was no longer trim in his baggy woolen civilian clothes, which drooped from his shoulders and his seat like a parachute hastily gathered after being ripped from the treetops behind enemy lines. He gave us only his name, rank, and serial number; his teaching credentials were never presented. Not that we asked for or cared about them. He seemed to know algebra.

Of all the material we were studying in high school, that in algebra was by far the most interesting to me. It was like puzzle-solving, which I had always enjoyed, especially jigsaw puzzles, in which you had to look for a clue on every piece and match it to the picture on the box. I made puzzles into games and games into puzzles. I loved to play hide-and-seek, and I enjoyed being It as much as hiding from It. Either way, I could turn the game into a puzzle by trying to figure out what the other children were likely to do. I could never get enough of riddles, especially the kind that involved numbers. "What has 2 wings and 22 legs and can be found on a field?" It was fun discovering that what I had assumed was a single insect was a collective football team.

So solving an algebraic equation was like solving a riddle, only much easier. "What number times 2 equals 22 and 2 more?" I enjoyed the interplay of words and numbers and looked for deeper meaning in phrases like "baker's dozen." Wasn't it interesting that 12 could equal 13? When Mr. Duncan showed us how to misuse algebra to prove that $2 = 1$, I was in heaven, if a confusing heaven.

One day we overheard Mr. Duncan being called Lambie by one of his faculty colleagues, and that was what we started calling him out of earshot. To his face he was still Mr. Duncan. His lecture style was to show some new concept on the blackboard during the first five minutes of the class period and then to sit down at his desk and have us open our textbooks to the day's page of exercises. Students would be asked to work a problem in their notebooks and then present the answer orally, Mr. Duncan leaning back on his chair toward but not touching the blackboard, directly below the crucifix that adorned the cinder-block walls of each classroom. He had developed a technique of writing on the board from that position, holding the chalk awkwardly in his hand and scratching out equations backward over his head, aiming for the unknown x like Annie Oakley firing a gun over her shoulder using a mirror to find the tin can. His manner was very practiced, and his chair was very precariously tipped. To the best of my knowledge he never fell over, though there was always the anticipation, even if I would not be present to watch.

I sat in the second row in algebra, just to the right of Mr. Duncan's desk, and so I could see clearly everything that he wrote on the blackboard, even when it was distorted by his unorthodox style. One afternoon, several weeks into the school year, after lecturing on quadratic equations, he took his customary seat and began to quiz the class on the subject. He asked successively harder questions about the roots of the quadratic he had scratched on the board behind him. I volunteered the answers and got them all correct. I liked solving equations and had paid close attention to his lecture, but he didn't seem pleased that I appeared to have absorbed it so completely.

Mr. Duncan stopped me after class and asked where I had learned about quadratic equations. I told him I had learned about them from him in class that day. He said he thought it was too hard a subject for a student to learn in a single day and asked me where I had gone to grammar school. When I told him Sacred Heart, he asked where it was. When I told him Cambria Heights, he asked me where that was. He had never heard of it. What did I like most about algebra, he asked. I told him it was like solving puzzles and riddles.

The next afternoon, Mr. Duncan wrote some different quadratic equations on the board, and their roots were not immediately obvious to me. I kept having to take the square root of a negative number, which didn't make sense. Then I remembered that he had said that happened when there were imaginary roots. I didn't fully understand the concept at the time, but I took Mr. Duncan's word that he would teach us how to handle such roots by the end of the semester. Still, why was he asking us today about things he said we would learn later in the course? I sat quietly and didn't say anything. No one else in class did either.

He called on "Herman Peterson" to tell him the roots of the equation on the board. I didn't recognize the name. There was no Peterson in our class, I thought. Was Duncan mixing us up with his other algebra class? But he kept calling on "Herman Peterson," looking up in the air as he did so, as was his manner. The class was dead silent. What was going on? Then he looked in my direction and called on "Herman Peterson" again. Still there was silence. Finally, he looked directly at me, stared in my eyes, and said, "Herman Peterson, what is the answer?" I didn't believe that he had meant me, and so I just sat there. It was only after he threw his piece of chalk at me and said, "You, Peterson, what's the answer?" that I and the class were sure whom he meant. I corrected him politely about my name and then answered his question.

After class, I didn't think much about what made Lambie misspeak my name. But at lunch, one of my classmates told me that he had heard that Petroski meant "son of Peter." Did I think that Lambie was trying to be clever by translating my name into English? Was he teasing me with a puzzle? I hadn't thought of it, I said, but then what about the "Herman" part? Neither of us could figure that out. Did "Herman" mean "Henry" in some other language? Was it a reference to my mother the way "Peterson" seemed to be one to my father? What was going on?

I had heard my father called "Hen" and "Hank," but never anything that didn't seem affectionate. Still, I didn't like being called either of those. Names were such a puzzle in themselves. My brother's given name, William, was seldom used, and it was never shortened to the obvious, Will. When we shortened my sister Marianne's name, we changed the *i* to a *y*. Why? As for my mother, as perhaps a lot of girls were in the wake of the queen's long rule, she was christened Victoria. She didn't seem to care for the name, always signing my report cards with what looked like a little letter *v* to me. She usually introduced herself as Vicki, but mostly she was called Vic. Her sisters back home called her Beckie and Beck, which she once admitted was a childhood name given to her when a boy at school told her that she reminded him of the girl in the movie *Rebecca of Sunnybrook Farm*. Why were names so complicated? Why did everybody have so many different names?

The very next day in class, Mr. Duncan called me "Herman Peterson" again. This time I knew he was calling on me, and so did the rest of the class. Some giggles were coming from the other side of the room, but Mr. Duncan ignored them. He continued to look at me and call me "Herman Peterson." I looked straight at him but ignored him. He threw a piece of chalk at me, hitting me in the forehead, but I remained silent and still. If he wanted to ask me a question, I wanted him to use my real name. He refused. After a staring match that seemed to last for several minutes, he told me to go stand out in the hall for the rest of the class period.

Out in the hall I had plenty of time to work on puzzles, and Mr. Duncan's behavior toward me was a puzzle like none other I had encountered. It seemed to go beyond fun; it seemed to have a purpose that was more than recreational. But what was his purpose in refusing to call me anything but Herman Peterson? I couldn't figure it out.

Rather than complain to Lambie, to the principal, or to my parents, I would see who would give in first, he or I. The puzzle would become a game. My fellow students were already calling me Herman Peterson, and I enjoyed the distinction. I was no longer just one of six hundred Holy Cross men, I was Herman Peterson, *the* Herman Peterson, who was in but not in algebra class.

Out in the hall, I wandered over to the bank of lockers and

looked at their numbers: 3022, 3023, 3024, and so forth. I wondered
how many lockers there were in the entire school. There was not
enough of a clue in these locker numbers to tell me. Were there
just enough for the students then enrolled, or were there enough
for the entire student body when the school would be at full enrollment? There were parts of the halls that I had not yet seen, and so I
didn't know if they had lockers or holes in the walls where the lockers would be installed later. The bell rang before I could devise a
plan to count the lockers. I went back into Lambie's classroom to
retrieve my books. He ignored me, and I ignored him.

The third-floor hallway during classtime was a quiet and lonely
place, as I discovered during the great amount of time I was to
spend out there throughout that semester. The small number of
staff members were almost all teaching, and the students were
almost all in classrooms being taught. When exiled for the period, I
usually sat down on the floor and leaned up against the wall just
beside the door, listening to Lambie's lecturing, badgering, and
ranting, waiting for him to fall back on his ass. He never did. He also
never let me take a book out into the hall, and I felt it was too risky
to go around the corner to my locker to get one to study another
subject. If a brother caught me, he might insist on following me
back to the classroom that I would have to say the book was for, and
the game with Lambie might be up. I took to stuffing some folded-
up loose-leaf paper in my pocket to have something to write on so
I could stay close to Lambie's room and work out the algebra problems I overheard him pose to the class. This not only gave me
something to do but also kept me prepared for quizzes and exams,
which I was always allowed to take. I signed my exams with my real
name, but Lambie always returned them to "Herman Peterson,"
dropping on my desk the paper clearly signed "Henry Petroski." I
knew by this that he knew my real name, which emboldened me to
continue the game. I never raised my hand or reacted to "Herman
Peterson" in any way, but Lambie dropped the test paper on my
desk, without commenting on its usually high grade. Instead, he
told me to leave the room, since I wasn't paying attention.

As risky as it was to be stranded in the hallway formulating plans for all contingencies and thinking about how I might infer the total number of lockers from a small sample, I knew I was better off than at Andrew Jackson. My parents had taken great consolation in seeing me attend Holy Cross instead of the likes of Jackson and Jamaica High, with their reputations for gang fights and knives, or even the new Van Buren, which would surely be like the other public schools. MARTIN VAN BUREN H.S. OPENED. Ironically, years later my mother herself ended up being assigned by the local political machine to spend entire days working at the polls in Jackson at election time. She was relieved to learn that the students kept away from the voting area, even if they seemed well-behaved enough.

The reputations of New York public high schools had come to us not from direct experience but from friends of friends and from the *Press.* On one occasion the paper carried a story about the condition of the boys' locker room at Jamaica. JAMAICA HIGH BOYS ROUGH ON LOCKERS. Of 2,400 lockers, only 300 were usable, according to the story. It told of how the contractor hired to fix them was appalled when he showed up at the school in the summer to do the work on a contract he had been awarded at the beginning of the school year. The condition of the lockers was so bad, in fact, that the contractor was released from his $2,300 contract with the Board of Education when he discovered that of those lockers that were still standing, "some have no doors, and the others could be forced open with a toothpick."

Though we had had to wait a couple of weeks for lockers to be installed at Holy Cross, when they did become available to us they were brand-new, as I had plenty of time in the hall to ascertain. So was the gym floor and the mats that were laid upon it. Things pretty much stayed in good shape also, which was probably not remarkable in a school where students were required to wear jackets and ties to class.

The new lockers that were installed in the hallways did present diversion for me in their numbers, but they provided no refuge for someone exiled from algebra class. On those rare occasions when a brother did come down to the remote wing of the school where I was stranded in the hall, I made as if I were going to or coming from the rest room, though I had no pass to do so. If the brother asked to see a pass, I had to admit that Mr. Duncan had sent me out into the hall. Some brothers nodded and let it go at that; others gave me a detention.

Detention was served after school, in a large room overseen by Brother Amos, the dean of men. Everyone but him called Detention Hall "jug," for its jail-like qualities. When a student had multiple jugs, as I sometimes did when Mr. Duncan also gave me a detention for a wisecrack in front of the class in addition to casting me out of his room, they had to be served on successive days. At one point I had accumulated so many unserved detentions that Brother Amos sent home a note to my mother, who at great transportational inconvenience dutifully went to school one afternoon for a conference. Nothing much seemed to come of it, and as long as I kept my detentions within reasonable numbers, I was let alone by the brothers—and by my mother, who did not like her son being singled out for punishment by an algebra teacher or anyone else. I told her I would take care of the situation.

Why Mr. Duncan refused to address me by my proper name continued to puzzle me. I believed that he was playing a game, so I looked for patterns by way of explanation. No one else's name, no matter how many syllables it had, was ever mispronounced by him, let alone transmuted. Granted, my name was unusual among Holy Cross students, as it had been among those at Sacred Heart. Most of my classmates had surnames that were obviously Italian or Irish, with appropriately matching first names. Their nationalities began with *I*; my name ended in *i*. It was not the vowel, I reasoned, for many an Irish kid had a name that began with *O*, and many an Italian name ended in *i*. I was being discriminated against for reasons I could not fully fathom. No one seemed to ridicule the couple of blacks in our class, the first I had gone to school with, but their names were not as unusual as mine. In fact, judged by their names alone, they could have been Irish or English. The one other student with a Polish surname was never ridiculed, at least in my presence, but he was not often called upon in algebra either.

Perhaps, I thought, it was because of my height. I had shot up over the summer and at almost six feet was tall for my age. I towered over Mr. Duncan and stood out in a line, usually projecting a full head over my peers. I was always directed to the last row for class pictures. My classmates called me "Protrusion"—and "'Trusion" for short. The name irritated me at first, but in time I began to wear it proudly, as if it were a badge of distinction. But the opposite happened now. If at first I reveled in the distinction it gave me, I could no longer stand being called Herman Peterson, especially by Mr. Duncan. Knowing that, my classmates avoided calling me Herman, unless they wanted to get me angry, though they did start calling me Heinrich and Hein, which did not bother me so much because they were not of Mr. Duncan's creation. In time, I would care less about what I was called, and I took it as an indication of my popularity that my yearbook would be signed affectionately to "Herman," "Hank," "'Trusion," and the like. The only thing I didn't like in my yearbook was when one of my classmates signed "Best of Luck, Karl" across my picture. I can't remember if I signed his picture "Good Luck, Herman."

But that was still years away. In freshman year, in spite of all the problems with my name, I earned the top grade in Algebra I, which seemed to be especially irritating to Mr. Duncan, because I was seldom in class to benefit from his instruction. He gave the grade grudgingly, I thought, and not to Herman Peterson, because it turned up on my report card. The animosity between us became an open battle, and Lambie appeared to go out of his way to taunt me. On the first day in Algebra II, in which I as student was reunited with Mr. Duncan as teacher, he again singled me out as Herman Peterson, warning me not to disrupt class as I had the previous semester. I was flattered, on the one hand, that I was distinguished from the rest of the class, but I was irritated on the other hand that it was done by giving me a polyglot name. One afternoon, as we were filing out of his classroom for a fire drill, Lambie called after

me, "Peterson, be sure to duck when leaving the room." I turned
angrily toward him and said, "Stop calling me Peterson. My name is
Petroski, Henry Petroski." He had won: I had broken first. He let
my outburst go without a detention for breaking the silence, which
I took to be an acknowledgment on his part that we were playing a
game. But why did he choose me to play the game with, or against?
I refused to think that it was because I had the same name as my
father. Perhaps it really was just a game. Or perhaps it was because I
played back. But why did he now continue? Perhaps he was bored
with civilian life. Perhaps he picked on me because I showed him
that I could learn algebra without him. Perhaps he was trying to
break me the way a drill sergeant does a green recruit. Perhaps
someone had made fun of his name in the army.

If Lambie expected me to be the bad boy in class, I continued to
oblige him in Algebra II. My having to remain out in the hall so
much during the new semester prompted Brother Amos, whose
office was just down the hall from the new classroom, to ask Mr.
Duncan why this was so. I cannot imagine he had a good answer.
Could he say, "Because Peterson was insubordinate in not respond-
ing to his incorrect name," or, "Because Petroski did not respond to
me when I called him Peterson," or, "The student who got the high-
est grade in Algebra I could not handle Algebra II"?

After that, my exile began to take a new and different form: I was
no longer kicked out into the hallway but was assigned to sit in the
extreme right rear of the room, with a buffer of empty desks
between me and my classmates, as if we were separated by a moat.
I could only think that I was being treated like this because I did not
answer to Herman Peterson, which Mr. Duncan continued to insist
was what he knew to be my name, and I was disrupting the class
with my stubbornness. As a final insult, he ceased calling on me
entirely, even when no one else in the class knew the answer to a
question. I felt I was like Lenny, the stable boy I had sat next to in
seventh grade, but I did not think I smelled of horses.

If I was separated from my classmates in body and spirit, I
would reach them in other ways than notes or whispers. I began to

bring a water pistol to class, following the example of many of the boys sitting on the other side of the moat. At the beginning of class, we had water fights in the back of the room while Mr. Duncan was writing at the board. I am sure he knew what was going on, but a water fight took at least two students, and he seemed to wish to discipline only one.

Surely I did something other than have a Polish-sounding surname—or did he think it was Russian or Jewish?—and a less-than-common first name to deserve the discrimination I experienced in Mr. Duncan's class, but he never hinted at what it might be. The discrimination was, in fact, largely innocuous, for he never gave me a lower grade than I deserved. He knew and acknowledged that I knew algebra backward and forward. After I had behind me the two algebra courses with Mr. Duncan, I moved into more advanced math classes taught by teachers who treated me as one of their favorites. I chalked up my experience with Mr. Duncan as one of pure play, though I was never completely sure. He seemed to enjoy the game for its own sake, as in fact did I, but was that all there was to it? My best guess is that he was bored to death by teaching algebra to thirteen- and fourteen-year-old boys in jackets and ties. He didn't want to face a routine class each day. He wanted to be behind enemy lines, living on the edge, feeling the adrenaline pumping in his veins, knowing he was alive but not knowing for how long.

Other aspects of school were of little interest to me. I did not care for my English or history courses, and Religion—to be called Theology, Morals, Ethics, and Marriage and the Family in successive semesters—was familiar, foolish, or obvious stuff. Biology was too diffuse in its content for my liking. After-school activities seemed too political, with leaders of clubs spending most of their energies thinking about who was to hold what office. I joined the chess club, which appeared to have the least structure, but I found that it too was more for its officers than for the game. Interpersonal relationships and team concepts came to me with some difficulty. I much preferred the one-on-one challenge of the classroom, the chessboard, and the paper route. There were no officers in the *Press* office, and unlike Mr. Duncan, Mr. Vitalis never embarrassed us in front of the other boys. In the *Press* office, I had an independence among independent paperboys that suited me fine.

If delivering papers had seemed to be becoming predictable, routine, and pointless during the previous summer, once the capriciousness of high school had been established I began to see my paper route as a refuge of rationality and stability. Each afternoon, I looked forward to getting home, picking up my bike, and delivering my paper route, preferably before dark. The predictability of my life was reassuring.

Another predictable thing was the Brooklyn Dodgers, who were famous for dashing their fans' hopes. The Dodgers were often in the running for the National League pennant, and they had captured five flags since 1940. They had started off the 1955 season by winning twenty-two of their first twenty-four games, and they clinched the league championship early in September. Dodger fans began to think to themselves the unthinkable. When it came to the World Series, however, the Dodgers were the Bums. They came close time after time, but in the end disappointed Brooklyn over and over. The rallying cry had become "Wait till next year!"

Ironically, the *Brooklyn Eagle,* the newspaper that Walt Whitman edited from 1846 to 1848, had folded just before the 1955 season began. The joke was that now Brooklyn was the only major American city that didn't have a daily newspaper, a railroad station, or a left fielder. Who would play left field in the series was a major problem for Dodger manager Walter Alston. He played the percentages, starting a right-handed hitter against a left-handed pitcher, and vice versa. This alternated the right-handed batter Junior Gilliam with the left-handed Sandy Amoros, a Cuban who understood little English but much baseball.

New York City actually had three major-league baseball teams in the early 1950s, but none of them called Queens home. The Dodgers played in the Flatbush section of Brooklyn; the Yankees had their stadium in the Bronx; and the Giants played in the Polo Grounds, located on Coogan's Bluff in Manhattan, just across the

Harlem River from Yankee Stadium. Ebbets Field was just ten miles on a line drive from either of them, no more than a dozen express subway stops away. Yankee Stadium and the Polo Grounds were separated by only a single stop on the Independent Line, the IND. A World Series between any two of the New York teams was thus called a subway series.

Cambria Heights harbored fans of all three New York teams. Immigrants from Brooklyn, like our family, were naturally Dodger fans, and we had been used to living among other Dodger fans. Our fathers were used to mixing with Giant and Yankee fans at work, but in Brooklyn we children had been accustomed to being among the like-minded. In Cambria Heights, we found Yankee and Giant fans outnumbering us among our friends, and it took some getting used to. Jim Wall and his brothers, for example, none of whom had been born in Brooklyn, each rooted for a different team. Regardless, everyone listened to the games on the radio, but we usually did so in the quiet of our own beds, where there were no opposing fans but also no shared misery or joy.

This year's was a subway series, with the Dodgers playing the Yankees once again, and the odds-makers had manager Casey Stengel's Yanks 13–10 favorites to take the crown. CASEY SAYS HIS CHAMPION YANKS WILL CLOBBER 'BUMS' IN SERIES. The Bums had disappointed their fans before, but this year it was the Yankee fans who were worried. Mickey Mantle and Phil Rizzuto were sidelined with injuries on the eve of the first game. YANKS STILL SERIES FAVORITES AS CASEY JUGGLES HIS LINEUP. Dodger fans had hopes, as they always did. Perhaps this was next year.

The Dodgers took an early lead in the first game, but the Yankees won 6 to 5. The Dodgers also scored first in the second game, but the Yankees won that game, too, by a score of 4 to 3. Later editions of the *Press* carried the inning-by-inning score of afternoon games, but the Queens paper took no apparent side. When a baseball legend spoke, however, the *Press* reported it. TY COBB SAYS: 'YANKEES BORN TO WIN.' "They never make the dumb play . . . they always have the good hitters." It was like a death knell for Dodger fans, who knew in their hearts that it was likely that they would once again be denied.

The third game was played at Ebbets Field, and the Dodgers came away with an 8-to-3 victory. DODGERS, COCKY NOW, PREDICT '3 MORE.' They took the fourth game 8 to 5, and the *Long Island Press* reported proudly that it was the third-inning homer of Roy Campanella, "of St. Albans," that sparked the Dodgers to overcome an early Yankee lead in the game. DODGERS EVEN IT UP!

The fifth game was played on a Sunday afternoon, and every Dodger and Yankee fan who could not get into Ebbets Field tried to watch it on television. (One fan said he came to the ballpark to see a game in color instead of on black-and-white TV.) Most everyone else listened on the radio.

Since the game of the previous day or night was hardly news for an afternoon daily, the early editions of the *Press* carried feature stories on that afternoon's upcoming game. The *Press* ran a retrospective story on Brooklyn's center fielder, Duke Snider, who played in his first World Series in 1949. He struck out eight times in five games that year, tying a record, and the fans were not too kind to him. He, in turn, called Dodger fans "the worst in baseball." Six years later the remark was still remembered, but his having hit his eighth and ninth World Series home runs in the previous day's game, which the Dodgers won 5 to 3, had put him in a reflective mood. DUKE STILL HAUNTED BY SERIES OF 1949.

The sixth game of the 1955 series did not help. Snider hurt his knee when he stepped into a hole in Yankee Stadium. And even without his center-field counterpart, Mickey Mantle, who was spending most of his time in the Yankee dugout with a pulled muscle, the Yanks jumped off to a 5-to-0 lead, giving pitcher Whitey Ford some good insurance runs to work behind. The Yanks won, 5 to 1. CASEY SALUTES FORD: 'HE WINS BIG ONES.'

So Brooklyn's chance at a World Series was coming down to the wire. No team that had lost the first two games of a best-of-seven series had ever taken the series crown. Dodger fans were still hopeful, certainly, but they had learned from experience not to be overly so. The seventh game was an afternoon contest, at Yankee Stadium. The Yanks had the odds on their side.

Transistor radios were still a new technology, but there were plenty around New York that fall and their tinny speakers were all blaring the series finale. At schools across the city, teachers kept the students apprised of the progress of the game, some even turning their own radios toward the class after the Dodgers gained a 1-to-0 lead in the fourth inning. Clubs and other after-school activities were given over to following the closing innings of the game. Having to get home to deliver my paper route, I hitchhiked in the hope of getting a ride in a car with a radio on. I did, and I heard the Dodgers get a second run in the top of the sixth.

By the time I got home, it was the bottom of the sixth, and my brother and sister were sitting on the floor in front of the TV. Sandy Amoros had come in to play left field for the Dodgers, Walter Alston having juggled the lineup in the top of the inning. The Yankees already had runners on first and second with no outs. Yogi Berra was up, and he hit an outside pitch down the left-field line. It looked to be a certain hit, driving in at least one run. The left-handed Amoros raced toward the foul line, extended his gloved hand out, and caught the ball on a full run. He turned and threw to Pee Wee Reese, who relayed the ball back to Gil Hodges at first. The runner at first, Gil McDougald, was doubled up and the Yankee's rally was snuffed out. We cheered so loud that all the Yankee and Giant fans located within three blocks of us must have heard.

It was now the top of the seventh, and Johnny Podres, who had not been able to finish his last thirteen regular-season games, was still on the mound. The rest of the game was easy. Podres went all the way and shut out the Yankees. The Dodgers won the seventh game and the series. Unbelievable. But the street outside was quiet. The Yankee fans in the vicinity far outnumbered us, and the Giant fans were just not involved. Bill and Mary and I danced around our living room, not daring to go out in the street.

Dodger fans seemed generally to be in shock, but business came first. Telephone lines between Manhattan and Brooklyn and Long

Island were overloaded. It was the heaviest calling since V-J Day, according to the phone company. Speculation was that many of the calls involved bet collection or dinner arrangements; perhaps husbands were calling wives on the Island to meet them in Brooklyn that evening. As the *Press* reported the next afternoon, it took over ninety minutes for the victory to become apparent in the streets of Brooklyn, but when it did, the borough erupted in revelry that lasted well into the night. Though they were not practiced in such celebrations, they did their best. It was the time that I most wished that I was back in Brooklyn, if only for a few hours. AH BROOKLYN! WHAT A PARTY!

12

COMMUTERS HERDED ON BUSES LIKE CATTLE

HOLY CROSS HIGH SCHOOL was farther from Cambria Heights than it had appeared to be on the maps in the application literature and acceptance package. We had taken it for granted that there were buses and subways to get from anywhere in New York City to anywhere else in New York City, and there were. That is not to say it was easy. To get to and from school by bus, we in fact had several options, all of them involving at least three different bus lines.

It was possible, for example, to board the Q4 bus at the corner of Linden Boulevard and 229th Street, less than two blocks from my home, transfer in Jamaica to a bus that went to Flushing, and then transfer there to another bus, which went right by Holy Cross. Bus transfers were free, and so the fare was the same whether we went five stops on a single bus or fifty on three. The problem was that to the transit time on the individual buses had to be added the time it took to wait for the next bus in the line of connections.

The total travel time was at least an hour, if there were no long waits at the transfer points. Since buses ran every five minutes or so during the morning rush hours, when we would be going to school, the time of the trip could be counted upon, but the comfort level could not. Chances were that all the seats on the Q4 would be taken by the time it reached the 229th Street stop, and a passenger getting on there would have to stand in the aisle all the way to Jamaica. There would be no guarantee of getting a seat on the other two buses either, and so the trip would be devoted mainly to maintaining one's balance through all the stops and starts and turns in rush-hour traffic.

The balancing act had to be performed while we carried all our books, which contemporary fashion had it were never to be contained in a book bag or a knapsack, or even cinched with a belt. The books were arranged according to a scheme as rigid as the code that dictated that they be carried under the arm. The base of the stack of books was a two-ring—or, more rarely then, a three-ring—loose-leaf binder, into which were inserted like shims spiral-bound notebooks until the covers of the binder formed parallel planes. Onto this pallet were laid the half-dozen or so textbooks, arranged crosswise to the binder to make two piles of nearly equal height. The assemblage was grasped around its bottom edge and the books held in place by the pressure of the inside forearm. When a lunch bag was carried also, it was held in the same arm, either dangling beneath the binder or held atop the textbooks with a pressure light enough to not squeeze the jelly out of a peanut-butter-and-jelly sandwich. The free hand was used to drop the fifteen-cent fare into the coin box or to hand over to the bus driver a green or yellow transfer slip. When necessary, the same arm was also used to grasp one of the straps hanging down from the ceiling of the bus. The entire ride was taken standing sideways, so that the legs could be set in the best position to counter the acceleration and deceleration of the bus.

Needless to say, it was not easy to read or study on the bus while standing in the aisle. But inventive commuters had devised a way to hold a broadsheet newspaper in one hand while standing on a crowded bus or subway car.

The New York commuter fold was usually prepared while on line at the bus stop or waiting on the subway platform, where there was room to open a paper like the *New York Times* to its full size. With the entire front page facing him, the reader creased the whole newspaper vertically down the middle and folded the left half back behind the right, thus putting on opposite sides of the tall, narrow and now doubly thick newspaper the title words "*The New*" and most of the "*York Times.*" (The period was still part of the title in the mid-1950s. When the punctuation mark was deleted with much fanfare in the growing ecological consciousness of the 1960s, the amount of ink saved by the move was a point of note.)

In the refolded configuration, the paper had a stiffness that kept it from flopping around and encroaching on another commuter's space. The newspaper could be held up with a single hand and easily manipulated to bring either side of the front page into view. Some readers stayed on the front page for a while, reading the beginnings of the dozen or so stories there, but most readers followed one story to the inside of the paper before proceeding on to another. Since the *Times* then told readers not only on what page but also in what column the continuation appeared, the commuter could refold the paper to see the rest of a story without having to search the whole page for it.

To turn to a story continued on page 5, column 7, for example, the reader would use two hands to hold up the narrow paper with the "*Times*" side facing him and open it to the right side of page 5. The reader would then fold the couple of tall half pages being held in the left hand back behind the remainder of the paper, which was being held in the right. The move exposed the rest of the story. Or, if the straphanger wanted to turn from the front page to page 10, column 8, he would open the vertical half paper to that page, fold the earlier pages back, open the refolded paper so that the right side of page 10 and the left of page 11 were spread before him, and then fold the one side behind the other. At this point, the front page was buried deep within the multiple folds and creases of the paper, but it could be returned to by merely reversing the process of fold-ing and double folding.

As a beginning high-school student, I seldom tackled the *New York Times*, either physically or intellectually, on the bus or any-where else. But as students we quickly learned how to stand on a moving bus with a spiral-bound notebook or paperback in one hand and a full armload of textbooks under the other. We devel-oped a one-hand technique for turning the pages of what we were reading for homework or studying for a quiz, which involved a lot of pressing of the book against our chest. We also developed a sixth sense of when the bus was going to stop so that we could stuff the book under the other arm in time to grab the strap. We soon learned to move to the back of the bus and put our stack of books on the floor between our feet, especially during morning rush hour, when the packed bus became a de facto express between Cambria Heights and the transfer depot on Hillside Avenue in Jamaica.

A seat on the Q4 could be more or less guaranteed by catching the bus at the first stop, which was at Linden Boulevard and 234th Street. But this stop, being just across the parkway from Elmont, also attracted a lot of commuters who walked over the parkway bridge from Nassau County. The first forty or so people on line would board the bus, but the rest would step aside for the benefit of anyone behind them who wanted to board as a standee. Since most at this stop knew they could get a preferred seat by waiting for the next bus, or at most the next two buses, even at the peak of rush hour, there were hardly any takers. For me, getting a seat on the Q4 required my walking the extra five short blocks down Linden Boulevard—seeing a bus or two pass me going the other way, toward Jamaica. In other words, I had to budget still another five minutes or so of travel time. Because there were no shelters at the bus stops, in cold or rainy weather most riders wanted to get on a bus, any bus, as soon as possible, seat or no.

In all weather, New York commuters were a very regimented lot, and the lines at bus stops were highly organized. It was strictly first come, first served, and a seasoned or even a novice commuter knew not to break into a bus line. A series of stories in the *Press* described the bus line as THE CONGA LINE, though I never saw anybody deliberately touch anybody else and certainly not dance and kick with anyone while waiting for or boarding a bus. A queue of commuters resembled a conga line only in that once the bus arrived and the door was opened, the line moved as a unit to a single drummer, snaking around into the bus, following the leader up the stairs and back toward the seats. It was only when someone on line inexcusably fumbled for the right change to drop into the coin box that the line's forward progress was halted and a few necks were craned and a leg or two reached out to the side and assumed an impatient pose.

The *Press* series was more credible in its description of the cutbacks in bus service—as much as 14 percent as an economy measure—being made by the New York Transit Authority. YOU'LL HAVE TO SHIVER AND WAIT FOR BUSES AGAIN THIS WINTER. "It stinks," one commuter was quoted as saying of the situation. Another suggested calling his bus line the "Q-8-Ball Line."

Once the five of us from Sacred Heart parish who had enrolled in Holy Cross came to realize the complications of commuting by bus, our parents got together and agreed to take turns driving us to school in the mornings, at least on a trial basis. The drive, which was mostly straight up Francis Lewis Boulevard, could be made in as little as fifteen minutes in good traffic. Still, whoever was driving had to allow thirty minutes for traffic and another ten or fifteen to drive around Cambria Heights collecting the passengers, both the prompt and the tardy. In all, the round trip could be expected to take well over an hour for the parent.

Since at that time my mother did not drive, it was my father who pulled chauffeur duty on Tuesdays. He disliked the buses and subways intensely, and so preferred to drive his car to his job near Long Island City. Still, to drive five boys to Holy Cross was no minor inconvenience to him. In addition to having to drive about ten miles out of his way, he had to leave home a couple of hours earlier than he normally would. (He worked a later shift because the freight bills he rated did not become available until trucks began bringing them in later in the afternoon.)

The car pool included David Velasquez, who lived on my paper route. He was a tall, quiet boy with black hair and eyes. Like mine, his family name was anomalous among the Irish and Italian names that dominated the rolls of Cambria Heights and Sacred Heart and now Holy Cross. One Tuesday morning, my father asked David about his name and was told that it was Spanish. None of the other kids in the car pool had to be asked: Michael McMann, Edward Garvey, and Robert Pellegrino had names of a familiar ring to my father, and to David and to me.

David's house was as distinctive as his name. It was the only one on my paper route with a front porch that extended the entire width of the house, and it had a wrought-iron railing around it. Like the house, the railing was painted stark white and enclosed some neatly arranged white iron furniture that I never saw anyone use. The house and its front yard, which sloped up from the side-walk, were perfectly kept up. I liked delivering to the house because the large porch, a real porch, even with its railing and gate that required I toss the paper higher than for any other house on my route, gave a wide target on which to land the paper. I never had to get off my bike and go back to retrieve the Velasquez paper from the bushes.

David reminded me of his house, even though he was as dark as it was light. He was always neatly dressed and well groomed. His pitch-black hair was always in place and his manner always proper. He was also distinguished from the rest of us by seeming older, with the faint sign of a dark beard appearing to shadow his face. I had always enjoyed collecting for the paper from the Velasquez house, for his mother was kind and pretty, her face neatly made-up and her hair pulled back and held tightly in place. She always gave me a generous tip. But in the car pool, she was distant and never acknowledged that I was her paperboy.

The car pool had not lasted more than a month or so into the school year before it began to disband. It was inconvenient for some of the mothers, their sons told us, to have to drive on the same day each week, and the logistics of arranging who would be driving on what day had become too confusing and burdensome. But the principal problem appeared to be that the drive to and from Holy Cross simply took too much time. One of the mothers looked for alternatives to the car pool and found that there was a way for us guys to get to school by taking only two buses, the first of which was caught in Queens Village. Since that bus stop was about a mile from my house and even farther from the Velasquezes' and the other boys', the car pool continued in a modified form. Once dropped off at the bus stop, we were on our own to take the bus to downtown Flushing and there catch another for school.

There were a lot more boys going to Holy Cross from Queens Village and its environs than from Cambria Heights. As more and more of them began to use the bus, it became increasingly crowded with Knights, which became obvious to the other passengers later in the fall. It was then that we began to wear our newly purchased green-and-gold jackets and other insigniaed paraphernalia, all recently designed and put on sale in the bookstore. We did not always wear the colors proudly, however, and our verbal and physical scuffles with each other became increasingly obnoxious and frequent. Whether or not because the regular passengers or the school complained, in time a special express bus was put on the route just for us, a bus that took us directly from Queens Village to the front steps of Holy Cross High. The morning transit time from home to school was reduced to thirty minutes.

The usual bus driver, who looked like Ralph Kramden but acted like Ed Norton, sat stiffly behind the steering wheel as if he were sitting inside a fortune-teller machine in a Coney Island penny arcade. His arms moved around the rim of the horizontal wheel as if selecting the card that would determine our fate. When he got caught in a traffic jam, he lifted his hands from the wheel and flicked them over it as if he were getting ready to write a check on a table before him. After a while, he became familiar with us and we with him. He kidded us about all the books we were carrying and we kidded him about all the lunch he was carrying in the box by his side. He was never viewed as the enemy, but was seen as the agent of our getting to school on time each morning. He was just doing his job, he told us. This did not please those of us who had become used to blaming our tardiness on a traffic jam on Francis Lewis Boulevard or a missed bus connection in downtown Flushing.

One morning, the school bus broke down while rounding a corner, and we all had to get off and wait for another bus to arrive to take us the rest of the way to school. As we stood on the sidewalk beside the disabled vehicle, we saw that its front end was listing at an unnatural angle. The bus driver told us that the right suspension had broken because of the years of service the bus had seen on busy commuter routes before it had been retired to carrying high-school kids who couldn't care less about getting to school on time. The mishap caused us to miss the entire first and part of the second period, but the bus breakdown was our perfect excuse, and there were no detentions for lateness.

As we grew accustomed to riding to school with each other, we boys began increasingly to develop a collective mind-set. Instead of studying for our individual quizzes and exams, we looked for activities to engage in as a group. The day after three or four dozen of us had stood beside our fallen bus, it was obvious to all that a bus brought to its knees meant a free pass into school at any hour we arrived. The thought was too appealing not to be pursued, and the bus driver, perhaps daydreaming on this kids' route with no stops, gave us our opportunity when he rounded a corner suddenly and too quickly. Without warning, the bus tilted to the right and boys on the left side slid off their seats and onto those of us on the right, crushing us against the windows. Instead of being upset, the busload of us cheered and asked for more.

As if in response to a great play in a ballgame, we were a crowd focused on a single thing. By throwing all of our weight to one side of the bus, we might be able to replicate the previous day's failure of the suspension system. One boy, who couldn't wait to take

physics, tried to explain what was happening by describing centrifugal and centripetal forces. Most of us knew instinctively what
we were doing and continued to do it without the benefit of theo-
ries, equations, or calculations.

When the bus turned right, we all rushed to the left side of the
bus; when it turned left, we all moved to the right. The bus driver
seemed to find all this very amusing, and he began to play with us,
faking turns and taking real ones more suddenly and sharply than
on a normal run. Sitting four to a seat made for two, we were enjoying the ride but not accomplishing what we wanted. The bus was
tipping, but not toppling. It was clear that we wanted to concentrate
as much of our weight as possible on the outside of a turn, and we
began to stand on the seats and on the floor before them to get as
many bodies as possible right next to the windows. We shifted from
side to side of the bus as the driver continued on his way with obvious glee. On one especially long turn, the sound of the front tire
rubbing on the wheel well gave us a sense of accomplishment and
progress for which we all cheered.

We didn't achieve fully what we had set out to, however, and we
arrived at school with ten minutes to spare. Over the next few
weeks, we continued to work on the bus assigned to our run, and we
imagined that its suspension was definitely beginning to feel the
effects of our horseplay. The ride became progressively softer, and
the tilting of the bus around corners became more and more
severe. No one would admit it, but the thought crossed not a few of
our minds that the bus could topple over completely on a turn and
we might all die, or at least get hurt. Would that be worth it to get
out of school? The thought passed quickly as the side-to-side rock-
ing motion of the bus became increasingly softer and more intoxicating. One morning, when rounding one of the sharper corners,
the bus did not right itself. SCHOOL BUS PLUNGES INTO RAVINE,
3 CHILDREN DIE. We had succeeded in breaking the vehicle, which
happened with a loud crack, and we cheered. The right front was
down, which was obvious when we exited the bus with a very short

step to the pavement. Looking back over our left shoulders, we saw that the right front bumper was resting on the street.

No replacement bus came to pick us up, and so we had to take a regularly scheduled one to Flushing and transfer there. We missed the first three class periods that morning, but when we arrived at school there was no dedicated bus driver to tell the dean of men what had happened. The story of a bus breaking down just as one had a few weeks earlier was not credible, and we were warned that if such tardiness happened again there would be a serious investigation.

None of the kids on the bus seemed to have the damage to the bus on his conscience. No one talked of what we had done as being wrong, or of its having to be confessed to a priest. The destruction of property was the cost of our having fun, but we did not think we would have to pay for it in any way. $6 MILLION ASKED FOR NEW BUSES. Who we did think should pay for our behavior was never discussed with us or among us, if it even occurred to any of us. We did know that we had gotten away with something, but it was not a lesson. Even I, whose bicycle spokes had been cut in front of the *Press* office, did not make the connection that what we did complicated life for the bus driver and cost the city time and money, not to mention its being just wrong.

My actions showed me to be as conflicted about the world of things and my relationship to it as I was about my responsibilities to the world of people and nature. The Church provided doctrine on how we related to living things, how we had dominion over the animals. But there seemed to be little guidance about our relationship to inanimate things, to made things, to artifacts. Who made them? How were they made? What respect did we owe them? There were no catechism questions or answers.

I enjoyed discovering and understanding the workings of mechanical things, but, like unfolding a folded newspaper, dissecting them often meant just rendering them harder to put back together and not necessarily easier to understand. The closer I looked at things, the more complicated they became. I tried to take care in disassembling things and then reassembling them, but the process was all too often like trying to reassemble into a neat package a paper that had been read on the bus. Not fully understanding things, I abused them. My bike, which I had put together initially with such care, was now something I let fall on the sidewalk when I got to the *Press* office. I was increasingly careless with the bike, letting it deteriorate in appearance and operation as I used it as a mere wheel on which to deliver papers. Ends and means were interrelated, I knew, but exactly how and to what extent remained to be learned. It was not something that would be easily learned in a high school or even a college classroom.

If getting to school was an ordeal, an adventure, a crime, or a sin, getting home in time to deliver my paper route was a challenge. BUS COMMUTERS NEVER KNOW WHEN THEY'LL GET HOME. There was no longer any special school bus back to Queens Village, because in the second year of Holy Cross too many students had developed too many different after-school schedules. High school was supposed to provide the opportunity to engage in extracurricular activities, and we were made to feel that if we did not participate in them we were not being complete students. But having attended three different schools in the previous three years, I was not used to competing for leadership roles, and had become more accustomed to observing than participating. Also, the obligation to deliver my paper route had given me an after-school activity that did not require me to stay at school. In fact, it discouraged it.

During the winter months at least, to get home, pick up my bike, and deliver my papers before dark, I had to leave school right at the last class bell and catch the regularly scheduled buses, which did not run as frequently at that time of day. Alternatively, I could hitchhike down Francis Lewis Boulevard, walking the last mile home, if necessary, and make it in a half hour. Hitchhiking was strictly forbidden by the brothers, and we students had some vague sense that it was illegal also. Nevertheless, each day after school several of us from Cambria Heights would walk over to Francis Lewis, get out of sight of the school building, and stick out our thumbs. At first we hitched in pairs, thinking that would make it less likely that we would be picked up by some pervert, kidnapper, or murderer.

One of the fellows I hitchhiked home with frequently was Ed Garvey. He and I had known each other by sight in eighth grade, and we got to know each other better when he started a paper route right after graduation from Sacred Heart. He was going to give it up right after the coming Christmas, he told me, so that he could spend more time staying after school. Ed and I had become closer through our car pool, and I learned that he lived on a wedge of a block just east of Springfield Boulevard. The front of his house faced 114th Road, but his garage was entered from 115th Avenue, an arrangement that intrigued me, because almost every other garage in Cambria Heights had a driveway that encroached seriously on its front or backyard. Even Jim Wall's driveway was long enough to fit the family Oldsmobile. The entrance to Ed's garage was right at the sidewalk, and so it had no driveway to speak of.

Ed was a chunky guy who looked clumsier than he was. His full face had a funny, asymmetrical look to it. His right eye was permanently black-and-blue and was always almost closed, as if he were caught in a painful wink. One day he told me he had been born blind in that eye. I wondered later how he could ever get a driver's license, especially because he would need the help of someone else's eyes to back his father's car out of the garage into the busy traffic on 115th Avenue. He told me he could see fine driving straight ahead.

Ed was also different in his taste in music. Like most of my peers, I had begun to assemble a sizable collection of 45-rpm records, starting with Elvis Presley and adhering to the canon of rock and roll as played by Alan Freed on WINS. Ed would listen to a different kind of music, and his favorite singer was Johnny Mathis. "Wonderful, Wonderful." At first I was incredulous that anyone our age could like that kind of music, but it was all Ed played when I visited his house. I never admitted to him that in time I grew to enjoy Johnny Mathis, as I never admitted to Bob Pellegrino that I also came to enjoy the mellow sound of his favorite, Perry Como. I didn't think I would ever buy their records, though, because I feared I would never live it down before friends like Jim Wall, with whom I had learned the lyrics of "Rock Around the Clock" and "Hound Dog" and went to Alan Freed's Brooklyn Paramount shows.

Ed was also unusual in that he smoked in his own house. We were sitting in his bedroom one afternoon, listening to the latest Johnny Mathis song, when he pulled out a pack of Pall Malls and offered one to me. I asked him if he wasn't afraid his mother, who was in the kitchen, would smell the smoke. He said she would rather he smoked cigarettes at home than took dope on the streets. "It's Not for Me to Say." I took a cigarette and he lit us both up. I saw immediately that he was inhaling, something I had not yet done, and I tried to fake it, as usual. But inhaling is not something you can fake, and so I had to admit to him that I didn't know how to inhale. He told me it was nothing, and showed me how to take a puff of the cigarette and just breathe it in like air. I tried it and choked on the slug of smoke, coughing for several minutes. Ed said that happened to everyone the first time, and he told me to drink a glass of soda and try again. I did, with as small a drag as I could take in his presence, and I did inhale it without coughing. But my head was light for a few minutes, my throat was sore for days, and it was several weeks before I tried to inhale again.

One Friday afternoon, Ed and I hitched home from school, catching a ride right away from someone going all the way to Murdock Avenue, which would put us within a five-minute walk of his house. This meant that we would get there early and would have plenty of time to get to the *Press* office. There was a White Castle hamburger stand on the corner where our ride left us off, and Ed suggested that we get some hamburgers to take to his house to eat as a snack before we picked up our papers. I loved the diminutive White Castle burgers, with their square shape that meant there was no wasted space on the grill or on the matching square bun. When the perforated patties were almost ready, the cook sprinkled the griddle with finely chopped onions, dropped a dollop of ketchup from a small hopperlike device on top of each patty, and scraped them off the greasy griddle and onto the small buns that were steamed almost to disintegration. Because the hamburgers were so small, it was customary to order three or four at a minimum, and so we each ordered four.

We carried our bags of hamburgers to Ed's house, where we were going to get a soda and eat them in his room, while listening to Johnny Mathis. When we got to his house, we found Ed's mother at home, and she asked us what we had in the bag. When we told her White Castles, she said, "Did you forget today is Friday?" We had, and we had the dilemma of what to do with the hamburgers for which our mouths and stomachs were so ready. Friday was fish day, we knew, and we offered to throw the hamburgers away. Ed's mother wondered out loud if it was better for a hungry Catholic boy to waste food that starving children would love to have than to eat it and confess the sin. Picturing our souls smudged as black as the White Castle logos emblazoned on the moist warm white bags that sat before us, we pondered the dilemma only momentarily. We ate the hamburgers and enjoyed them with a clear conscience that we could tell our transgression to a priest the next day. How convenient it was that Friday fell the day before Saturday, the day that confessions were heard. In exchange for our telling the priest we ate four hamburgers he would tell us to say a dozen "Hail Marys" and the "Act of Contrition."

The more we hitchhiked without incident, the more we grew confident that it was not something fraught with danger. When Ed and I did not leave school together, I would often hitch home by myself. The ideal ride was one all the way down Francis Lewis to Linden Boulevard, from where I could either walk or, if one was coming, catch the Q4 bus to 228th Street. Linden was too much of a commercial street to hitchhike on, because there were always cops patrolling it.

Most guys who picked up hitchhikers wanted to talk, and because I considered it a fare of sorts, I did a lot more talking riding in strange cars and trucks than in most other social situations. The conversation was usually easy and innocuous, mostly about where I went to school and what courses I was taking. Sometimes the driver would talk about himself, giving himself advice about how he should have stayed in school and studied harder. Occasionally, though, a driver who stopped for a hitchhiker had other things on his mind.

One afternoon, I was picked up by a guy who seemed neither young nor old. He asked where I was going. I told him Linden Boulevard and asked him if he was going that far. He said, "Sure," and we drove off. The conversation began on a familiar note, his asking me where I went to school and how old I was. After a few blocks he began to talk about how he had lots of friends who were my age, and he told me he had some pictures of them in the glove compartment. I could look at them if I liked, and I figured it would be rude not to look at the pictures.

I opened up the glove compartment and saw a thick pile of photos sitting right on top of some maps. The first few were of young teenagers, boys and girls, sitting on a couch, looking as if they were at a party. When I got farther down into the pile of pictures, they changed. The teenagers had no clothes on and were lying stiffly on a bed, a boy between two girls. 'HE MADE ME POSE IN NUDE!' I had never seen anything like the photos I held in my hands, and I was at the same time both curious about what else was in the pile and fearful of what I was getting into. The next picture was of a naked girl kneeling before a naked boy, and there were dozens more pictures behind it.

By the time the driver asked me if I would like to meet some of the boys and girls, I had definitely caught on. I had heard about guys like this. He continued to drive along Francis Lewis, now going along the stretch where it passes through Cunningham Park. The traffic lights in this area are far apart, and my ride asked me if I knew what kinds of things happened in the woods beside the road. BOY LOST IN PARK FLEEING SEX PROWLER. I was becoming more uncomfortable, not knowing exactly what this guy wanted to do, and I began to look for a way to extricate myself. I told him I did not want to look at his pictures, and I put them back in the glove compartment, slamming it shut for emphasis. We were now driving down the long slope toward Hillside Avenue, in heavy traffic that was backing up at the light at the bottom of the hill. I could see that he could not make a U-turn and had to stop at Hillside. I told him, "Let me out at the next light." He did, and he watched me walk toward a policeman on the corner. The guy in the car didn't seem to panic. He probably knew that kids like me would be too embarrassed to tell the cop what had happened, or hadn't happened. I asked the policeman what bus I could catch from there to get back to Cambria Heights.

13

THE HONEST BOY, A CHRISTMAS STORY

WHAT STARTED AS SOMETHING to keep me busy during one summer had developed into a major focus of my life. I had delivered the *Press* throughout eighth grade at least in part as an act of defiance against Sister John Michael, and after graduation, I had seen no reason to quit when I had before me another summer and all the time in the world. Even the prospect of an hour's commute to and from high school had not weakened my resolve to carry my paper route through another Christmas. Delivering the *Press* had become as routine as going to sleep and waking up.

It is remarkable how we tolerate the stark quotidian for the rare day of joy. Paperboys lived for the holiday season, and no paperboy would willingly give up his route late in the summer, even if he had to trudge through snow and sleet for the entire month of December. It was an unusual occurrence indeed that a boy would pedal his bike through the heat of June, July, and August and not coast through the fall to the winter. I did not realize this when I sought out my first *Press* route in midsummer, equidistant between two Christmases. My route became available when it did only because the previous carrier learned with little warning in late July that he had to move in early August. Christmas, especially Christmas in New York, was the high season of holiday tipping, and paperboys expected to be the recipients of many generous tips from their customers. The boy who made fifteen dollars in a regular week could pocket an extra hundred dollars.

As Christmas approached, some of the *Press* boys talked of ordering greeting cards. There were several schools of thought in the circulation office as to how the cards should most efficaciously be distributed to customers. One group swore that you should deliver a card inserted into the paper a day or two before collecting on the weekend before Christmas. Another group insisted that the card should be slipped separately through the mail slot on a rainy or snowy day when all the papers were doorknobbed. Still other boys believed that the card should be handed directly to the customer on collection day. Whatever the mode of delivery, there was overwhelming agreement that an investment in greeting cards was repaid many times over in increased tips.

In spite of all the anticipation at the *Press* office, I was unprepared my first Christmas delivering papers for just how generous my customers would be. Because of the great amount of change I had had to deal with even on ordinary collection days, I had begun to wear on my belt a bus driver's change dispenser, with its three slots and three tubes and three levers for nickels, dimes, and quarters. (Pennies had to be kept in the pocket with the half dollars.) This had worked especially well as the days had gotten shorter and I found myself collecting after dark on Friday evenings. If a customer gave me a dollar bill to pay for a daily and Sunday subscription, I single-clicked on the quarter and nickel tubes and triple-clicked on the dime, thus shooting sixty cents in change into my palm. Like Mr. Duncan leaning backward on his chair and showing off by writing the equation $60 = 25x + 5y + 10z$ on the blackboard behind him, I thought I was being clever. I was giving the customer the choice of returning to me as a tip anything from five to sixty cents, in five-cent increments.

Some of the older boys in the *Press* office told stories about how they made extra money by giving change for a five-dollar bill whenever a customer gave them a ten, or by giving change for a ten when given a twenty. I thought they were kidding. First of all, it was very, very unusual for me to have to change a five, let alone a ten or twenty. I also didn't believe anyone would have the nerve to really give back less change than due, until I found myself short-changed in a barbershop. After getting a haircut (Frank O'Connor would always ask, "Why didn't you get them all cut?"), I gave the barber a ten-dollar bill, which he put on the shelf of the cash register. He rang up the amount of the haircut and gave me change for a five. I was about to pass him back a tip when I realized that I had been short-changed. I told him I'd given him a ten and only gotten change for a five. He turned to the cash register and picked up my ten on the shelf. He said by God I was right and immediately gave me the rest of my change, apologizing profusely. Who could say that he did not make an honest mistake? If he had really wanted to cheat me, would he have left my ten out in plain sight? I pondered this for a long time and concluded that he probably intended to bilk me. It was a perfect scam. If I called him on it, he had covered himself by leaving the bill on the shelf. How could I accuse him of being dishonest if he left the evidence out in plain view? At the same time, he should not have given me change for a five with the ten lying on the shelf right in front of him. I doubt he would have called me back if I had tipped him and headed for the door without realizing I had been taken.

The *Press* office was the forum for a debate on the ethics of a different situation when, a couple of weeks before Christmas, the paper carried a story about an "honest boy" who had found a creased and soiled envelope beside some railroad tracks along which he was walking. When he saw that it was an undelivered piece of mail that looked like a check, he took it to the address he saw through the cloudy window. The man to whom the check was addressed had not even missed it, according to the story, but now he had the money for the Christmas dress that he had hoped to buy his daughter for the holidays. The picture of the smiling man holding the twenty-six-dollar check that arrived six years late attracted the attention of the *Press* boys. If the man had not missed the check, one of the older boys asked, did he really deserve to have it delivered to him now? The paperboys were divided on the verdict. Most said the boy was a fool to turn over the check, even though he could not easily have cashed it. I sided with the boy's decision to return it.

In my first year as a paperboy, Christmas fell on a Saturday, which meant that I was collecting on Christmas Eve, when the giving spirit was especially high. Most of those customers who gave me a dime tip throughout the year gave an extra dollar tip at Christmas. Some even gave two or three dollars. Even the nickel tippers tended to give a dollar. I was lucky to have my coin changer, I thought, because I was collecting so much money that my pockets would barely have been able to hold it. As much as possible, I kept the bills representing payment for the paper in one pocket and those representing tips in the other. But my pockets were also bulging with odd coins and the overflow from my changer. I entered each payment and tip separately in my route book. By the end of the evening, during which I tried to collect from all of my customers, I was carrying about $140 around with me, about a fourth of it in coins. I had also collected a fair number of cards and even some wrapped presents, which I had put into the *Press* bag in my bicycle basket.

Prior to my first Christmas as a paperboy, I had seen the inside of the houses of my customers only as far as I could see from the front door. On occasion, especially when collecting on very hot or very cold days, I had been invited to stand inside the door while the subscriber brought me lemonade or hot chocolate. I relished those times and the kindness of the people. They were invariably the same people who were generous tippers and who expected no special service. The customers who expected the most, the people who required that I doorknob every day and collect only every two weeks, were more often than not the nontippers and the ones who complained whenever the paper was late. They never invited me to stand inside the door, even when it was freezing cold and they couldn't find their purse.

I enjoyed standing in a vestibule or a hallway especially because I got to see what someone else's house looked like. I had been inside a lot of my friends' homes, but almost always we entered through the side door and went right downstairs into the basement, hardly ever seeing the kitchen, let alone the living room. All basements were certainly not the same, I soon learned, and I inferred that neither were the upstairs rooms.

Although so many of the houses on my route looked to be the same shape on the outside, inside they were all different. It was not just that the walls were painted strange colors or the carpets had unusual designs. There was something less obvious to describe, something sensual. Standing just inside a front door made music that was muffled through the storm door come alive. Often it was surprising music: classical in the house with the motorcycles in the driveway, opera where an Irish family lived, and country-and-western in an Italian family's house. At dinnertime I could tell when something unfamiliar was cooking in the kitchen, and I wondered what it was and how it was prepared. Some houses were so dark that I could not read my *Press* book; others were so bright that I was embarrassed by my dirty shoes. I had heard that dogs shared a resemblance with their masters, and I began to realize that homes also took on the personality of their owners. Warm people had warm homes, at least on my paper route. Though I was not welcomed inside the doorway of the grouchy people, from what I could see through the front door their homes looked grouchy too, and cold.

Most homes had a mirror near the front entrance, either on a closet door or on the wall opposite. Especially in the nicer homes, the ones that I just knew had a beautiful living room and a formal dining room, I looked in the mirror, patted down my hair, and straightened my shirt. I wondered if these homes also had a fireplace, and an oil painting over the mantel. If they did, I never smelled any smoke.

During the holidays, a few customers invited me into their living room to look at their Christmas tree, under which they found the present they had put there for me. The more homes I was invited into and the farther into them I was led, the more I realized how different they could be. I had certainly known this to be the case with the homes of my relatives who lived farther away than Lynbrook, but the concept did not strike me with force until I saw what could be done with a modest home in Cambria Heights. The furniture in our home and in Aunt Jean's had become so familiar to me that I no longer noticed it. It was mostly where it always was, and I didn't have to think about where I walked to avoid it or how much it would give when I sat down in it. In a strange living room, I had to watch where my feet stepped and had to be prepared for a sofa being anywhere from extra firm to extra soft.

The overwhelming part of the time, however, I was not invited into a customer's house and so had no surprises. Standing on a stoop, I was on familiar territory, and I could relax—usually. On one occasion, I noticed while standing there a yellowed folded newspaper lying behind the bushes, visible only from my particular vantage point. It embarrassed me to think that this was an afternoon's *Press* from weeks ago that evidently had not been found. I had not received any complaint about the paper being missed, and I could tell from my collection book that I had not noted any less in payment or tip for any week's paper. After that incident, I paid special attention to getting that house's paper on the stoop.

Over the course of my first year and a half of delivering the *Press,* I went through five collection books and countless pencils. By the last book, delivering and collecting had become routine. I knew my route by heart and had stopped carrying any lists at all, though I did continue to revise the ones I kept at home as subscribers were added and dropped. Even the *Press* book was carried only on Fridays and Saturdays, when I collected, and sometimes on Mondays, if there were still outstanding payments due. My last book still looks almost brand-new, having been used only six weeks.

After my second Christmas as a paperboy, I kept the route only two more weeks before calling it quits. RETIRES AT RIPE AGE OF 13! My last were long but easy weeks. The paper carried few ads and so was thin. There was no school and so no homework. It was usually too cold to play touch football on the street, and so my main outdoor diversion occurred in the twilight after the papers were delivered. Frank O'Connor and I rode up and down the streets looking for discarded Christmas trees, their tinsel glinting under a streetlight. When we found a particularly full one with no people or cars in sight, we would pull the tree into the middle of the street and set it on fire. The crackling blaze was as close as either of us had been to a fire in a fireplace, but instead of warming our hands before it we rode our bikes as fast as we could to the end of the block. Safely there, we hid in the shadows and watched until the fire subsided, leaving a charred skeleton of a tree in a puddle of melted snow.

Though the snow and ice lingered where it had been plowed beside the curb, the street had dry paths cut by the automobile traffic. Virtually all the sidewalks and driveways were shoveled immediately after any snowfall or storm, and so there was little impediment to delivering papers. The rare sidewalk that was not shoveled seemed always to be in front of a house that did not take the paper. In any case, I showed my successor the route my last Thursday on the job, and I gave him the route list on Saturday. He was a seasoned paperboy who had just moved from Long Island City, and he knew the drill.

Without a paper route, I was going to stay longer after school, joining clubs and being a model high school student. I planned to come home on the newly organized school bus that was scheduled to leave Holy Cross in the late afternoon, after all the extracurricular activity periods were over, and not worry about having to hitchhike to get to the *Press* office before dark that evening. Without the obligation to deliver papers, I would spend time with Jim Wall until we heard our mothers call us for supper. He was still in grammar school, but our nonacademic interests continued to parallel each other's. Our latest to maintain its intensity was rock and roll.

We rode our bikes to the music store on Linden Boulevard and flipped through the bin of 45s, looking for something we wanted. We took our latest purchases to Jim's basement and played them on his portable record player. We mumbled the words, but seldom sang. Jim and I each had our favorite songs, favorite artists, favorite flip sides, favorite record labels, and we talked incessantly about them. We studied the records as we had studied baseball cards, striving to know and order the data they contained. WHAT IS THIS ROCK 'N' ROLL? We committed to memory the labels, the flip sides, the songwriters, the times, the lyrics. Our involvement with rock and roll grew with the popularity of it.

Elvis Presley was the most frequently represented artist in our collections. The oldest record of his that I had was "Hound Dog," on a scratched, chipped, and brittle 78-rpm disc, and my goal for some months was to buy an unbreakable 45-rpm version. All the newer records I had were 45s, each kept in its dust jacket, in mint condition except for the small number I had written in blue-black ink in the upper-right-hand corner of the jacket, corresponding to the number written on the record label itself. No longer occupied with having a route list to keep up-to-date, I prepared lists of my records, arranged by the numbers that represented their order of acquisition. My master list was prepared on my father's Remington, with column headings typed using the red half of the ribbon. ROCK 'N' ROLL SIMPLY A FRANTIC FAD.

In the meantime, Elvis had become "the King of Rock 'n' Roll." PRESLEY ROCKS AND TEENSTER $$ ROLL IN. The increasing number of stories about him had led me deeper into the newspaper than I had been accustomed to delving. I learned that he was making forty thousand dollars a week, which made my *Press* boy's earnings seem pretty puny. There I had been, making a couple thousand times less per week than Elvis and contributing disproportionately to his wealth. It didn't make much sense, but I continued to buy his records with enthusiasm, even though I no longer had the income from a *Press* route.

Another story in the *Press* about Elvis was accompanied by a picture that showed him in a familiar pose: standing behind a microphone, legs spread apart, left foot turned up and in and right foot out, strumming a guitar, and curling his upper lip. When asked by the reporter if sex had anything to do with his popularity, Elvis denied trying to be sexy: "My movements, ma'am, are all leg movements...I don't do nothin' with my body." Beside the picture of Elvis was one of Pat Boone, wearing a sleeveless sweater and white bucks, leaning back against a wall with his legs crossed casually in front of him. He had "graduated from Rock 'n' Roll" to ballads, the caption said.

Where Jim and I fell between Elvis and Pat Boone was hard to say. Our dress favored neither, though the functional black leather motorcycle jacket that had kept me warm and dry on my *Press* route made me favor Elvis. In time, we would acquire some of Pat's ballads for our record collections, including "Love Letters in the Sand" and "Why Baby Why," and we would enjoy listening to Johnny Cash's "Ballad of a Teenage Queen" and Marty Robbins's "A White Sport Coat (and a Pink Carnation)." But, unlike Robbins, we didn't even go to dances. We didn't know how to dance, and we made no pretensions about wanting to learn. All of our listening to music was in a seated or leaning position. The few times we had gone to Friday-night socials in the basement of Sacred Heart, we hung around the chairs on the periphery and spent most of the time in the boys' bathroom and out in the alley, smoking.

The closest we got to girls was at these socials, but all we did was watch them sit on the other side of the room and dance with each other. Neither Jim nor I had a big sister to teach us the rudiments of dancing, and we never spoke to each other about learning. Unlike Elvis, we never really tried to be sexy. Our movements actually were all leg movements. Sitting in a folding chair, we kept our upper body and head motionless as our legs pumped up and down almost in unison, as if pistons driving an invisible crankshaft. In time with the music at first, soon our leg motions became accelerated to a rate beyond any dance beat. When we were synchronized, even the terrazzo floor seemed to bounce beneath us. It was time to go out for a smoke.

Our legs were also the pistons of our bicycles, their reciprocating motion converted to linear by the ingenious crank-and-
sprocket drive that took the wheel to another level. Early on
Sunday mornings, when riding along 115th Road in the dark, paying
no heed to cross traffic that was seldom encountered at that time of
day, I had been used to getting my legs moving in such synchrony
with the pedals that the bike glided true as a sled on ice. I rode in
the middle of the road, where there were no potholes, and I let go
of the handlebars, letting the front wheel find its natural course.
Sitting straight up in the seat, hands on my thighs, I rode the bike in
its purest form. Sometimes I closed my eyes for blocks at a time. I
was not trying to be tough or sexy; I was trying to be one with my
bike. It was all in my legs, and my upper body just went along for
the ride. It was a ride I had been missing of late.

I had been without my *Press* route for barely six weeks when a
new circulation manager called me to say that a route he thought I
might be interested in was becoming available. It was Route 4710,
which comprised 218th Street between 115th Avenue and Linden
Boulevard, which meant that it started only about four blocks from
the *Press* office, which incorporated District 47 in addition to 58.
The route was small, with sixty daily and forty-five Sunday papers,
which meant that it could be done easily even on Thursdays and
Sundays. Unlike my old route, which had grown to a hundred daily
papers and ninety Sunday, the new route would not take two trips
from the *Press* office on especially thick-paper days, which had
become increasingly common. I had long thought that a route this
size would be a pleasure to have, and now I had the chance to have
one.

I had missed the camaraderie in the *Press* office and the occupation that a paper route had given me after school. The sober silence
of the chess club was just not as exciting as the banter that accompanied pitching pennies with the paperboys. Getting home to
deliver the new route would be relatively easy with the regular bus
now running in the afternoons, and having a route again would give
me the steady income I had begun to miss, having already spent

about half my collection of Liberty coins. It would also give me the excuse to drop out of after-school clubs, which I was not enjoying. I agreed to take the new route and started in late February.

There was no initiation this time, for I was considered a veteran carrier, and, other than getting used to a new list of subscribers, there was no learning curve. I knew how to fold, pack, flip, and collect, and I could do them all efficiently. Since the route was small and closer to the *Press* office, I could spend more time there and even return to it easily after delivering my papers to pitch pennies and play handball until suppertime. The *Press* office became the locus of my most enjoyable activities. School was just a place to spend the day.

I had been delivering my new route only two months when a second new route became available just two blocks away, on 220th Street. The route I had been delivering was so modest and easy that I had come to be a bit embarrassed at the lightness of my load and the ease with which I could ride my bike up the hill on 115th Avenue. The second route, which would double the number of papers I drew to about 120 daily and a hundred on Sunday, would give me one of the largest combined routes in the district, which now appealed to me. Even on the heaviest-paper days, the short return trip to the *Press* office would be easy. I agreed to take over the second route in early May. If Holy Cross did not capture my interest in or after the classroom or provide role models in the form of upperclassmen, my double *Press* route would provide plenty of challenges, and I would be a role model for the younger boys.

A substantial test of my resolve arose shortly after I began to deliver the second route. A Sunday paper came in at 146 pages. It was definitely one that could not be folded with its insert in place, and so it had to be stuffed, and even that could not be done easily. In addition, it was difficult to get more than sixty of the papers into a bag, and so I had to use two bags, which veteran carriers kept in their baskets as a matter of course. Instead of delivering half of my papers and then returning to the *Press* office to get the second half, as I had reasoned I would do in such circumstances, I decided to take all the papers at once. This was what I had seen other boys do on only several occasions. My hubris knew no bounds.

I squeezed the first bag into my bicycle basket as well as I could and then pulled out a line of papers to act as a lip against which I could rest the second bag, so that it wouldn't slip back on me as I rode up the hill. I stacked the second *Press* bag on top and, to prevent it from falling forward, I wrapped its strap around my handlebars, which had been raised like Lenny's in what was now the style of the times. With the handlebars pointed up toward the sky, a paperboy could ride more upright and so flip from a more appropriate position, though he did have to raise his arm sufficiently to clear the bar ends.

The raised handlebars also allowed a paperboy carrying a single bag to get away without a basket. The shoulder strap of the *Press* bag could be wrapped around the ends of the handlebars in such a way that the whole bag was suspended from the strap a safe distance above the front wheel, which was seldom protected by a fender. Such a scheme worked fine with a route half the size of mine, but it was no longer available to me. I had delivered without a basket for a while when I started my lighter route, having discarded the old beat-up basket when I quit Route 5812. With the addition of the new second route, however, I had bought a new basket, without which I could never have attempted what I was doing this Sunday morning.

Getting the two bags in position had been difficult, and the sixty-pound load taxed my ability to steady the bike when I had to stop for a car before crossing Springfield Boulevard. The ride up 115th Avenue was near-impossible, and I had to stop about halfway up and get off the bike to walk it. When I did so, the back wheel lifted off the ground, the front wheel turned back toward me, and the top bag fell off to one side, pulling the whole bike down with it. Since the bag was wrapped around the handlebars, the papers came out of it and spilled all over the street, and I had to put the bike down and retrieve them before they were shredded by passing cars.

With the papers repacked in the bag, I left it at the curb and rode my bike up to the beginning of my route, which was on level ground. I left the one bag there and rushed back to retrieve the other one. Having done that, I delivered papers down the even-numbered side of 218th Street to Linden Boulevard and then up the odd side back to 115th Avenue, where I was relieved to find my second bag of papers still in place and untouched. I loaded it into my basket and rode over to 220th Street to finish delivering. On subsequent thick-paper days, I delivered one route before returning to the office to claim the papers for the second. My hubris had been tamed by failure. I had learned.

14

EVERYONE TAKES COVER
IN CD TEST

IT WAS MY MOTHER WHO was usually home when the men came
to read the water, electric, and gas meters, and she would let them
in the side door and show them down the stairs, remaining uncomfortable in her kitchen until they left. The meters were located
beneath the fuse box, which was my father's province. Whenever a
fuse blew, he looked for one of the correct amperage among those
arrayed across the top of the box. For an inexplicable reason, he did
not discard old blown fuses but mixed them in with the new, perhaps on the odd chance that what appeared to be a broken filament
was not really broken after all. Trying to find in this array a fuse that
worked was like playing a shell game.

Every time a utility bill came, it provided an opportunity for my
father to repeat the story that my Uncle Joe had told him about the
men's store in Brooklyn that was stealing power from the barbershop next door. It seems that the basement wall had been broken
through and some electrical sleight of hand had been performed.
The ruse apparently had been going on for years before the barber
who was being victimized saw his electricity bills go up instead of

down during the couple of months his shop was closed after a fire. When he went into the basement to look at his electric meter, he noticed the line tapped into by the haberdasher. The illicit wiring was undone, but there was not enough evidence to convict anyone of a crime. That in itself seemed to me to be a crime.

My mother called the man who read the meters the Meter Man. With the same anonymous distancing, she referred to the vegetable peddler down the block as the Tomato Man, the guy who ran the laundry on Linden Boulevard as the Dry Cleaner Man, the fellow who worked in the meat market as the Butcher Man. If her dealings with the adult world were with categories of people—even her husband was referred to as "the father" to those outside the family—her dealings with us children were highly personalized. When Bill, Mary, and I were all coming home from Sacred Heart every lunchtime, our times of arrival were perversely staggered by our different rates of walking and by the whims of childless nuns who did not all release their classes promptly at the sound of the bell, but each one of us could count on our favorite foods being made to order.

Mary and I were seldom home at the same time, but I expect she was treated to her favorites, what my mother called roly-polies, but which might have been called crepes in a fancy restaurant or blynas in a Lithuanian one. Billy enjoyed fried liverwurst and fried baloney sandwiches, my mother nicking the edges of the slices of meat to form four quadrants so that the disks cut by the butcher did not inflate like balloons in the frying pan. For Bill, the crust was cut off the bread and just the right amount of mustard was spread on the sandwich. My favorite lunches were soups. In cold weather my mother made, from scratch, split pea and ham, lima bean, and cabbage soups. In warm weather I could count on beet soup, cold and full of cucumbers, sour cream, and dill. We never called it borscht.

After school, while having milk and cookies before going to the *Press* office, I often watched my mother work on preparing supper, even as she was still cleaning up dishes from lunch. The mechanical implements of the kitchen fascinated me: the open gearwork of the eggbeater, the reciprocating base of the flour sifter, the broad wheel of the rolling pin, the loose, slotted blade of the potato peeler. To my mother these were essential, specialized tools, but I marveled at the operation of these simple things as if they were toys, not guessing that this fascination was a manifestation of the mechanical bent that marked me as an engineer long before my school counselors did.

I was particularly drawn to the meat grinder, which had to be assembled before use and afterward disassembled for cleaning and storage in the cabinet below. Whenever I saw that my mother was going to grind meat, I would ask if I could set up the contraption. A large clamp secured the grinder to the countertop, and I derived great pleasure from tightening the large wing nut beneath the counter's lip until the wood creaked. The guts of the machine consisted of a heavy cast-iron base that ended in a trumpetlike shape. Inside was a large helical screw that was turned by a long-handled crank. The screw fit snugly inside the grinder's casing and, when the crank was turned, pushed the cubes of meat about the size of children's small alphabet blocks that were fed through the flared mouth into the body of the beast. As the crank continued to be turned, the screw advanced the meat toward the exit, which was covered with a die through which the ground chuck or pork was extruded. I found the mechanics of the simple appliance hypnotic. It was a mechanical model of the human digestive system, I thought, but dismissed the idea as disgusting. Operating the meat grinder was as fascinating to me as assembling it, though I did not like to imagine what could happen to a finger that was caught in its grip.

For hamburgers, the beef came out in marbled spaghettilike strands. A very fine die was usually used for pork, because my mother wanted it more finely ground or shredded to mix with onions and stuff into what she generically referred to as "little pies." I enjoyed helping my mother make her little pies, but I preferred them filled with mashed potatoes and cheese more than with meat. Whatever the filling, they were all wrapped in the same dough. After she had prepared it, I was allowed to roll the dough out on a floured board. I approached using my mother's rolling pin as I did using one of my father's tools. Like any tool, the rolling pin worked best when the correct force was applied in the correct direction. Otherwise, the dough would not be of uniform thickness and so not cook evenly. Once the loaf of soft dough had been rolled into a sheet, it was time to cut circles out of it. This was done with an upside-down Welch's grape jelly jar that was ordinarily used as a glass, and I thought through different arrangements first to get as many circles as possible out of the irregularly shaped dough. A small mound of filling was spooned onto each circle and the edge moistened with a finger dipped in water. The dough was folded over in two and, with the edges matched, pinched and given a little twist all around the semicircle. That having been done, the pies were ready to be boiled and, ultimately, fried in butter with diced onions. We never called the little pies by their Polish name, pierogies, as if using that term would make us less American. (My mother, whose ancestors had come from Lithuania, and who learned to cook Polish food from her mother-in-law, considered all food made in America to be American.)

When I went to high school, I missed working at the kitchen table in the afternoons. I also missed coming home at noon, but my mother made sure that my lunch bag always contained a sandwich that I liked—peanut butter and jelly or American cheese and mustard—and never something I had to look to trade. She packed desserts with some reluctance and always under protest. My mother felt that we got enough sweets over the weekend, when my father brought them home after a clandestine excursion to Ebinger's for fresh bread, rolls, doughnuts, crullers, or a coffee cake; or, on special occasions (special by his own declaration), a Boston cream pie or chocolate layer cake. (Heard once at the bakery: "Are Ebinger's franchised?" "No, I think they're Jewish.") My mother detested these store-bought desserts, and she was hurt that her own pies and cakes, complete with homemade crusts, fillings, and toppings, which had been good enough for Schrafft's customers, did not satisfy my father's sweet tooth.

Regardless of what my mother thought of it, I enjoyed accompanying my father to the bakery, where the clerks were dressed all in white and resembled nurses. As in my mother's kitchen, I was fascinated by the simple and functional technology of the place. When a customer ordered a loaf of rye bread ("Seeds or no seeds?"), the clerk asked if he wanted it sliced. My father always selected seeds and sliced, and I watched the loaf put whole into the back of the slicing machine and come out the front sliced. There was what looked like a series of knives separating the front from the back, but the transformation of the bread was as mysterious to me as a magician sawing a woman in half. The loaf of sliced bread was taken up by the clerk as she might take a concertina and then balanced vertically on the palm of one hand while the other hand dropped a clean white bakery bag over it. With a motion practiced to perfection, the bag of bread was flipped upside down, closed, and placed on the counter. "Anything else?"

Packing the softer and sweeter treasures was very labor-intensive. Unlike a loaf of rye or pumpernickel bread, whose crust was its armor, the stickier goodies were easily damaged by human hands. The women who worked at the bakery used a small square of waxed paper to grasp the doughnuts from the display tray and put small numbers of them into a white waxed paper bag without ever directly touching them. When the customer announced that he was going to select a dozen doughnuts, an irregularly cut sheet of white cardboard was first pulled from under the counter and folded into an open-ended box with the same assurance with which a paperboy handled a Wednesday paper. The box being almost fully formed, it was lined with a waxed sheet and held like a printer's composing stick in one hand while the other grasped jelly, glazed, iced, sugar, and cinnamon doughnuts as if from a drawer of type. The lines of doughnuts were justified in the box, but never packed too tightly or too loosely. When the order was filled, the waxed tissue in the lady's hand was left on top of the doughnuts, for the customer to use to reverse the process at home. The box was fully folded up and its top brought down with the side flaps hanging out like wings. The flaps were never put inside the box, lest they cut the doughnuts or scrape the icing off a cake.

Tying the box with string was the part of the operation that most transfixed me, for it was a highly evolved *tour de force* that was done with a speed and aplomb that, as in handling newspapers, came only with experience. Bakery string had a distinctive pattern of green and white twisted strands. The lady behind the counter pulled it off a giant spool that rotated on a spindle beside her or was suspended from the ceiling, though in some bakeries the spool was out of sight under the counter and the string was pulled out through a grommeted hole. When a bakery clerk wrapped a box of confectioneries, she did so with a motion even more complex than that of the baling machine in the *Press* building, first going around one way and then at 90 degrees to that. The box danced on the counter like it was full of Mexican jumping beans. It never fully left the countertop, and the string was whipped under it like a jump rope under an overweight girl. The tension in the string was just right to hold the box firmly closed and yet provide enough slack to allow the customer to get his fingers under it and carry the suspended sugary treasures home. When more than one box of bakery goods was bought, a tower of boxes was tied together with a generous length of string so they could be carried like hatboxes with a single hand.

Cutting the string was the *coup de grâce,* and it was done with a simple tool that I coveted, though I had absolutely no need for one. Each woman at the counter wore a steel band of a ring that was topped not by a stone but by a small crescent of a blade across which a length of string was pulled to be cut. The sharp knife-ring was as important to a bakery lady as a pair of wire cutters was to a *Press* stationmaster, and it was used as unobtrusively and as expertly. In all of the diverse motions it took to get a box assembled and filled with doughnuts, neither the box nor the doughnuts it contained were ever sliced, scratched, or punctured with the ring's blade. Nor were the fingers on the bakery lady's other hand. Watching her work with her dangerous gem of a tool, absorbing the soft and appropriate technology of her performance, was for me a high-light of a trip to the bakery.

As delectable as confectioneries were to my father, it was ice cream that we children craved, even we children who had seven-day-a-week jobs delivering newspapers. For all of our responsibil-ity, paperboys were young boys still, kids really, basically children who melted at the thought of an ice cream freezer. When the Good Humor truck came down 229th Street on a summer afternoon, we were as eager to meet it as our smaller brothers and sisters were.

Unlike pies and cakes, ice cream was not something my mother made, and so she was not opposed to our buying it from a vendor. She usually found money in a cookie jar, if there was none left in her purse, for Billy and Mary to have an afternoon treat. I was on my own with my paper-route money to buy an ice cream bar or a Popsicle anytime I wanted, and my mother knew that I did just that, and often and then some, at the soda fountain.

My mother called the Good Humor man the Good Humor Man. Unlike the Bakery Lady, who dealt in soft technology, the Good Humor Man dealt in hard. I also learned from watching him that he was much more distant from his goods and technology, it being more advanced and more powerful and obviously more mechanical. His hard desserts, being iced and frozen, required that he drive a truck that appeared to be little but an adjunct to a boxy white freezer whose thick doors reminded me of those of a bank vault. Lest the warm air devalue its contents, the truck's doors could be left open only for brief periods of time. As long as he observed that caveat, the Dixie cups, ice cream bars, sandwiches, sundaes on a stick, Fudgsicles, Creamsicles, and Dreamsicles could be handled with an iron fist. Since they came prepackaged, there was no need for waxed-paper tissues or finesse when dealing ice cream out of a steel freezer box. The Good Humor Man reached through the carbon dioxide cloud of melting dry ice deep into the arctic dark of the white box—looking away, as if ashamed of his wares—to pull out a child's choice. He tossed as much as handed the prize from a large cold hand to a small warm one, and it was a frigid day in August when he had to take it back because it was the wrong thing.

The Good Humor Man who serviced our neighborhood was known to all the kids as Mike, and he knew all of our names too. Mike would let some of his regular customers ride around the neighborhood in his truck, but only one at a time. The white Ford was as rectangular in shape as the Good Humor bar pictured on the sides. Except for the bite taken out of the corner of the bar, the truck's only circles were its tires, lights, and steering wheel. The cab was open on top, like a convertible, and it had only one seat—for Mike. There was a space beside him in the cab where a single kid could crouch down beside the trash receptacle built into the truck, as if he were taking cover underneath a desk during a civil-defense air-raid drill at school. CAN YOU ESCAPE ATOMIC FALL-OUT? Mike's rules were simple: no standing and no feet showing in the doorway. There really was no door, just an opening where one might have been, and this was apparently why we had to be so careful.

We could always hear the bells on Mike's truck when he was around the block, on 228th Street, and we knew from much experience that he would be coming down 229th in no more than a couple of minutes. Once around the corner and off the avenue, he drove no more than about three miles an hour to allow time for any kid who wanted to to get money and to stand out in the street, as if flagging down a taxicab.

Mike made plenty of sales every time he stopped in front of our house, but there were always a few kids who did not have a nickel or did not choose to spend one that day. When Mike saw that he had sold as many treats as he could on a stop, he did what every kid had come to expect of him. He took a two-sticked Popsicle out of the truck and skimmed the cherry or lime sled across the pavement toward the crowd of kids waiting for their chance to get one on the house. Everyone would scamper for the treat, some holding the Popsicle they had already bought up in the air as they dived to the ground for the redundant treat. Usually only one kid would come up with the prize. On rare occasions, two kids would get their hands around it, and while it was still in its polka-dotted white paper bag one of them would grasp the Popsicle like a holy scroll and, as if cracking the spine of a book, break it down the middle into two halves.

My mother never ate a Good Humor in my presence. Her pleasures, while we children were growing up at least, seemed to be few and her world simple. What she knew of its geography was prescribed largely by lines on a map—not lines outlining a state or a city but lines connecting one location to another, walking lines, bus lines, subway lines. Since she did not drive then, she must have done a lot of walking up to Linden Boulevard while we were in school, for there was always plenty of food in the cupboard and in the refrigerator when we got home. She did not buy soda, telling us it was bad for our teeth. Besides, she told us, we got plenty of soda on our weekly visits to Aunt Jean and Uncle Joe.

The fact that my aunt and uncle had no children confused me, because they seemed to like their nieces and nephews and kids generally, as long as they stayed out of my aunt's garden and off my uncle's driveway. I couldn't believe that my uncle was like the man in Cambria Heights who kept our Spalding whenever it went into his yard, but I also couldn't explain otherwise why there were so many old rubber balls on a high shelf in my uncle's garage.

Whenever Uncle Joe knew that we were coming to visit, he left the gate to his diminutive compound open, if he did not wait there himself to wave us into the driveway and close the chain-link gate behind. Soda flowed in Lynbrook like water in a stream. Uncle Joe bought it by the case in an assortment of flavors that he selected himself to accommodate our differing tastes: orange, lemon-lime, cream, root beer, cherry cola. One quart bottle of each flavor awaited us cold in the refrigerator. The wooden case was in the basement; whoever drained the last glass out of a bottle had to take the empty down and bring a fresh one up.

My favorite activity during visits was to haunt my uncle's basement, where I lingered and studied its arrangement and its contents. The oil burner was located dead center in the bright basement space, efficiently positioned to heat not just a corner but the entire cellar. It being equidistant from all walls of the squarish house, it sent warmth efficiently up to the first floor, where my aunt and uncle lived, and to the second floor, which they rented out to a young couple. The rental income paid a good part of Uncle Joe's mortgage, if not the whole thing. He was neither poor nor cheap, but as an accountant he knew the importance of the bottom line, spending his own money only when he had to or wanted to.

The extreme sensibleness of the location of the heart of the heating system was symbolic of my uncle's preference for rationality in all things, but the scheme did not allow much room for model train platforms. Every aspect of my uncle's house and its contents appeared to have a serious purpose. In fact, there seemed to be little in my uncle's life that was frivolous, save for an unpredictable impishness or a practical joke now and then. One family picture shows him putting his hand over my father's balding head, so that it would not reflect the flash. He loved getting a new gag for a Christmas or birthday present, and Billy was equally happy to find one to give him. The man who was so Spartan that he shaved himself with cold water at the kitchen sink before going to bed each night lowered his guard when confronted with a joke. Hand buzzers, trick matches, dribble cups, rubber vomit, fake dog poop, whoopie cushions—all amused him equally. He would watch transfixed as my brother cranked a magic device that turned one-dollar bills into fives, or just plain made them disappear. He insisted on learning how it worked.

Of my uncle's work as an accountant, about the only thing we knew was that he changed employers on a seemingly regular basis. Why he did this was never clear to me, but moving about did not seem to hurt his chances of getting a new job whenever he left his last. The fee of the employment agency was always paid by the hiring company, we were told, and he got to see a great deal of the commercial world by moving from place to place.

He must also have seen a good number of the storerooms and supply cabinets of the commercial world, for it was understood that the proliferation of stuff in his basement was brought home piece by piece, day by day, on the Long Island Rail Road. Around the periphery of the basement were odd cabinets and chests of drawers taken out of service upstairs. They contained everything from nuts and bolts and electrical fixtures to books and office supplies. The only thing besides his car and his house that I knew him to be proud to have actually bought was a new-model ballpoint pen, when it was still a novel and costly thing and so unstocked in most offices. He showed an inordinate pride of ownership in the pen and showed it off to us kids, clearly pleased that over a lunch hour he was able to get one of the few hundred that went on sale in New York City that day. I doubt that he ever bought another pen or pencil or a piece of paper in a stationery store. When I later became an engineering student, he supplied me with a number of pocket slide rules and many pads of quadrille paper, his own stationery of choice.

What confused me about my uncle's behavior was my family's response to it. Why was it seen as humorous, or at worst just mischievous, to bring home office supplies from an accounting firm but criminal to bring home stalks of bananas from the docks, as our longshoreman neighbor did, to my parents' clear disapproval? Since Uncle Joe was Protestant, I couldn't ask if he had to confess what he did, but our neighbor was Catholic, and I wondered what he said in the confessional.

One corner of my aunt and uncle's basement was walled off to form a separate room in which she kept the canned fruits, pickles, jellies, jams, and other preserves that she prepared in her small and hot kitchen every summer. If Uncle Joe's part of the basement was a hardware store and stationer's, Aunt Jean's was a grocer's. She shared freely of her gardening and canning efforts, and it was a rare Sunday indeed that we did not go home with a basketful of screw-top Ball jars full of tomatoes or peaches, and wax-sealed jars of jams and jellies that she had preserved in her kitchen. I puzzled over why she said she was canning when she was obviously putting things in glass jars.

I never knew Aunt Jean and Uncle Joe to go on a trip. Perhaps he never worked long enough in one place to earn any vacation time, or perhaps he and she saw little need or freedom to leave their well-provisioned compound at the end of their cul-de-sac. The crawl cellar at the rear of the house was certainly not a fallout shelter, but it would serve in a pinch. When civil defense tests did occur, my aunt spent the time in her pantry and took stock of what she had and what she needed to put up the next summer. She listened for the all-clear only to know that she could then go out to her garden or walk into the village.

Lynbrook itself looked as if it was as far from Cambria Heights as the latter, in turn, was from Brooklyn. Still, I found it difficult to believe that we would not all suffer the destruction that the *Press* reported would take place during the ten minutes that all Long Islanders were required to take shelter for an upcoming simulated attack:

Everyone Takes Cover in CD Test Wednesday

Sometime Wednesday afternoon the "Apple Jack" red alert will sound, signaling the beginning of "Operation-Alert-1055."

For 10 minutes, until the "Snow Man" all-clear is sounded, all Long Islanders will be required to take shelter in accordance with civil defense instructions.

During this period a hydrogen "bomb", several thousand times more destructive than the A-bomb that fell on Hiroshima, will be theoretically exploded along the East River in the Williamsburg section of Brooklyn.

The blast will create an area of total destruction more than 10 miles square and

> kill or injure more than 6,000,000 people in
> New York City alone.
>
> Of these casualties, more than 400,000
> will be in Queens, or about one dead or
> injured by the bomb out of every four bor-
> ough residents.
>
> Although Nassau and Suffolk theoreti-
> cally will not suffer any casualties from the
> explosion, CD officials in these counties
> will contend with the deadly effects of
> atomic "fallout."

The story was reported in an edition of the press that had a
curiously mutated banner reading, *Press Sunday Long Island*. It
wasn't exactly a reversal of the words, and I wondered how it could
have happened. The clues were in the composing room of the Press
Building that we had visited in eighth grade, but I didn't figure out
how the mistake might have happened until years later. Because the
Press had a different name for its daily and Sunday editions, the
logo had to be reset once every seven days. The common compo-
nents of the paper's name were *"Long Island"* and *"Press,"* and these
were cast as ligatures of type, so they could be set quickly with the
appropriate *"Daily"* or *"Sunday"* ligature between them. Type is set
in reverse order to how it is read, of course, and so on this day an
inexperienced, careless, or mischievous typesetter had put the
"Long Island," "Sunday," and *"Press"* ligatures into the page form
in reverse order. The banner typo was corrected in a later edition. It
would not have been so easy to correct the effects of atomic fallout.

Even if Lynbrook was not a safe haven from nuclear war, there
was little need to leave home, except to go into the village or the
city for food and supplies, trips which could be made on foot and
via the Long Island Rail Road. My aunt and uncle did have a car, a
1949 Mercury that I coveted, thinking it was the most perfectly pro-
portioned automobile ever made. I dreamed of owning such a car
one day, but in a chopped and channeled version with Frenched

FINAL ★★★ Press Sunday Long Island 10¢

| 135th YEAR | NO. 161 | SUNDAY, JUNE 12, 1955 | 156 PAGES |

'Anyone Who Saw Her Would Want Her!'

Founding Home Nurse Catherine Reichel and Sister Genevieve Mary get acquainted with "Little Miss Hill."

Ike Urges Atom $$ For Allies

UNIVERSITY PARK, Pa. (IP)—President Eisenhower recommended yesterday the United States put up atomic nuclear materials and "know how" for her new atoms-for-peace program where they believe the progress subject to approval by Congress, provide for keeping such nations abreast of atomic power and research reactors. The President pledged them as the pathway to a broad horizon of progress in which atoms could be the servant of man...

65 Killed As Race Car Hits Crowd

LE MANS, France (IP)—A speeding sports racer crashed and exploded yesterday, spraying wreckage on crowds watching the Le Mans 24-hour road race. It was Europe's worst racing accident since the war. At least 65 persons were killed and 50 others injured, police said. Other estimates of the injured ranged up to 150.

Order Probe Of Vaccine 'Mix-Up'

WASHINGTON (IP)—Chairman of the Senate-Commerce Committee ordered a full investigation of the Salk polio vaccine manufactury (snafus) clearance issued yesterday of one plant producing two lots of vaccine and tossed it out and several weeks later.

BONITA TENT

Donita Winning Polio Fight

Little Bonita Tent is winning her game fight against polio. The plucky little girl who — and defeats which and now must make her legs run. The father, Donita, and The Press yesterday afternoon was...

Turncoat GI Falls In Love

OKLAHOMA CITY (AP) — Samuel David Hawkins, Oklahoma City turncoat soldier who pleaded with the Communists after being repatriated to Korea, has fallen in love with a San Angelo girl in China and hopes to marry her, his mother said yesterday.

GM and Union Meet In Deadline Talks

DETROIT (IP) — Negotiators for General Motors and the CIO United Auto Workers met for a crucial bargaining session yesterday as the eve of the union's strike deadline against the world's biggest auto maker. Traditionally the gap that would come up with a new contract.

10 Crewmen Die In Air Disaster

STUTTGART Germany—(IP)—All 10 crew members of a B-29 Superfortress were killed when their plane plummeted and crashed into a field near a residential area here yesterday.

Train Hits Bar, Islander Hurt

CHATHAM Set (P)—The Brook-ville railroad yesterday...

2 Little Girls Still Missing

Have you seen the little children? The girls—Diane, 13, and Clarolyn, 8, have been missing since Thursday morning when they left their home at St. Delana Pl. Investigators for the Nassau Avenue police...

Court Reverses Assault Verdict

The State Court of Appeals has reversed an assault conviction...

No Break Yet In British Strike

LONDON (IP)—Hope for a speedy settlement of the two-week-old British rail strike...

Everyone Takes Cover In CD Test Wednesday

Today's Chuckle

The Weather

A confused masthead

headlights and a hood and trunk lid stripped like my plastic models of all ornaments and chrome. I rode in the Mercury only on rare occasions, for it was almost always kept inside the garage behind the house and was moved more often for maintenance than for travel. The garage had a grease pit built into its floor, which enabled my uncle to change the oil and do other things beneath the car in a semiprofessional way. He had for years, we knew, spent weekends working at a gas station in Brooklyn while saving up the money to buy a house on Long Island.

Uncle Joe hired Billy and me to do odd jobs for him, and he once engaged us to paint the chain-link fence around the entire perimeter of his property with aluminum paint. We had to do both sides of the fence, which meant being careful not to step on the neighbors' flowers or trample on Aunt Jean's rhubarb plants along the side of the house. Being as thin as water, the paint splattered easily on plants and dirt and the concrete driveway, something which made Uncle Joe cross, and so we had to work our brushes very slowly. Too vigorous a motion also splattered one or the other of us on the other side. Painting the fence behind the garage was a special challenge, since there was barely enough room for even one of us kids to squeeze between the building and the fence. Uncle Joe couldn't easily inspect how well we had done in that tight space, but he did see clearly that we had not performed the job to his satisfaction along the driveway. Since I was deemed the more mature and careful painter, the one who splattered less and covered more, it fell to me to go over the entire fence a second time to fill in the spaces missed, which my father and uncle alluded to as "holidays." As I toiled in the sun, I wondered if Billy, who was inside watching television, had been the wiser painter.

There was never a rigid schedule of weekend plans, but almost invariably when we didn't go to Lynbrook, my aunt and uncle would come over to Cambria Heights, especially if my father had a project to work on. When that was the case, they came early on a Saturday morning, and Uncle Joe brought his tools with him.

His abundant tools were arranged in several toolboxes in his basement the way his supplies were arranged in the several cabinets and chests. "A place for everything, and everything in its place," my father liked to say, but as his own toolbox attested, he didn't practice what he preached, at least with physical things. Though his tax records were impeccable and he had the reputation for being flawless at his work, he could not keep his ashes in an ashtray. My uncle, on the other hand, was supremely organized with everything, thoughts and things alike. He would bring to a job only a selection of specialized tools, chosen specifically with the nature of the project in mind. He always used all the tools he brought and never needed any more than he had with him.

One of the projects that captured my interest was the building of a closet in our attic, in which my mother wished to store our winter clothes over the summer. Uncle Joe arrived early in the morning, and he and my father went upstairs to determine what materials they would need for the job. There were no plans or drawings, and all that was written down was the number of two-by-fours, planking, finishing strips, and pieces of hardware that would be needed. They took my father's car to the lumberyard and came back with the wood sticking out the left rear window and tied to the door handles on the passenger side of the car, requiring my uncle to slide out through the driver's seat to help untie it and carry it up to the attic.

Uncle Joe did almost all of the measuring, marking, sawing, and hammering. My father was his assistant, holding one end of the tape, steadying the unwieldy boards, bracing the incomplete frame. I watched from a respectful distance on the stairs and marveled at how the structure took shape from its parts. What had started as my mother's wish for a place to keep heavy winter coats had been transformed in my uncle's mind into a plan to buy lumber and assemble it into a thing—a closet with sides and top and doors that kept dust and moths at bay. This was design and engineering, words that were not yet in my vocabulary, but processes with which I was clearly fascinated and to which I was drawn.

It was from my uncle that I learned most to admire machines

and to build things. Under his tutelage, even before I learned to drive, I used the grease pit in his garage to change the oil in my father's Dodge, and it was there I eventually tackled more ambitious projects, like replacing an entire driveshaft. Neither my uncle nor my father seemed to have any interests or special tools when it came to bicycles, however, and I had to rely on Sam the Bicycle Man and my own instincts to maintain and fix my Schwinn.

Working on my bicycle was a source of great satisfaction for me. With the machine upside down on its tripod, I loosened the nuts holding the front wheel in place and lifted it off the frame. The wheel had to be disassembled every now and then to clean the innards, especially the ball bearings, of accumulated grit and grime. Each part was removed from the axle and dropped into an old tobacco can full of kerosene or turpentine. The thin liquid had turned thick and black by the time I had the bare-bones axle to drop into the soup. I didn't actually drop it but rather lowered the axle into the dirty solvent with my hand, swooshing it around but being careful not to bang it against the nuts and cones and bearings sitting on the bottom of the can. I fished out the pieces one by one, gently agitating the solvent with my fingers to get a cleansing action. Each piece was laid out on an old copy of the *Press,* until it was ready to be dried off with an old towel or T-shirt my mother had consigned to the rag barrel in the basement. The axle was reassembled with clean grease and the cones and nuts adjusted until the wheel spun freely and without rub or wobble.

Disassembling the rear wheel was a much more complicated and delicate procedure, for the New Departure coaster brake had to be dealt with. Usually I didn't take the brake apart, it not being necessary and I not wanting to risk misassembling so critical a part of my bike. The adjustments to the rear of the bicycle were much trickier and more crucial to safety than those to the front, and so I usually convinced myself that the back wheel was running fine and did not need any maintenance. In truth, I was intimidated by the brake of my bicycle, with its curious exposed angle arm that was attached to the frame with what looked like a too-delicate metal strap held together by a screw from an Erector set. The one time I did begin to disassemble the brake, I reversed the aborted procedure with a great deal of anxiety and difficulty. I would have needed more instruction from Sam before I felt sure of myself in plumbing deeper into the insides of that thicker hub. As much as I liked machines, I was not as thorough or self-confident a mechanic with my bicycle as I should have been.

In other situations, my mechanical confidence could be more than the circumstances warranted. On one occasion, my mother showed off her new electric frying pan, something she had long wanted for deep frying and making pancakes. The squarish aluminum pan stood on four black plastic feet and had a receptacle at its base into which an electric cord fit. It was a marvel of modern technology to my mother, who had always cooked with coal or gas, but I was most attracted to the little light on the control panel. I had never seen such a small bulb, and I wanted to know what made it click on and off with the heating element. There were a couple of screws on the underside that I removed with a Phillips screwdriver.

The inside of the control unit held what looked like a rheostat, which attached to the knob by means of which the cooking temperature was set, and a lot of wires. The control unit was on the inside as much of a black box to me as the outside had been, but I did see that the bulb was larger than its visible tip had indicated. It was not unlike the bulbs that were on the new set of tree lights my father had brought home from work the previous Christmas. I ended my quest for understanding at that and proceeded to put the gadget back together. In reassembling the frying pan control, I caught the tip of the little bulb between the top and bottom parts of the housing and pinched it when tightening the screws. The bulb shattered, and I had ruined my mother's new appliance after only a single use. Though it still worked, the absence of the light diminished its magic. I thought we could get it fixed or replaced, but my mother chose to keep it in the bottom of the pot cabinet and use her old frying pan. I was never officially punished for my carelessness, but every time I saw my mother make grilled cheese sandwiches on an old cast-iron griddle, I lost my appetite. If my principal vice was taking things apart that I couldn't put back together, my mother's most hurtful virtue was her ability to hold her tongue. Like a book's, her thoughts were inside.

The only vices Aunt Jean and Uncle Joe seemed to have were her smoking and their joint passion for cards. Playing pinochle or poker was a favorite feature of our Sunday-afternoon visits to Lynbrook, and there was always a certain amount of betting, which naturally required plenty of change. When I couldn't change it at the candy store, I carried my paperboy's weekly take of coins to Lynbrook to convert into dollar bills. My aunt and uncle didn't need any more change than they already had in the heavy coffee tin and cigar box they brought to the table, but they always gave me bills for coins, my aunt usually short-changing herself, my uncle never. The mom and pop who ran the candy store could never be counted on to take my change, and the candy store lady certainly never made a mistake in my favor.

To me, playing cards was like disassembling a home appliance. The shuffled deck was like a black box, even though usually colored red or blue. I often studied the back of the deck of Bicycle cards to see how they could be marked. It was not that I wanted to mark the cards, nor did I suspect that they were marked. I had just heard that it was done in big games, and I was curious about how, in theory, it might be done, if a person was so inclined. The pattern engraved on the back of the cards was complicated enough that I could see how an unsuspecting player would not detect that a different little crevice was filled in on different cards. At the same time, I wondered how a card shark could pick out a little tick here or a missed line there as the cards were being dealt around the table. He would certainly have to have better eyes than I, or maybe wear glasses.

The hands dealt were disassembled parts of the deck, but they might as well have been bicycle parts that could not be seen in the grease-darkened solvent. The idea in poker was to ask the dealer for some replacement parts, hoping that he would give you those that meshed with the parts already in your hand. Sometimes they fit and sometimes they didn't. A card game consisted of a half-dozen or so people sitting around a table trying to get the dealer to reach into the murky can of parts and pull out a washer or a bearing or a cone nut. Not only did he not know where those parts were in the can, but also he did not know what parts you were asking for and so could not choose them even if he wanted to. The mechanics of playing cards was at the same time fascinating and frustrating. It was a game of chance, I knew, but I wanted it to be more than that. I began to excuse myself from the game and explore the books in the cabinets in my uncle's basement.

Books, I was beginning to learn, could be as much treats for the mind as cake and ice cream were for the mouth. At home, almost all the books my father and mother owned were kept on the three glass-enclosed shelves of the upper part of the secretary in the corner of the living room. There were three sets: a red-spined encyclopedia bought in installments at the grocery store; a complete black-and-gray set of Dickens purchased through the mail; and a gunmetal-colored picture history of World War II bought by subscription through a newspaper. I read the encyclopedia as I needed to, the Dickens on assignment from school, and the war history from cover to cover. There was no text as such, the story being told in captions to the news photographs, but my image of war was formed through the graphic carnage I turned quickly through to get to the pictures of tanks and planes.

My uncle's library, if that is not too grand a term for books stacked up like groceries in old kitchen cabinets in a basement, was rich in illustrated Victorian editions of novels and poetry and in well-worn how-to books. I didn't read the books at first; I looked at the pictures. The fiction and poetry books offered idyllic scenes, captioned with what I took to be précis of chapters and verses. The how-to books, obviously the more used, were full of diagrams of how things worked and how things could be made. I passed quickly through *Magic Casements* to hunker down beside the oil burner with *The Boy Mechanic: 700 Things for Boys to Do.*

In many of the books I found notes my uncle had made on loose sheets of paper, folded to fit neatly into a volume, perhaps as a bookmark. Most lists were on quadrille paper, and all were in his tightly controlled hand and bore an accountant's sense of column. There were lists of presidents, state capitals, dates in history, definitions of words. Finding these incongruous lists in my uncle's books was like finding a cryptic diary. At one time, I imagined that he had compiled them to help someone pass a citizenship test. Certainly he did not need to pass one himself, having been born in Brooklyn.

Increasingly, I spent a good deal more time downstairs than up, even though Aunt Jean had plenty of bulk ice cream in her freezer, and we were always free to help ourselves to seconds and thirds. Opening up the large freezer door, we saw an array of flavors that we could identify simply and precisely by what was printed on their cartons. It was not at all like selecting a book with an enigmatic or enticing title and finding an entirely different world inside. I much preferred the gamble to the sure thing. Playing cards, as much of a gamble as it was hand by hand, had become predictably boring in the aggregate. Opening up Aunt Jean's freezer ourselves was just not the same as watching Mike nonchalantly turn his head to the side as he reached into the dark of his Good Humor truck to produce a lime Popsicle from among the vanilla Dixie cups. Could he, I wondered, also deal an ace of clubs from a blue deck of Bicycle cards? Could I, I wondered, draw a winning hand?

The game of life in which I found myself was being played with a marked deck, I suspected, but how could I tell for sure? The hand I had been dealt was from a familiar deck, albeit one with a complicated background, and I was expected to draw all of my future cards from that same deck. Would my situation have been different had I started with a different deck? In my dream game, I would be in Nevada, where everyone was gambling. Some were playing for higher stakes than others, but only a few were winning. I certainly wanted to win, no matter how small the stakes, but did I know how to do so? Was I being taught to know how?

The casino in which I found myself was so separated by distance and money and heat from the other casinos on the Strip that it was hard to change venues. I was stuck with dealers who were men and women dressed in black and white, who didn't reveal their true colors to me. My education consisted of my being dealt random parochial cards, which once taken were hard to discard. All the kibitzers around the table told me to play the numbers and the mathematics, always working with the cards I was dealt. It was my fate to want to draw to an inside straight.

15

A BROKEN SEWING MACHINE
LEADS TO A BROKEN HEART

CAMBRIA HEIGHTS WAS WHERE I expected to grow up, work, and die, possibly in an atomic war. The city was my father's bread and butter, as my mother constantly reminded us, and it should not surprise us if it became ours. It was not what you knew but who you knew that got you ahead, she told us, and we didn't know anybody important.

The location of our house just five blocks from the city line meant that we could not really move any farther east and still have the ineffable security of the city that we did. As long as my father worked in the city, even if only across the East River from Manhattan—the real City—my family was never going to move farther out on the Island. As it was, we were pushing the envelope of escaping the ills of New York, while not fully leaving it. Some bad had to be expected with the good. CITY, SUBURBIA SEEK CURE FOR 'GROWING PAINS.'

That is not to say that my mother and father did not dream of things being better. My father worked two jobs, which kept him away until past our bedtime at night and, if he did not have carpool duty, kept him in bed until after we left for school in the morning. He did not work on weekends, but he was restless around the house and so went off on excursions to the bakery and elsewhere for much of the time on Saturdays. Some of those excursions, I suspected, were to play the horses. My father always hoped to win big, but he never managed to do so. When we got together with my aunt and uncle to play cards on Sundays, the stakes were penny-ante, but winning was still exciting.

My mother had not worked outside the home since I was born, but she did on occasion take in "homework." That use of the term seemed to have entered her vocabulary during World War II, when she sewed aviator goggles and gas masks in our Brooklyn apartment on Prospect Avenue. The heavy-duty khaki-colored thread she used had come on four-inch-high wooden spools that must have been liberally distributed during the war, for leftover spools remained in drawers and boxes throughout our house. If my mother the pessimist saw them as half empty, as a pragmatist she kept them for their being half full. If my father the optimist saw the spools as half full, as an idealist he argued for their being discarded as half empty. The pragmatist had prevailed, and half-full spools of "homework thread" served as our staple thread, string, and cord well into my teenage years. It was used to sew patches on dungarees and to repair sneakers and, double- or triple-wound, to tie up packages for the post office as if they were boxes of doughnuts from the bakery.

My brother and I had used homework thread to belt together pulleys on our Erector set creations, and we used it as telephone and power lines strung from plastic poles on our electric-train layouts. In Brooklyn, homework thread had been the line of choice for lowering a weight faced with chewing gum through a subway grating to the coins lost below; in Cambria Heights it was used for flying kites along the parkway. At Christmastime, the khaki thread steadied the tree in the living room and formed clotheslines for greeting cards hung like laundry from corner to corner of the dining room. It was well into the Cold War before our supply of homework thread began to run low, and it was at about the same time that my mother found a new source of money for a rainy day. A friend had told her about how much she could make addressing envelopes at home. My mother signed on to give it a try.

My father had years earlier brought home an ancient Remington typewriter that his office was going to discard, and it had been kept on the bar in the basement, where, sitting awkwardly on a stool, I had used it to compose my lists of rock-and-roll records and updated route lists. Now it was set up on the dining-room table. The job of addressing envelopes involved typing names and addresses on blank envelopes from the minuscule print on a page torn out of a telephone directory for a town in Minnesota. The envelopes came in boxes of five hundred, and the pay was half a cent per piece. In other words, for executing the motion of taking a blank envelope from the front of the box; inserting it into the type-writer; ratcheting it down to a prescribed position on the platten; typing out name, address, city, state; ratcheting it out; and putting the finished envelope in the back of the box, my mother was paid five mils. For repeating it five hundred times, she was paid $2.50. We kids thought it was a thrilling job, and we all wanted to help type envelopes. We soon tired of it and quit; once committed to it, my mother couldn't. Compared to addressing envelopes, delivering the *Press* was a dream job.

At least my mother was paid the $2.50 a box that she was promised. There were a lot of "gyp artists," according to the *Press,* who preyed on women who wanted to make money at home. Women all over Long Island were receiving postcards reading, "Would you like to earn $25 a week knitting at home? If so, put your phone number on the card and mail it back to us." One woman, who wanted some extra money to buy things for the baby she was expecting, responded and was visited by a well-dressed salesman who showed her "beautiful knitted baby sweaters and baby booties," which she could make herself on a knitting machine he would sell to her. His company would buy the things she knitted.

The price of the machine was four hundred dollars, payable in installments. She could pay ten dollars weekly and still net as much as fifteen dollars a week. Unfortunately, the machine worked only until it was almost paid off, and the woman could not locate the salesman to get it fixed, let alone to sell him the baby sweaters and booties she had accumulated before the machine went dead. The woman was heartbroken.

Aunt Jean found that story devastating. Though gardening was her summer passion, sewing was her year-round one. Besides a good cigarette and a better cup of coffee, what she loved most was working at her sewing machine. It sat center stage in the sunroom at the front of her house, and she spent hours of each day before it. She sewed dresses for herself, my mother, my sister, and my aunts and cousins "back home." The west-facing sunroom was the brightest and most open room in the house, with a wall of windows looking out on a street that no Good Humor driver would waste his time on, its six houses holding no more than three children total. One of those, who lived in the house directly across the street, was the only child of immigrant Germans who dressed him in lederhosen and kept him behind a fence, to protect him from the nonexistent traffic on the dead-end street.

My aunt at her sewing machine, behind the sheer curtains she had sewn, watched the boy and waited for the milkman and for the mailman and sewed and sewed. Behind her, against a windowless wall, there was a barrister's bookcase, a legacy from one of my uncle's uncles. To the best of my knowledge, not one of the books jammed into it had been removed for decades, until I had been through the books in the basement and began to read through this upstairs collection of poetry anthologies, *fin de siècle* novels, and histories of war. My aunt's reading, like my mother's, seemed to be limited to *TV Guide*, the *Family Circle* magazine brought home from the supermarket, and Simplicity, Butterick, and Vogue pattern books read at the yard-goods shop. She also read *Newsday*.

Newsday was the other Long Island newspaper, serving, as it did

then, Nassau and Suffolk counties. It had been founded in 1940 by
Alicia Patterson, the daughter of Joseph Medill Patterson, founder
of the *Daily News*. For a while, she worked as a reporter for the *News*,
but she did not succeed at the job. In fact, she was fired by her
father, who nevertheless promised that she would eventually come
back to that paper in a position of power. In the meantime, she married her third husband, Harry Frank Guggenheim, who wished to
help her overcome her playgirl ways. He purchased for her the
printing plant of a defunct paper, the *Nassau Daily Journal*, so that
she could start her own paper and prepare herself for bigger things.

The name of the new paper was the subject of a contest, which
the first issue declared had been won by a mechanical engineer
from East Hempstead. In fact, the name *Newsday* was suggested first
by a staff member and then the contest entries were searched for a
match. The name was a closely guarded secret until the first issue
was out, the editors fearing that the news magazine *Newsweek* might
seek an injunction against the upstart publication.

To me, *Newsday* was a curious-looking paper. Like the *Daily
News*, it was a tabloid, but it was wholesome, like the *Press*. Innova-
tive in its use of color, *Newsday* also attracted attention with such
gimmicks as running a center section of features that was inserted
upside down in the paper. Before it was ten years old, the paper
achieved a circulation of 100,000 and the International Circulation
Managers Association recognized its carrier boys as the best in the
United States and Canada.

When I was not playing cards or haunting the basement in Lynbrook, I sat on the couch or in Uncle Joe's recliner and read *Newsday*, which was full of local news, if "local" meant anything in a
circulation area that stretched a hundred miles out to Montauk
Point, on the easternmost tip of Long Island. Every now and then I
found the day's *Newsday* still in the state it was delivered in, rolled
like a set of blueprints and held together with a rubber band. The
only time I rolled a broadsheet paper like the *Press* up that way was
when I wanted to make a tall paper tree to amuse a small cousin at

a family reunion. With the paper held together with cellophane tape, I ripped it the long way every half inch or so around the tube. Then I twisted the inside backward, so that as I pulled it from the center it helixed out of the paper trunk a multitude of branches. The demonstration usually ended with the tree being used to swat away some older cousins.

I wouldn't dare make a paper tree out of my aunt and uncle's *Newsday.* Not because the paper was too short, but because in their house nothing was destroyed frivolously or thrown away casually. Kitchen waste was used to fertilize the garden, wood scraps to make a fire for cooking hamburgers. The disposal of trash was treated as a rite. There was a large wire basket sitting on a circle of concrete in the backyard, and in the fall Billy and I were treated to watching my uncle burn the leaves. He crumpled up some old *Newsday*s and placed them in the bottom of the basket and filled the basket with leaves. The flames shot out in all directions as the smoke rose over the house. When Lynbrook banned leaf burning, the basket disappeared without a trace. The concrete pad remained as a monument to the practice, and as a place to set the grill.

Aunt Jean was never in the yard when the leaves were burned. She stayed inside and smoked a cigarette over a cup of coffee. Though she said she much preferred making things to destroying them, she never admitted that smoking cigarettes was exactly like burning leaves. Mostly she did make things, however, including the crocheted doilies and antimacassars that were on every end table and soft chair. In fact, she had crocheted so many bedspreads and tablecloths that she gave them away to every niece who came of age. Her latest projects exploited her new sewing machine, an electric model to replace the treadle one she had used for years.

House dresses and aprons having long since been mastered, and with no children for whom to make lunch, Aunt Jean now looked to ever more difficult sewing projects. She found her ultimate challenge at the high school that she walked by each day on her way to and from shopping in the village. An adult-education class in tailoring was accepting applications, the message board declared, and after several weeks of reading the announcement, my aunt entered the school and enrolled. Her "sewing teacher" became her mentor and her guru, as she took increasingly advanced classes in tailoring. Class projects included shirts and trousers for my uncle, which he appreciated for their economy. Even with the cost of the class and the material, these were good but inexpensive clothes. In time, my aunt had sewed everything she could place with or fit on a relative.

Since the unheated sunroom became the coldest room in the house in the winter, the sewing machine was moved into the north-facing dining room, which was directly over the furnace. The move was always cued by the first freeze, the day after which the machine was set before the double window overlooking the rhubarb plants. The dining room was the hub of the house. Off of it were the kitchen, through which we usually entered, the living room, and the single bedroom, through which we had to go to reach the single bathroom. Because of the traffic that flowed through the central room, the dining-room table was normally kept leafless in a corner of the sunroom, retrieved each Sunday for the noontime dinner and postprandial card game. One year, the table remained in the sunroom all winter, because a new picnic table and benches were moved from the backyard into the dining room to protect them from the elements. Whenever any table was moved, usually by Billy and me, we had to be careful not to bang it into any walls or furniture or, especially important, the sewing machine. Aunt Jean's sewing machine was her mechanical love, as my bike was mine.

I was saddened by the abuse the bike had had to take at the *Press* office and on my paper route. My years-old birthday present was showing its age: its tires balding, its seat sagging, its paint dulling, its chrome pitting, its kickstand limping, its brakes fading. My bike had grown older so much faster than I. It was ironic, I thought, that I might outlive this steed of steel. But for all of its ailments, my bike was still my most compatible companion. As its parts loosened and its springs softened under my weight, my body adapted to them, fitting into a seat that leaned to the left, and getting used to hitching

*A Sunday in Lynbrook, with Marianne between Aunt Jean and
Uncle Joe and with author behind camera*

up the kickstand every third or fourth turn of the pedals on Sunday
mornings. The bare handlebar ends, whose plastic grips had long
since been scraped through by so many encounters with the sidewalk, had inadvertently been sharpened like a brass belt buckle.
The handlebars were best grasped at the attached crossbar, one of
the few accessories that still remained in place and functioned as
intended. The steel tube was cold in the winter, but in delivering

my paper route I wore one glove only to keep my flipping hand unencumbered.

I had come to mount my bike as easily as I switched from a walk to a run. I joined it in a single fluid motion that carried my right foot over the back of the seat to land on the right pedal, which had been rotated into position by a nudge of the left one, at the same time that my arms were turning the fork to point the wheel forward and my left foot was pushing off from the ground and in the same sweep raising the kickstand and catching the left pedal just as it was passing through its topmost position. My bike and I moved off with a gliding motion that belied the weight it carried.

Sometimes my bike was a vessel moving effortlessly across the trackless black asphalt sea. The motion created its own wind, and my shirt caught it like a backward sail. The front-ruddered vessel plied the sidewalk as if it were a river channel between banks of grass. The ballast of my legs keeping the ship upright, I moved my body in compensatory ways to stay the course as I gradually jettisoned the cargo of newspapers from the forward hold. Like wedges of wood thrown overboard to measure a ship's progress, the flipped papers drew my attention to their regress backward. The papers twirled out like vortices in my wake. Like knots on a line let out astern, the number of papers left behind on the stoops marked the speed of my journey.

Whether imagined as romantic or viewed as prosaic, delivering papers was above all a repetitive thing, as so much of life is. Repetition, especially mechanical repetition, is part of the human condition. Our hearts beat and pump, our lungs inflate and deflate, our eyes blink and stare, our heads turn and droop, our legs rise and fall, our arms extend and retract, our bowels fill and empty, our bladders swell and void, our bodies sleep and wake, our minds leap and lie, our hearts pump and beat, pump and beat, pump and beat. Repetition is part of our nature and in the nature of things, and we succeed in our human endeavors by mastering the art of repetition.

Delivering the *Press* had become so repetitious that the only things that kept it interesting were the occasional new subscriber and the frequent missed stoop. Missing the stoop pulled my mind back into the job, for the errant paper called me back to consider its lie. If it landed on the walkway or the steps leading up to the stoop, I usually left it there, it being in full view of the front door. If it landed on the lawn, I was torn between going back to center it, or going on knowing that it was not really lost to view. Which course of action was taken usually depended upon whether the grass was damp with a morning dew or wet from an afternoon shower or a lawn sprinkler. The paper that landed in the bushes beside the stoop demanded an epicycle of the bicycle to extract the daily planet from its eclipse by the greenery.

A paperboy on a bicycle spent a lot of time looking backwards, watching the fate of the last paper flipped even as he was reaching into his bag to grasp the next paper to flip. Like a baseball pitcher on the mound looking back at a ball hit into the outfield, while at the same time considering the next batter, the paperboy wanted to know the result of his last toss and what it meant for his next. If his job did not exactly depend upon it, it could certainly affect the statistics that only he kept, or his weekly tip.

For all the papers I flipped that missed their mark, and for all the times I retraced the tracks of my bicycle to root through a forsythia bush, I never experienced the cliché of the paperboy: the errant paper landing on a roof or shattering a window. If these things happened to anyone, they must have been rare, or deliberate acts of frustration or anger. There wasn't a *Press* boy in the office who couldn't hit a milk bottle on a stoop thirty feet away if he stopped his bike and concentrated on the throw. Perhaps the doubtful stories came from the Midwest, from the same never-never land where the Newspaper Boys of America association composed our route books.

In any case, what most caused us to miss was our ennui. The routineness of the task led us to dream of the perfect route, one with a subscriber in every house and a pretty girl at every window.

A route on which no one asked us to doorknob, and on which it never rained or snowed. A route on which every Friday evening a beautiful woman in an open bathrobe waited at the door to give the *Press* boy his forty cents plus a quarter tip. A route on which the next week the woman's equally pretty daughter waited for us to work our way down the block and ask her out on a date. Just as routinely, our dreams were shattered, and our hearts were always broken.

And it was just as well. The dream route would be a sure route to total and permanent boredom. As with everything else in life, the totally predictable is indistinguishable from the totally boring. In a perversely fortunate way, tedium and weariness lead to a lack of attention and carelessness, and these to errors and mistakes, which in turn give us a new goal to pursue. Seeing a pretty girl in every window would cause a paperboy to misflip his papers, not because their watching made him nervous, but because their being in every window made him care less. His weariness and dissatisfaction at the perfection of his route, even if it was only in a dream, would lead him into error and failure.

Even a little self-satisfaction could be a dangerous thing, for with it hubris returned. With every successful day—save for the odd paper that missed its mark not because of the paperboy's error but because of a dog on the lawn (DOG CATCHERS ON STRIKE) or a crack in the sidewalk or a child in the street or a ball in the air or a shift in the wind—with every successful day, a veteran paperboy became more convinced of his talents, which admittedly were superior to those of a novice. And because an experienced paper-boy could count his draw faster, fold his papers faster, pack his bag faster, ride his bike faster, flip his papers faster, finish his route faster, he could deliver a larger route in the same time as a smaller. So he usually acquired a second route to make more money, faster.

An overconfident paperboy also believed he could read the weather better than the weatherman, and so he believed he knew when it was not going to rain even if the *Press* weather box said it would and it looked to everyone else that it would. He flipped his 120 papers on days that younger boys doorknobbed their fifty. On the one day he was wrong, half of the papers he delivered were not taken inside before the sky exploded. 'THE STREET IS LIKE A RIVER.'

Telephone service was out in Cambria Heights, and so customers could not call the *Press* to complain and the circulation manager could not know to call the paperboy to save the customers, some of whom stopped the paper the next weekend. Many of those who did not stop it stopped their tipping for it. The paperboy had to reestablish his reputation not from square one on the Monopoly board but from the corner jail. If delivering papers had become as routine as addressing envelopes, sewing sundresses, or knitting booties, the tedium was undone in the time it took the sky to change.

The sky might as well have been changing from blue to grey for Brooklyn fans, as talk of the Dodgers moving out of Ebbets Field, once so unthinkable, became increasingly credible. Ebbets Field, where the team had played since 1913, had a capacity of just over 32,000 at a time when the Dodgers could fill 50,000 seats easily. The team president, Walter F. O'Malley, who called himself The O'Malley, began talking up the need for a new stadium in Brooklyn.

The O'Malley, who had studied engineering at the University of Pennsylvania, was known to be a genial man, but one who conducted business as if it were a mean game of poker. When Charlie Dressen, the Dodger manager who had led the team to National League pennants in 1952 and 1953 but lost the World Series to the Yankees, was offered a one-year contract for 1954, he told O'Malley he wanted "three years or nothing." He got nothing, and O'Malley hired Walter Alston, who did bring the world championship to Brooklyn the next year.

Even in the midst of that magical season, there were rumors of where the Dodgers would be playing in years to come. The O'Malley had already arranged for the team to play seven games in New

Jersey in the 1956 season. With Ebbets Field sold to a real estate
developer, from whom the Dodgers were leasing it back, there was
little financial incentive for the club to stay in Brooklyn. A new stadium, however, might do the trick, but no land on which to build
one seemed to be readily available in Brooklyn. O'Malley had
appeared to be moving ahead with plans to buy a site formerly
owned by a Forest Hills gambler and most recently occupied by a
veterans housing project. It was on Horace Harding Boulevard,
next to the Grand Central Parkway, and just east of Queens Boulevard—in Rego Park, Queens! LOOKS LIKE DODGERS WILL BE IN
QUEENS BY '58.

The move made sense. The Rego Park location satisfied O'Malley's important criterion that a new ballpark would have to be
within thirty minutes of any Brooklyn fan. The *Press* reported that
the players were "100 percent for the move," noting that many of
them already lived in Queens. Hell, The O'Malley himself lived on
Long Island, in Amityville, and so the new park would be more
convenient for him. Like a lot of rumors, this one made a lot of
sense.

But shortly after the Dodgers won the 1955 World Series, The
O'Malley turned up the heat. There was increasing talk about moving the club to the West Coast. Recent New York legislation had
given the mayor of the city authority to issue as much as thirty million dollars in bonds to build a new stadium, and sites began to
become available. A grandiose plan had been devised for a fifty-
thousand-seat monument to Mammon with a sliding glass roof
over the infield. The proposed stadium was to be built in downtown
Brooklyn, within blocks of a half-dozen subway lines and the
nearby Long Island Rail Road station. Fans, who were already used
to taking public transportation to the ball games, could come to this
new location from all corners of the city and from the Island. But
the stadium plan was complicated and by no means universally to
the liking of influential factions within the city. The O'Malley said
he himself would not invest in it. He was also concerned about

timetables. His choice for a site was not far from the city's, on land already largely owned by the Long Island Rail Road, which he expected would be favorably disposed to joining the Dodgers in investing in a new stadium that could be built more efficiently. Like many other things, it was all a matter of money and timing.

16

DOESN'T NEED A LICENSE
BECAUSE HE CAN'T DRIVE

DURING THE SUMMER I WENT frequently to Jones Beach with Jim Wall, his brothers, and their cousin. Since none of us was old enough to drive and getting public transportation from Cambria Heights out to the beach was inconvenient at best, we often hitched a ride with a lifeguard named Kevin, whose shift started at eight in the morning. We returned with him in midafternoon, in plenty of time for me to deliver my papers, which for all its tediousness and repetition remained a highlight of the day.

The beach was no more than a thirty-minute ride along the Southern State Parkway. Rumor had it that New York's master builder Robert Moses had the Southern State designed and built with limited-clearance overpasses, so that buses could not take low-income people from New York City to the parks and beaches on Long Island. NOT ENOUGH PARKS? LUNDY'S FAULT, MOSES CHARGES. The story didn't make sense.

The parkways were designed to exclude trucks and buses, granted, but as far as I could tell, not for any deliberate social or political reasons beyond providing a pleasantly landscaped highway that automobile drivers and their passengers could experience without having the scenery obscured and the ride rendered hectic by larger vehicles. To this day, when I am behind a truck or bus on a scenic highway or behind a massive sport-utility vehicle or minivan on an interstate highway, or even at a red light, I long for the parkway experience of Long Island. The overpasses were not only kept low to maintain the roadway's ambient geometry and minimize the intrusion of approaches into surrounding neighborhoods, but also were faced with stone to give them a finished, permanent look. Driving on the parkways in and around New York City was a pleasurable and relatively relaxing experience precisely because they were restricted to automobiles. I didn't believe they were designed with any more insidious social or cynical political motive in mind.

But what in fact was an automobile and not a truck, and thus eligible for use on the parkway, came to be somewhat a matter of definition. Panel trucks, which were used by many a small business for a delivery or service vehicle, were forbidden. Yet if, Jim told me, windows were cut into the side panels of a truck, and if it had no obvious commercial markings, it might be classified as a personal vehicle and so be driven everywhere. As a result, many an anonymous deliveryman's, plumber's, or electrician's truck had a small window cut into each side panel. Pickup trucks, even though they were more open in the back than panel trucks with windows, were considered unabashedly commercial and so definitely forbidden from the parkways. With the advent of minivans, sport-utility vehicles, and pickup trucks with shells enclosing their bed, distinctions between cars and trucks, between business and pleasure, became even more blurred, and eventually, long after I left Cambria Heights, a new New York State law began allowing "personal-use pickup trucks" to be registered as passenger vehicles. This meant they could obtain and display the license plates that marked them as legal on the parkways.

In the 1950s, except for those windowed panel trucks that drove through the loophole, the profiles of vehicles on the parkways were

more or less uniform. During those summers, Jim and I used to
spend a great deal of time on the grassy aprons of the Cross Island,
sitting in the shade of crab-apple trees whose sour fruit we tried
once and then rejected forever, just watching cars go by, calling out
their year, make, and model. Often we would engage in friendly
competition; we would each choose a make of car and then we'd see
who could count more going by on the parkway. Jim, ever loyal to
Ford, invariably chose it. I alternated my choices between Chevro-
let and Plymouth, not because I liked them but because only they
were competitive with Ford in their numbers on the road. When I
did not care about the contest, I chose Mercury.

Jim knew cars better than anything else. He made no pretensions about being a student and prized more highly than books the
colorful new-car catalogs that generous dealers gave out to kids
like us, who obviously were years away from making a purchase. As
talk of the new model year began to accelerate in *Motor Trend* and
other automotive magazines, it was a ritual for Jim and me to ride
our bikes a good distance into Nassau County to the car dealer-
ships on Merrick Road and ask them for the newest brochures. The
new car models did not come out till October and November, but
well before their announcement dates we knew about as much
about them as it was possible to know.

Each fall I also read the inside pages of the *Press* more carefully
than I did during any other season of the year. I combed each day's
paper for car advertisements and stories about the new models,
clipping them out carefully to paste into scrapbooks that just the
previous spring had been unpretentious school composition books
or spiral-bound notebooks. Some of my car books still bore the
label "Religion" or "Social Studies," with the few pages that had
been used for class notes ripped out and the remainder salvaged for
a better cause.

I especially prized the fall issues of *Parade,* the rotogravure section carried in the Sunday *Press,* in which the new automobiles
were pictured in colorful advertisements, showing off chrome trim
and two-tone paint jobs to best advantage. Using the sharpest scis-

sors I could find in my mother's catch-all kitchen drawer, I carefully cut out the images of the new machines, separating them from
the advertising copy and female models that surrounded them. The
result was irregular polygons circumscribing the soft curves of the
streamlined and large-finned beauties. There could never have
been a more blatant conflict between the machine and the garden
than in my old English notebook, where pastoral poems were
pasted over with the portraits of chromed and sculpted internal
combustion machines. The rigid blue rules and red-lined margins
of composition books printed in classical form were boldly overlaid
with aerodynamically curved Fords and Chevys raked at defiant
angles, as if they were brand-new cars parked diagonally across
several spaces in a parking lot to protect the finish. Misaligned as
they were, the cars fit snugly into the tight spaces of a student's
dreams.

Jim and I took the bus and subway into Brooklyn and New York
for only three things: Dodger baseball games, Alan Freed rock-and-
roll programs, and the Auto Show. At Ebbets Field, the Bums somehow never won when we were present, and I became increasingly
more engrossed in the steel structure of the upper deck than in the
game on the field. At the Brooklyn Paramount, we waited on long
lines to get inside to watch Chuck Berry do his duckwalk across the
stage, Bo Diddley coax the most unnatural sounds from his guitar,
Jerry Lee Lewis pound the piano keyboard with his heel, Frankie
Lymon and his Teenagers sing as fast as they could, and Screamin'
Jay Hawkins come out in a flaming coffin. Screamin' Jay wore a gar-
ish cape and sang "I Put a Spell on You" while brandishing his cane,
which was capped with a cigarette-smoking diminutive skull
named Henry.

After a hiatus of sixteen years, the National Automobile Show
was held in the fall of 1956 in the newly opened Coliseum at
Columbus Circle in Manhattan. At the show, where we saw our first
high-finned Plymouth Golden Fury, we collected brochures from
each display and stuffed them in the shopping bag we wouldn't be
caught dead carrying at any other time. The show had some exper-

The '56 Ford Thunderbird—latest version of the fabulous car that inspired the styling of Ford's full line for '56.

NEW '56 FORD

Page from a car scrapbook

imental vehicles and cars of the future, but these interested us less than the brand-new models that we had yet to see on the Cross Island. We sat in the cars we could sit in and we watched the others rotate untouchable on their turntables, guarded by buxom and leggy models whose curves we tried to see around.

We were not completely oblivious to the young women who ran their fingers along the sharp fins of the new cars and brushed their hands ever so lightly over their bulging hoods and bulleted bumpers. But we focused on them only after we had understood the subtle differences between last year's and the coming year's automobiles, between a '56 and a '57. As a result, we usually made at least two rounds of the car show, and it was on our second round through the Coliseum that we focused on busts and butts in addition to grilles and taillights. We were not looking at re-creations of the car ads that appeared in the Sunday paper, in which an attractive mother sat next to her husband in the front seat, accompanied, sometimes, by two children in the back. At the auto show the cars were under the control, supervision, and spell of beautiful models. The cars turned on cue and doors and hoods opened at the graceful wave of the gloved feminine hands of women who were dressed much more seductively than the mothers in the newspaper ads. Jim and I were still car fans, but we also were beginning to appreciate the accessories, even if they were out of reach of young teenage boys.

When we were not looking at cars, we were coveting them. The natural extension of this desire was, of course, the wish to drive them. There were plenty of stories around the *Press* office of boys having taken a car for a joyride early on a Sunday morning, before delivering their papers. ANOTHER JOY RIDE ENDS IN JAIL. I had never witnessed this directly, but I certainly could imagine it.

One Sunday morning, when I was going out to the garage to get my bicycle, I was stopped by the presence of my father's car, parked in the driveway rather than put away in the garage. The unusual occurrence of the car being left out overnight prompted me to go back into the house to see if the keys were lying on the kitchen counter or on the telephone table in the dining room. They were in the kitchen, and I took them from the counter and went quietly out to the driveway with the intent of moving the car into the garage—putting it away to protect it, I would tell anyone who caught me. I

had never driven a car, but I was confident that I could do it, for I
had watched my father many times start up and drive the machine.
DOESN'T NEED A LICENSE BECAUSE HE CAN'T DRIVE.

I opened the driver's door as quietly as I could, emboldened by
the fact that my parents slept in the far front corner of the house,
and I got into the driver's seat. I pulled the door closed but did not
latch it, for fear that the noise would awaken my brother or sister. I
tried to put the key in the ignition, but it wouldn't fit. After several
attempts I realized that I was using the wrong key. When the right
one was finally inserted, I sat straight up and turned it with some
trepidation. The car started, leaped forward, and stalled immediately, having advanced only a foot or two toward the garage. The
car had been left in first gear, and I had forgotten to depress the
clutch. I startled myself but apparently had awakened no one in
the house. So I decided to try again.

This time I pushed the clutch to the floor and held it there
before doing anything else. Then I took the gearshift handle and
worked it up toward neutral, looking for the play that my father
always found before starting the car. Confident that the transmission was in neutral, I again turned the key to start the engine. It did
not run smoothly in the cool morning air, but I knew if I pulled the
choke out the engine would race and make more noise. With the
car sputtering, I slowly pulled the gearshift handle down and
toward me, seating it in the position I knew to be first gear, and
began to let the clutch out very slowly. The spring on the clutch
pedal took me by surprise, however, and it flew out the final inches
with great force, engaging the transmission and shooting the car
forward. Luckily the car again advanced only a couple of feet
before stalling. This time I had forgotten to release the parking
brake. My father, being a belt-and-suspenders man, in thought if
not in dress, always engaged the parking brake, even when the car
was left in gear with its front wheels turned toward the curb.

Since no one seemed to have been awakened by my false starts, I
decided to try once more. I was not going to make the same mistakes again, and so this time I held the clutch pedal in with a tensed

foot ready for any springback. With everything appearing to be in order, I carefully reached down to my left and slowly pulled the trigger on the emergency brake handle under the dashboard. I did it deliberately so that the handle would not fly forward with a bang the way it did when my father released it. The play on the brake handle had taken my arm well into the dark under the dash, pulling my body down so that I was looking up through the steering wheel into the trees. From that position I saw the leaves moving, which confused me because I did not remember there being any wind. As a paperboy, I had become very sensitive to when there was the slightest wind to alter the course of my papers.

Straightening up my body to start the car's engine, I saw that it was not the wind that was moving the leaves but the car that was moving under the tree. The driveway had an ever-so-slight incline down toward the street, and my holding the clutch in and releasing the emergency brake had allowed gravity to take its course. I was immobilized in the moving car, so taken by surprise that I could not think what to do to stop it. The car was picking up speed and, since I had turned the wheel slightly when reaching down to release the brake, heading into the neighbor's fence. I knew immediately why the parking brake was also called the emergency brake, but I was afraid to reach down for the handle because then I might move the steering wheel the wrong way. I tried to steer in the opposite direction, but then the left front fender was heading into the fence. My mind was working as quickly as the car was now moving, but my arms and legs were still immobilized. My arms were frozen on the steering wheel, waiting for a message from my brain about which way to turn. My right leg, which had been at the ready on the gas pedal, was so heavy that I could not get it to move to the brake. Suddenly, my left leg, numb from pushing down so hard on the clutch, shot up from the floorboard as if propelled by some external force. This engaged the transmission, which stopped the car so quickly that I thought that I'd suffered whiplash. Fortunately, I had forgotten to take the car out of gear.

The car had stopped just inches from the fence, so close that I would not be able to get out the driver's door. But I was afraid to try to start the car again, not wanting to push my luck. I slid across the front seat and got out on the passenger side. The car had rolled back a total of maybe six feet, not even reaching the grassy median, but at the steering wheel it had seemed to me that it was rolling for sixty. I walked around to look at the driver's side, confirming that I could not have gotten out and that my father would never get in from there. There was no way he would believe that he had left the car in this position, but I was afraid to try to start it again, realizing that I could not count on myself to remember to do everything in the right order and get the car back where I had found it. Even if I could start the car successfully, I was not sure I could steer it back into place. I had watched my father try to pull out of enough parallel-parking situations to believe that it would not be easy. I decided to leave the car where it was, hoping that my father would accept my suggestion that some teenager must have tried to roll the car out into the street without starting the engine. He certainly would ask me if I knew why the car was where it was. I returned the keys to the kitchen counter and rode my bike to the *Press* office, never again to try to move my father's car without his knowledge. He never asked me how the car got moved.

On another occasion I tried to move a stranger's car. The talk around the *Press* office had been about how easy it was to hot-wire a vehicle. There were these wires underneath the dashboard that had only to be touched together, according to the talk. Even without ever having looked under a dashboard, I was confident that I could find the wires, touch them appropriately, and know what to do next. My plan was to just drive the car around the block and park it exactly where I had found it. I didn't think it smart to take such a joyride in a car parked on my own paper route, so before going to the *Press* office on a moonless Sunday morning I rode down the next street over. There was a line of cars parked at the curb in front of some attached houses on this block, and I proceeded up the line trying each car's door. The first three were locked, but the fourth had been left unlocked, so I climbed in and angled my body to look under the dashboard. There was a small amount of light from a nearby streetlamp, but hardly enough to clarify the maze of wires that I found. I abandoned my attempt and got back on my bike, thinking all the way to the *Press* office about what might have happened to me had I been caught. BOY IN STOLEN AUTO KILLED FLEEING COPS.

What was a crime and what was not, what was a sin and what was not, what was safe and what was not, were not completely obvious to a boy of fifteen. That summer, there was a short-lived fad of taking the fancy ornaments from cars, especially the small, handsome, multicolored ones that appeared on the sides of newer Fords, and attaching them to the baskets and fenders of bikes. Given our auto-show knowledge of cars, Jim and I knew exactly which ornaments were most desirable and where they were located on the cars. Most were attached to a fender or hood by pressing two prongs into predrilled holes in the sheet metal until they snapped into place, and they could be removed by just reversing the process. Jim assured me that a medallion could be taken off without damaging either the car or the ornament by just sliding a thin pocketknife blade underneath the jewel and prying it up until it popped off. Jim showed me a few that he had taken off in this way, and I agreed to go out with him one afternoon looking for treasure.

When we found a parked car with a desirable ornament, one of us would straddle his bike as if taking a break from riding but would in fact be standing guard while the other crouched low on his bike and worked at freeing the prize. In my dreams, the first one I had tried was a snap to remove, and I had become immediately addicted to the ease at which the deed could be done—and without leaving any visible scars on the car other than two small empty holes in the body. In reality, I couldn't get myself to pry hard enough, fearful that I would scratch the car or break the ornament or bend the knife blade. Jim was always less queasy in the face of technological surgery, and so he took over.

At the end of the day we divided up about a dozen trophies, and we rode home to hide them. That we hid them assures me that we knew what we were doing was wrong, but the intoxication of the act to which I was an accessory kept me, at least, from immediately thinking about it on any moral level. I didn't think about the anger a new-car owner might feel when he noticed his Crown Victoria missing one of its gems. Since we had not scratched or otherwise defaced the car, I rationalized, he could easily remove the shadow of dirt and wax that was left behind with a bit of polish and elbow grease, leaving only the two insignificant little holes. If they bothered the car owner, he could buy a replacement medallion and restore the vehicle to its original condition. Anyone who could afford a car could afford to replace a missing ornament, I reasoned.

But we were responsible for the feelings of disgust, the inconvenience, and the expense our vandalism must have caused proud new-car owners. When I had slept on the act, I felt I had done a very bad thing, and I remained anxious about it until I went to confession the following Saturday. It seemed to take the priest some time to understand exactly what I was confessing to, but once he claimed he did he confirmed what did not need confirming—that what I had done was wrong. He told me I should return what I had stolen to its rightful owner, but this generic response was of no help to me. I told him that I could not remember exactly where the cars were parked, and, even if I could, I could not be sure the violated car would ever be parked in the same place again. What I really feared was attempting to replace a stolen medallion and getting caught in the act.

The priest insisted that I make restitution of some kind, and so he suggested that I put an extra amount of money in the collection box at the back of the church. THE PUNISHMENT CLEANS THE RECORD. The disposition of the stolen ornaments was never addressed further. I left my stash of them hidden in a brown paper bag in the garage, in the crevice between the top of the wall and the bottom of the eaves, nestled between two rafters. It was the same place that I kept my Daisy BB guns, outlawed in the city but bought legally just over the border in Elmont and smuggled into Cambria

Heights. I had put the guns to rest after I wounded a bird shooting my Red Ryder by the parkway. BOY, 14, HELD AS HIGHWAY SNIPER.

I never took the ill-gotten ornaments out of the paper bag, and I certainly never attempted to install any of them on my bike. I threw the unopened bag in the garbage one evening, as I took it out to the curb. The BB guns were forgotten where they were hidden, where they may remain hidden to this day. What Jim did with his medallions I never knew, but I do know that he did not attach any of them to his bike either. After we conspired in our deed, we never talked about it to each other. I suspect that he, too, had pangs of conscience, having defaced so many of the Fords he so loved. He probably also went to confession, but that was not something boys talked to each other about.

We didn't think about such stuff when we went to Jones Beach. When we got a ride from Kevin or some other lifeguard on early duty, we were the first ones on the beach and could lay down our blankets wherever we wanted. We usually settled as close to the water as possible, just behind the high-tide line, defying the receding surf to return. This was something we could not do when we were with my parents, who preferred their blanket well back from the still waters of Zach's Bay, which was adjacent to Jones Beach but protected from the direct sea by the comforting arm of a breakwater. In the bay the water was calm and predictable, and there were no undertows.

On the beach proper, the waves were high and unforgiving. Unlike the cars whooshing past Jim and me sitting by the side of the parkway, on the beach the waves broke and the water ebbed straight at and away from us. It was more like laying my head down on the tracks before an oncoming electric train, picking my head up, letting the train pass, and then laying my head down again, but in the other direction, looking at the receding caboose. Early in the morning, without people on the beach to distract the eye or ear, the surf was hypnotic. The air was also cool in the mornings, and so we raced headlong into the water, diving under the waves. We knew that the water, after an initial shock of cold, would calm our goose bumps. We felt warm as long as we stayed submerged to our necks in the water; when we emerged from it we wrapped ourselves in beach towels immediately upon reaching our blanket.

We had to wait for hours for the beach concessions and pool to open up, and we dug in the sand around our blanket, wondering what we might find that someone else had lost. We never found anything of any significance. In time we abandoned our treasure hunt and followed the beachcombers around, trying to get a glimpse of what they found. The littered and tramped-on surface of the beach was sifted and flattened by tractors dragging behind them large flat baskets, skimming the remains of yesterday off the top of today. The baskets were emptied periodically into the round wire-mesh trash cans placed all along the beach. Amateur beach-combers followed the sanitation crew and dug their smaller broom-handled baskets much deeper into the sand, almost to the dark, wet foundation sand in which we cooled our feet after walking across the hot top sand that burned them. We did not get to see most of the treasure that the beachcombers unearthed; it was secreted away into pouches that they wore around the waist, like barkers at a car-nival. Only rarely did a beachcomber hold something up to the sky to look at it in a different light. On those occasions we could see that what was being found was rings. Since this was the 1950s, the rings were still only the kinds worn on fingers, not the rings of alu-minum pop-top cans that became the bane of beach walkers in the early 1970s. Those, still attached to the curled sharp metal tongue pulled off the can top, and looking not unlike the bakery lady's string-cutting ring, would slice feet and toes left and right, until the detachable pop-top was banned.

If we could still walk through the sand with impunity, we respected the water greatly, avoiding it when the undertow got too strong because we knew that we were not practiced swimmers. When we felt the water pull the sand out too swiftly from between our toes and out from beneath our soles and when the current pushed and pulled at our shins and calves where we stood in the surf, we knew it was time to retreat to the bathhouse. There we played in the pool, acting like we knew how to dive and swim, things we didn't do very well. But we did know that the pool did not have the "towering waves and whiplash undertow" that I read about in the papers I was folding after returning from the beach one afternoon. HEAVY SURF TAKES 3 LIVES. On that occasion, according to the *Press,* it was a fifteen-year-old Cambria Heights boy, who was snatched in broad daylight. BOY DROWNS AT JONES BEACH. The boy had lived on 225th Street, just across from Montefiore Cemetery. We didn't know the drowning victim, but he might easily have been one of us. As late as the three-star final went to press the next day, the boy's body had not been recovered from the sea.

17

THE KID WHO DRINKS THE
MOST IS CHAMP!

THE *PRESS* OFFICE WAS MOVED one weekend, because its lease could not be renewed at a favorable rent. On Saturday afternoon we were told that the next day's papers would be the last to be picked up at the Colfax Street office; on Monday afternoon we should report to a different storefront, just off Springfield Boulevard, across from the Little Sisters of the Poor convent whose walls I had often passed but would never see behind.

Inside, the new *Press* office was almost indistinguishable from the old. The wooden benches, carved with initials, notched with cigarette burns, stained with newsprint, and polished by boys folding papers at the bench's edge and packing them against the wall, had been moved on Sunday afternoon and were installed pretty much as they had been on Colfax Street. The major difference was that the new office had no back door suitable for the delivery truck to use. This meant that the wire-bound bundles of papers would have to be unloaded from the street and passed by a brigade of paperboys through the front of the store to the back, where they were stacked behind the counter for distribution back out to the front.

We had a better handball court, in that there was a long unbroken brick wall between the new *Press* office and the Tip Inn Bar & Grill on the corner. The Grill part of the name of this and other like emporiums was an artifact of the law. To get a liquor license in New York City, an establishment had to serve food as well as drink, and so most saloons incorporated some reference to dining in their name and in their signage. Thus we took the bar-and-grill sign in stride, but we snickered at the neon sign in the window reading "Cocktails."

The handball court along the Tip Inn's wall mimicked outside the geometry we could see for the barroom inside. Against the near wall was a tabletop shuffleboard game, perhaps twenty feet long, which paralleled the bar, which in turn was set along the opposite, windowless wall. We *Press* boys came to know the layout of the place on afternoons when the papers were late and the bar was empty of patrons. The law allowed kids as young as sixteen to go into bars unaccompanied by an adult, but not to be served alcohol. We sat at the bar, as if it were a soda fountain, and nursed Cokes. The drinking age in New York at the time was eighteen, but few waited that long to experience beer and liquor. The older *Press* boys gave us younger ones detailed reports of what happened in a bar in the evenings, but we were not prepared for what we saw and heard on Sunday mornings. 'KIDS, STAY OUT OF THE GIN-MILLS!'

Bars apparently could serve liquor until the wee hours of Saturday night, which was really Sunday morning, and the last customers seldom left before four or five o'clock, having had a reserve of full glasses set up at the bartender's announcement of "last call." Riding my bike past the Tip Inn on Sunday mornings gave me the impression of a loud party, and on occasion I witnessed men and women staggering out into the waning dark or the breaking light. It was not uncommon to find, on rounding the corner, along our handball court, men sleeping, pissing, or throwing up against the wall. We didn't play handball on Sunday mornings, and inexplicably the wall always appeared to be clean, and so the slop forgotten, by Monday afternoon. In spite of the tawdriness of the Tip Inn and its patrons, just about every one of the *Press* boys wanted to experience the effects of alcohol.

Even though we did not as a rule read the stories in the papers that we folded and delivered, there was one investigative series that was followed with some interest in the *Press* office. For weeks, the paper ran articles under the rubric "*Press* Spotlight on Booze for Boys," reporting on growing unruliness in Rockaway Beach and attributing it to underage drinking. The trouble was centered along "Tavern Row," a collective name for the bars that were located between Rockaway Beach Boulevard and Ocean Promenade—the boardwalk—and stretched for twenty or so blocks, from what in Rockaway was designated Beach 95th Street to Beach 116th Street, near the amusement area known as Rockaway Playland. In this mile-long, one-block-wide area the *Press* reporter counted seventy-four bars, and nine out of ten of them were reported to sell beer to minors as young as fifteen, and some not even boys. IF MY MOTHER COULD SEE ME NOW, SHE'D KILL ME, SAYS TIPSY GIRL. The *Press* series rubric evolved to "Spotlight on Teen Drinking."

One story described the bar game of chugalug. This was heady reading for us younger *Press* boys, and we soaked it up. For the youngest among us, the article was a primer:

The Kid Who Drinks the Most Is Champ!

Teen tipplers along Tavern Row in the Rockaways have rediscovered an old beer joint game. It's called chug-a-lug and here's how it goes:

The bartender sets up a row of glasses filled with beer. The young toper picks up the glass and drains it without lowering his head. Then he goes on to the next glass... and the next... until he can't drink anymore.

When that happens, the next drinker tries his luck. Whoever drinks the most is the champ!...

There's also a variation to the game. The bartender sets up two or three rows of glasses and the young contestants race to see who finishes his row fastest....

One bar in the heart of Tavern Town has an honor roll. If you want your name inscribed, all you have to do is drink 50 beers there during a single day.

According to the reporter's calculation, assuming that "a day in Tavern Town usually begins at 10 at night," a drinker had about five hours to earn honors. That came to an average of ten beers an hour or one every six minutes, and at fifteen to twenty cents a glass, a bar bill as high as ten dollars. The older *Press* boys ridiculed this conclusion, for they knew that the bartender would serve every fourth or fifth beer "on the house," in effect giving a substantial discount to a frequent drinker.

With the *Press*'s spotlight on the problem of teen drinking, the New York State Liquor Authority came under scrutiny and an investigation was called for. State officials blamed the tavern owners for not following the law. TAVERN ROW BAR ADMITS IT COULDN'T SERVE A MEAL. But the barkeeps were defiant, and one even declared that anything should be allowed, "just like the old days." The paper carried stories of robberies and knife battles prompted by drinking. The father of a boy who stabbed another said to a reporter, "I don't understand why the newspapers are interested in such trivial incidents."

Judges began to be more strict in their rulings, one fining a waitress $250 for selling beer to a fifteen-year-old girl and in addition telling the girl that her parents should take her to a woodshed and use a big paddle. Another judge imposed a similar fine or thirty days in jail on a barkeeper who sold beer "to two boys who rode to his bar on bicycles, and stopped in for a drink."

No one that I rode bikes with had yet gotten up the nerve to try to buy beer. I did want to experience the effects of drinking, however, and I had my chance on one of the longer bicycle trips that on occasion I took with two of the *Press* boys I spent the most time with outside the office. On a Saturday morning, Frank O'Connor, Ron Orange, and I were to ride up toward Little Neck Bay, passing through Alley Pond Park. Since I had spent a lot of time with Frank, hanging out with him after delivering our *Press* routes, I thought I knew him. He knew Ron well, because they spent a lot of time together before delivering their routes, and it was Frank who asked Ron to join us on the bike ride.

Ron was the only Protestant boy that I spent any time at all with away from the *Press* office. His name was funny in a different way than mine, and Frank and I always mispronounced his last name by placing the accent on the last syllable, sometimes even calling him O'Range, just to avoid calling him the name of a fruit, which we figured was insulting. Anyway, Ron was shaped more like a pear than an orange; it was Frank who in his rotundity more closely resembled the citrus fruit. Both were heavyset, but certainly not fat. Both had lighter hair than I, and both were a lot more worldly. WATCH 'BAD APPLES,' SCHOOL KIDS ADVISED.

Our excursion was begun early on a Saturday morning so that we could travel some distance and still get back to the *Press* office by midafternoon. We rode north mostly on the east side of the Cross Island Parkway, quickly past Creedmoor, the mental hospital, and at a more leisurely pace through Alley Pond Park. By late morning we had gotten as far as the widest part of the bay, to about where we had planned to turn around and begin our way home. Wanting to come back on the west side of the Cross Island, we saw our chance at a rare pedestrian bridge. With some effort, we carried our heavy balloon-tired bikes up the stairs of the bridge approach to get them to the other side of the parkway, and once there we sat down to rest on rocks set in among some bushes on a hill high above the bay.

Frank and Ron each produced a bottle of Pepsi-Cola from their *Press* bags, and Ron took a tin of aspirins from his pocket. Each of them put two aspirins in his mouth and immediately took a large gulp of Pepsi. Ron told me that the combination gave the same sensation as being drunk, and I wanted to see what it felt like. I tossed a couple of aspirins into my mouth. They began to dissolve on my tongue, leaving a salty taste. As badly as I wanted to wash them down with the Pepsi that Frank offered me, I first held the bottle to my side and rubbed its mouth with the palm of my free hand. It was a reflex reaction that we all had, to cleanse the bottle of the previous drinker's germs, and no one took offense. In the meantime, though, the aspirin was effervescing on my tongue, and I took an extra-large gulp of Pepsi to wash it down.

Almost immediately, I began to feel, or imagine myself feeling, light-headed and blurry-eyed. Since I did not wear the glasses that I needed, I was probably close to being legally blind and in no condition to ride a bike, with or without the Pepsi and aspirin. KEEP ASPIRIN OUT OF THE REACH OF THE CHILDREN—IT CAN KILL!

My fellow *Press* boys, who through prior use must have developed a tolerance for the potential effects of acetylsalicylic-acid cocktails, got up quickly and took off on their bikes into the wooded park. I followed, or thought I was following, in slow motion. They were too far ahead for me to see clearly what path they were on or hear distinctly what they were yelling back at me, but I followed what I thought were the sounds of their voices and the rattle of their bikes. Soon I was lost in a thicket, and I found myself on a path that began to fall off steeply. I could not brake on the loose dirt, and I could barely control my bike to avoid hitting trees as it gained speed going down the hill. After some distance I ran out of hill and flew over a retaining wall and through the air, like a motorcycle daredevil launched off a ramp. When the front wheel of my bicycle hit the ground, I was thrown over the handlebars and landed on my face and forearms, scraping along the pavement to a stop, unconscious. BIKE RIDE'S END.

I awoke to strangers leaning over me, my head propped up on someone's folded jacket fitted against the curb beside a parking lot. A priest was among the strangers, but he said I did not need last rites. Soon an ambulance came and I was put on a stretcher. I asked about my bike, and what about my paper route, and I was told that my friend Frank had said he would take care of them. I passed out again, but woke up as the ambulance bounced over some railroad tracks. I kept going in and out of consciousness in the emergency room, lost to time. When my parents appeared, the doctor told them what he thought had happened, and after a few hours of watching over me, they were told they could take me home.

I slept in my parents' bed that evening. They must have slept in the living room, if they slept at all. My front teeth were broken, my nose was broken, and I had deep abrasions on my face, my wrists, and my elbows. My body had landed on a tripod of its own making. I complained of a headache. When offered an aspirin, I declined.

The next morning, Dr. Goldman, our family doctor, made a house call. He looked in my eyes with his small flashlight and diagnosed me immediately as having a serious concussion. I should never have been released from the hospital, he told my parents, and he had me admitted to Jamaica Hospital that afternoon.

I had a semiprivate room all to myself in the hospital, overlooking the Van Wyck Expressway. After a few days I began to feel pretty good, even though my broken teeth were sharp against my tongue and the abrasions under my nose were crusted over with a thick scab of a mustache that stiffened my upper lip and would leave a scar. It hurt when I tried to smile, which wasn't often. My parents visited me every day, and Aunt Jean came to see me a few times. When she asked me what I would like her to bring me, I told her the names of some new rock-and-roll records, even though I had nothing to play them on. The records sat on my bedside table, and I soon knew their labels by heart.

One evening, my English teacher, Mr. Murphy, came to visit with a couple of my classmates from Holy Cross. It was in Mr. Murphy's class that I was beginning to learn really to read. Prior to then, I had relied upon Classics Illustrated, the comic-book versions of the Western literary canon, to learn enough of the plot of a novel to pass a test on it or write a book report. Before Mr. Murphy's class, book reports had taken a familiar form: "The title of this book is _____. It was written by _____. The main character is _____. The action takes place in _____. The story is about _____. The lesson of the book is _____." The blanks were easily filled in from the comic-book précis.

Mr. Murphy had a different approach to books and reports. He wanted us to read—not to fill in blanks, but to picture ourselves as part of the story and to participate in the action, or at least to watch it from behind some bushes, within shouting distance of the characters. He thought books should be something to enjoy and learn from, not something to tick off on a summer's reading list. I heard him say all this in class, and I wanted to do what he said, but I had been having a hard time going from comic-book panels to pages of solid type. Though I had paged through my uncle's library, I had read few real books all the way through, save for an illustrated edition of *Treasure Island,* which I kept in my room. I had survived English by relying on the Classics. I couldn't tell this to Mr. Murphy when he visited me in the hospital and brought me a copy of the book the class had begun reading in my absence.

Mr. Murphy left me the book, *Heart of Darkness,* by Joseph Conrad, and told me not to worry about missing class. If I read this book, I would be all caught up, in his class at least, when I got back to school in a week or so. I planned to ask my mother to bring me the Classics Illustrated version of the book the next time she visited. In the meantime, since there was little else to do in the hospital room, and since I owed it to Mr. Murphy for visiting me, I began to read *Heart of Darkness.* The experience was entirely new and more intoxicating than the Pepsi fizz. The people and scenes in the book came alive for me, and I was able to follow the plot better than in a comic book and to see the action more vividly than in a cartoon. I saw the boat and the river and the jungle, and I savored every word on every page. Though I can't say that I fully understood it, I read the story to the end, and I was sorry that Mr. Kurtz died and that the story was not longer. So I read *The Secret Sharer*, which was bound with *Heart of Darkness*, and became equally engaged in it immediately. I went on to read more of Joseph Conrad, and was greatly saddened one day when my copy of *Lord Jim* fell from under my arm facedown into the puddle of muddy water that lay between the curb and the bus onto which I was climbing.

Once I became engaged in literature, I turned into a real reader. That is not to say that I stopped buying *Hot Rod* and *Motor Trend*, or ceased to enjoy them. Words on the page simply began to mean more to me than pictures in a magazine. I also continued to read the adolescents' favorite iconoclastic magazine, *Mad*, and I was thrilled to see on the newsstand the issue whose cover resembled a school composition book. THIS COMIC BOOK'S DESIGNED TO SNEAK INTO THE CLASSROOM! It was clever, and it was a great gag, but it was the words and ideas in *Mad* that were now more important to me than a camouflage cover or the toes of a Don Martin character drooping like Salvador Dalí clocks over the edge of the curb.

By my second week in the hospital I had begun to enjoy the comfort of the bed, though I was told to get up and walk around so I did not develop bedsores. I stood and sat for hours at the window, looking down on the traffic, learning its diurnal patterns. I followed individual cars, as far as I could see them, watching them weave in and out of lanes on the Van Wyck Expressway and disappear into and reappear out of underpasses. I also watched the movement of people on the sidewalk and on the elevated train platforms in the distance. Though the people and the cars they drove were free to go in all sorts of directions, they followed very predictable patterns throughout the day and night. There was an overarching order, even amid the disorder of people exiting and entering the trains, cars entering and exiting the expressway, buses stopping, starting, and turning onto the streets below. What I was watching was technology in motion, and what made it happen was the engineering of the machines and the transportation systems within which they moved. I could not have articulated it that way, but I was becoming equally attracted to the real world of things on the street and the imaginary world of ideas in books. Although I didn't know it, C. P. Snow had just published his first article on the concept of the two cultures, through which he expressed outrage that poets did not know thermodynamics. Like most of my peers, I would not know the term "two cultures" for years, but I was already trying to straddle the gap between them.

After two weeks in the hospital, I was released, and I went immediately to the dentist. My four top front teeth were broken off in jagged patterns, and one of the bottom ones was broken off clean just above the gum line. Their fracture surfaces were full of sharp edges, and I had learned from the first day to keep my tongue away from them. The dentist evaluated the damage and told my mother I would have to have root-canal work done on all five of the broken teeth, which then could be fitted with caps. He could do the work that summer. In the meantime, he did not think it worth doing anything else to my teeth. I was told to keep my tongue away from the teeth and to avoid anything too hot or too cold, precautions whose value I had already discovered for myself. For the rest of the school year I kept my mouth shut and my smile muted. I avoided looking at myself in the mirror, and I longed for the time when I had just a single chipped tooth.

When my accident happened, I had just become old enough to have my teeth permanently capped, and during the six-month process of repairing them I would pass from childhood into young adulthood. I would be taken from the sweet taste of a teeth-cleaning to the otherworldliness of root-canal work. At first, I would dread the repeated visits to the dentist, but the routine that was soon established numbed me to the pain. Each of my broken

From a photo-booth at the beach

teeth had to have the same multiple-step processes performed, serially, one at a time. What I would experience with the first tooth I knew had to be repeated on four more. The broken tooth had to be cut off at the gum line, the tooth had to be drilled into and its innards removed, stainless-steel posts had to be inserted into the space vacated by the roots, and caps had to be fitted over the posts. Plaster casts of my broken teeth had been taken before the work was begun, to record my occlusion, or what was left of it, and other casts were taken after my teeth were cut down and the steel pins had been put into place. The temporary caps that were to be fitted to my teeth in the interim would have to be sculpted without bene-fit of a true casting, and I was fortunate that my dentist was an artist. After half a year in the chair, I would be pleased to have teeth rather than stumps again, and I would treat my new bite with great respect, not carelessly eating apples or corn on the cob and cer-tainly not removing bottle caps with my incisors. I would have a mouth that was all bark and no bite.

For the two weeks I was in the hospital, Frank O'Connor had delivered and collected my paper route. I would reciprocate when he went on vacation and also while he recuperated from a slipped-disk operation. My first day back on the job was a Sunday, and my father insisted on driving me around my route. I put up no resistance, appreciating the convenience of being able to place the papers proper and the comics-clad inserts in separate piles side by side on the backseat. When we reached the first block on my route, I counted out the right number from each pile and, like a Midwestern paperboy with a Junior Carrier Seal, paired paper and insert as I walked across the lawns. I slid a completed paper under the corner of a welcome mat or inside a screen door. I was relieved that I remembered the route without a list; I took it as the final proof that I had not damaged my brain in my accident. My father was also impressed by my command of the route, and he took it as a sign that I could deliver it myself on Monday.

It felt good to get back to delivering papers again, but my bike was not what it had been. Frank had brought it back to my home, carrying the carcass like a dead deer slung across the basket of his own bike, and left it in our garage. My basket was a total loss, the front wheel was bent badly out of alignment, the fork was permanently skewed, there were deep gouges on the frame, and the handlebars were badly scraped and rusted. The bike reminded me of my own damaged wrists, arms, and upper lip, which were healing slowly and developing brown scars. I was told to keep putting cocoa butter on them. I didn't worry about the scars on my bike, but I did have to get it into working order. I adjusted what parts I could with my father's wrenches, but I had to go to Sam's to buy a new basket and to get the wheel fixed. He told me I needed a new rim, and he could install it for me in about half an hour. He advised leaving the fork bent as it was; I would get used to the bike pulling to the right. I was self-conscious about my teeth, face, and arms, and so instead of talking with him while he worked on the wheel, I roamed about the store, looking at the new and used bikes that had come in since my last visit. In the front of the store, behind a bunch of sixteen-inch children's bikes with training wheels, was one I had not noticed before.

It was out of reach, but I could see that it had a basically black frame, with red accents and chrome fenders. I asked Sam about the bike, and he told me that even though it looked new it was used. It was a Schwinn Black Phantom that had just been traded in for an English racer, and it appeared to be in excellent condition. He was going to put it out in front as soon as he had a chance to give it a good polishing. I had heard about this model Schwinn but had never seen one. It had a spring fork, and a horn console fit in between the top bars of its frame, mimicking the gas tank of a motorcycle. The front fender had a streamlined headlight faired into it, and a substantial black luggage rack was fitted over the rear wheel. The fenders were chromed, as were the wheel rims, and the tires were whitewalls. The light-colored tanned leather seat—the saddle—looked as softly upholstered as an easy chair compared to my old bike's tractor seat. The Black Phantom was the Cadillac of bicycles, and I wanted it.

I asked Sam how much he was going to ask for the Phantom, and he told me sixty dollars. I asked him if he could hold it for me for a few weeks, while I saved enough from my paper route, and he told me I could take the bike home if I would promise to pay him five dollars a week for the next ten weeks. We shook on the deal, and I carefully moved all the children's bikes out of the way to get at the Phantom. It was everything I hoped for in a bike, and it would be what I would ride for pleasure after delivering my paper route. The bike I had been given as a birthday present just three years earlier was fenderless, scratched, rusty, and now forever out of alignment. The chain guard had had to be removed when it could no longer be kept away from the chain, and the kickstand had not been functioning for some time. The basket, which I had just replaced, was now the best-looking part of the bike.

Although my workhorse Schwinn needed attention, it was the

A Schwinn Black Phantom

Phantom to which I gave my time. I polished the chrome of its fenders and rims, which to my disappointment were ever so slightly pitted with rust, something I hadn't noticed in the low light of Sam's shop. The rims were especially difficult to clean around the spoke nipples. I took the wheels off and disassembled the front axle, cleaning the bearings in solvent and laying them out on newspapers to dry. I tested the brakes and found them sound, so I only oiled the rear axle assembly. I reassembled the bike with pride, taking great care not to round the nuts with my father's adjustable wrench that did not hold its setting.

I rode the Black Phantom only when there was no chance of rain, and it stayed looking good for some time. In the meantime, my old Schwinn continued to break down. Its chain often came off the sprocket, and its dangling kickstand interfered with the crank when I pedaled backward to apply the coaster brake. On more than one occasion I had to stop the bike with the soles of my Keds. One

Sunday morning, just as I was jumping on the bike to go to the *Press* office, a link in the chain broke, and I did not have a replacement. I could have taken the chain off the Black Phantom and put it on the old Schwinn, but instead I took the Phantom out of the garage to deliver the day's papers on it. It looked to be a clear, dry day.

The guys at the *Press* office had seen the Phantom the day I rode it back to the office after finishing my route on my old bike, but they never thought I would deliver on it. I surprised them, and myself, this Sunday. The bike didn't have a basket, and so I would have to carry the bag of papers suspended from the handlebars, which was difficult to do with the spring fork poking into the bag like a knee in a back. I cinched the bag up very high, so that it cleared the fork spring underneath. After delivering that bag of papers, I returned to the *Press* office for the second. All worked well, the ride being much smoother and the seat much more comfortable than on the old Schwinn. For several weeks after that I used the new bike for delivering my route, but when I noticed it getting a bit rusty from riding through the drizzle on Saturday afternoons and the dew on Sunday mornings, I fixed the chain on my other bike and went back to using it.

I had surprisingly few bad feelings about the accident precipitated by the kid's cocktail, and I held no grudge toward Frank and Ron or the old bike over whose handlebars I had flipped. Even riding past the Tip Inn every Sunday morning made me feel no special animosity toward those who were inside enjoying themselves with beer and liquor. It would still be a couple of years before I would be eighteen and of legal drinking age, but it would be well before then that Frank and I would get up our nerve to stroll into a place like the Tip Inn, sit at the bar, and order a beer. By the time we were seventeen, we would know bartenders on a first-name basis, and they would serve us, no questions asked. The Tip Inn would become one of our favorite hangouts. Frank and I would sit and talk about what we were going to do with our lives. The talk would not get very serious, though, until we were close to graduating from high school.

In the meantime, we would play shuffleboard, getting pretty good at a game that involved the same feel for the puck on the polished wooden surface as pitching pennies did for the coin on the concrete. It was all in sensing how the disc would bite as it neared the end of the board or the base of the wall. Granted, more English could be applied to a sliding puck than to an arcing penny, but there was also a sameness to the games. In both cases, it was the marker out in front of all the others that was the winner. Frank and I began to talk about being such markers in life, but we didn't yet have a clue about how to go about pitching ourselves.

At various times throughout the night, the Tip Inn's bartender, Sal, would go to the back room and come out with a pizza pie, which he would place on a small table sitting right beside the scoreboard on the shuffleboard game. The pizza would be devoured by the patrons, who swore it was better than that served at the nearby pizzeria, and everyone would order another round of drinks. We would drink late into the night, not trying to make any honor roll, but just enjoying shuffleboard, pizza, beer, cigarettes, and the semblance of conversation.

One night, Ron Orange joined us at the bar. He was older than we, and he was now legal. He also knew the ways of bars, and so we looked to him for guidance on how to behave. He showed us how to drink boilermakers, which were surprisingly easy to down. It was only years later that I would learn the caveat "Whiskey on beer, never fear. Beer on whiskey, mighty frisky."

Ron was not a good shuffleboard player, and so he took part in only one game. We watched from our stools as others played, listening to his description of other bar games. Out of the blue he asked if anyone wanted to play Chicken Wings. None of us knew what it was, and so he explained. Two guys place their arms flat on the bar, elbow to elbow and wrist to wrist, as close as they can get them. A third person lights up a cigarette and takes a few puffs, getting it burning so it won't go out. When the cigarette is about a third smoked, it is dropped into the crevice between the two arms, and the first guy to move—to flap his wing—is the loser and has to buy everyone else beers. Ron challenged me to play Chicken Wings, and I accepted his challenge.

The cigarette was dropped by Frank. I felt it warm at first and then quickly hot. The hair on our forearms was already singed, and its odor filled the air around us. The cigarette tip was red-hot, and there was the faint smell of burning flesh. WHISKEY-FED BLAZE OUT OF CONTROL. Although there was a sensation of discomfort, I could not say that it was painful. I was not sure what to consider a threshold of pain, since I had had so much dental work done without novocaine, and I had come to expect that things sometimes hurt, but that there was nowhere to go to escape.

The cigarette continued to burn, and a crowd had gathered behind and around us. The crowd was very quiet, and all eyes were on the fault line between our arms, waiting for one of us to quake free and thus relieve the tension in the barroom. The cigarette was still only about half burned down, the rate of burning having slowed in the confined space. Time became suspended, and neither Ron nor I said anything after the initial bantering about who was going to move. We looked straight ahead and glanced down at our arms only when reaching for our beers. When the cigarette ash grew too long to support the butt in the position it had fallen, it broke free and the spectators jumped. Ron and I held our arms steady, neither of us wanting even to flinch and so give the other guy the chance to yell "Chicken!" Each arm was supporting the other in a sense, his against mine and mine against his, each providing a benchmark of immobility for the other. The cigarette continued to burn and had reached about one-quarter length when Sal broke the silence, saying, "You guys are crazy."

I can't speak for Ron, but I was in a sort of trance. It was not a trance induced by beer, for I had had only two or three glasses before we began the contest. Perhaps the shot of whiskey had affected me, but I would swear it had not. Rather, it was the kind of trance I had experienced at the dentist's. After the initial shock of pain, there was a cloak of numbness that surrounded me in the chair, as it was now surrounding me on the bar stool. Dentists must understand this, because they go on working on the teeth, seeing as they must the nerves they are exposing and exciting and burning with their drills.

Though everyone else was still and silent, Sal began to pace back and forth behind the bar and mutter how we were out of our minds—and in his bar. Ron and I asked onlookers to light up cigarettes for us and put them in our free hands, so that we could have a smoke, acting even cooler than we thought we already were. We also continued to sip the beers in front of us, nursing them. Our flesh was still being cooked, slowly, like a hamburger over dying charcoal, but the charcoal was sitting on the meat. We had been at it so long that the odor had become lost in the much stronger one of stale beer and urine and a fresh pizza burning. All of my senses but touch had become acute. Ron and I were stoic, each of our arms as rigid as a two-by-four. The only movement was a slight swivel of the bar stools now and then, when our asses got numb from sitting so still for so long. Our arms, though, remained motionless, neither of us wanting to give the other the opportunity to say "You moved!" and pull his arm away in victory.

The contest did end with a chicken, but it was neither of us. Sal, who knew that he could get away with serving beer to minors all night long, feared that there would be no escaping an incident of an arm having to be amputated for gangrene because of a bar game played on his watch. He asked us to call it a tie, but neither of us responded. He said he was going to tear our arms apart if we did not move them, now. Still we remained steadfast. Suddenly, he tossed a glass of water on the cigarette, and it sagged into submission. The game was over, and each of us could say that he had won.

Sal was the loser. He had chickened out. Though he expressed a lot of concern for our safety, he really didn't give a damn about what happened to us once we left his premises. We knew he was concerned for his profit and his liability, and nothing else. He sold beer to minors because it put money in his till. He sold lots of beer to minors because it put lots of money in his till. If he offered a beer on the house every three or four, it was because he knew we knew that the customer knew that he was not supposed to leave after the bartender had given him a free beer. Plenty of nights we left tipsy, but Sal didn't care as long as we didn't fall until we were out on the sidewalk. If we puked around the corner, he didn't care, as long as it was not too near the front door. He would flush it into the gutter and down the sewer after the last drunk had left.

Everyone but Sal wanted to see our arms, each of which bore a raw swath of skin where the cigarette had smoldered. Neither of us admitted to its hurting. Sal gave us beers on the house, no doubt relieved that he was off the hook. We were moving our arms as if nothing had happened, and I went back to playing shuffleboard.

That night in bed, I worried when my arm began throbbing. In the morning I saw that the area around the burn had taken on a green tinge, and the red center was oozing yellow pus. I told my mother that I had burned it on a radiator, and she put her nameless salve on it and bandaged it. The sore grew for several days, looking as if my flesh had been pecked at by a crow, but then the ugliness began to recede. My mother told me to leave it open to the air, so it could heal naturally, and not to pick at the scab, which was black and thick.

I trusted my mother's form of folk medicine. After all, it was she who had successfully dressed another wound that I had suffered seven years earlier on the same arm. I was climbing a high chain-link fence to get into a school playground when my Keds slipped out of the wire diamonds that my feet were beginning to outgrow. My forearm happened to be over the top of the fence at the time, reaching for the other side, and the sharp exposed end of the fence wire dug into my arm like a meat hook into a shoulder of beef. I was hanging from the fence by one arm, or rather the meat of one arm, my dead weight digging the spike deeper into my flesh. It was only when I pulled myself up with my other arm that I could unhook myself and back down the fence and run home. There was surprisingly little blood, but I could see the insides of my arm all white and pink and the flesh ripped and coming out the hole like feathers out of a torn pillow. My mother washed out the wound with peroxide and dressed it with her salve. Since it was summer, we went to the beach so I could take off the bandage and immerse my forearm in salt water, which she swore was the best cure.

Years later, whenever I gave blood, that inch-long lenticular scar on the inside of my left arm drew the attention of nurses, who could see that it had never been sutured. They invariably told me it should have been, but I knew that it didn't need to be. The nurses did not see my burn scar, the patch of smooth, hairless skin about an inch long and a quarter inch wide—cigarette-butt-like—on the outside of my forearm, which was lying still, as if on a bar. Like the opposite sides of a coin, the scars could not be seen at the same time, but taken together they suggested that my arm was pierced by a bayonet or spear in the wars of youth.

But that was all still in the future, after Frank and I would quit our *Press* routes, but before we would turn eighteen. We were lucky never to be caught. Whether we were drinking or only playing games, no policeman ever did come into the Tip Inn or any other bar that we would drink at, nor did I ever see a cop in the vicinity of the *Press* office, where some of the older boys still hung out. New York police were pragmatists. We kids were not the ones who ended up on the sidewalk around the corner. When we threw up, we did so quietly in our bathrooms at home, thinking our parents didn't suspect a thing. And we didn't get into fights. To intervene, the police had to be provoked or called, the way they were by the *Press* in the case of Rockaway Beach.

When beer-drinking became a regular thing for us to do, we spent an increasing amount of our pocket money on beer and cigarettes. Baseball cards, electric trains, 45-rpm records, and even car magazines had been left behind us, like papers flipped into the shadows at twilight. Late at night, whether to have another round or another butt was usually our most pressing question. Decisions about what to do with our lives were ahead of us, but not yet close enough for us to talk about too seriously at a bar. We wanted to enjoy the leisure life. We wanted to go to school, work a few hours a day, and talk about drinking on Friday and Saturday nights. That was the good life, even if the only girls we had thus far known were those whose faces we had glimpsed in the windows of the houses on our *Press* routes.

18

BINGO'S BACK AGAIN IN QUEENS

W E HAD GROWN UP WITH games of skill and chance. We shot marbles, flicked bottle caps, flipped baseball cards, pitched pennies, and even put our moons on the line in handball games. At home, with relatives, we played penny poker and nickel pinochle. It was no wonder that we later played shuffleboard for beers and blackjack for bigger stakes. Gambling was part of our experience; it was our recreation.

Games of chance were also a well-established means of raising money for worthy (and unworthy) causes, which is what has endeared them to groups throughout history. Many a medieval bridge was built by a trust that raised its money through a lottery. Princeton University's historic Nassau Hall was built with the proceeds of lotteries held in the mid-eighteenth century, which enabled the College of New Jersey to relocate from Newark. On mid-twentieth-century Long Island, a more recent form of lottery raised money to run Catholic schools and enabled other nonprofit organizations to carry out their charitable works.

A pure lottery is a raffle, in which there is but one winning number. The participant exchanges some money for a ticket. The stub of the ticket is deposited in a great drum with all the other stubs. The one stub pulled from among the thousands determines the winner. His lot had been drawn. But there was only one winner. Everyone else lost, and that did not encourage participation.

An alternative way to conduct a lottery is to have the contributors select a set of numbers, with the winning combination being drawn from a drum with numbered balls. In choosing the numbers, the player has more control over the game, or thinks he does, and there can be multiple winners. This is essentially the lottery, illegal in the 1950s, that so many states have subsequently come to adopt. As games of chance, these lotteries do require a degree of patience on the part of the players, who might well prefer to know more immediately than Saturday night whether they are winners or losers. Hence the instant lotteries of today.

The game of lotto, the word being Italian for "lottery," also introduced immediate gratification. Lotto is played with cards bearing a matrix of numbers, which are covered as they are called out. All the players are in the same room, playing the game in real time. The first person to cover a line of numbers is the winner. The winner collects a prize, and a new game begins immediately. Lotto has been played in various forms around the world. During gold rush days, a variation of the game was called keno, a word derived from the French *quine*, meaning a set of five winning numbers in a lottery.

Lotto was being played in America during the Depression. One night, a Brooklyn toy salesman named Edwin S. Lowe happened upon a small country carnival at which a group of people was engrossed in the game, using beans to cover the numbers on their cards. He was struck by their doggedness in playing until two o'clock in the morning, and he considered adding to his toy and game offerings a home version of what he called "beano." With a rubber-stamp set, he prepared a twenty-four-card prototype of the game to try out on a group of friends. One of the players, upon hearing called the last number that she needed to complete a line, yelled out, "Bingo!"—which became the name of the game that Lowe sold for home entertainment.

When a priest from Wilkes-Barre, Pennsylvania, approached Lowe looking for a way to raise money for his church, the toy salesman suggested bingo. But a lot more than twenty-four different combinations of numbers were needed to make the game pay off for the church, and so Lowe hired a mathematician to come up with more number arrangements and yet keep the game from having too many winners. He devised six thousand unique bingo cards, and Lowe produced a booklet explaining how prizes should be valued so that the game could be run for a profit. By 1934, more than ten thousand bingo games were being played each week, and Lowe's company had a thousand employees and sixty-four printing presses, running twenty-four hours a day, using more newsprint than the *New York Times.* "Bingo," meaning "I've got it," was once a simple interjection yelled by scholars and savants, in the tradition of Archimedes' "Eureka!" In 1950s America, "Bingo!" had become a poor people's "Eureka!"—not because they had found a new way to measure the amount of gold in a crown but because they thought they had found a new way to win enough money to be able to afford some simple luxuries.

By the time we moved to Cambria Heights, bingo was being described as one of the most popular forms of low-priced gambling in the world. It had come to be played at least weekly in church basements and school auditoriums all over Long Island, with the priests and nuns usually keeping a respectable distance from the game. It was not lost on them that here was a steady source of revenue that did not depend on some lucky sweepstakes winner turning up in their parish and tithing. But the fact remained that bingo was illegal. Actually, New York State's antilottery laws forbade gambling of all kinds.

In spite of its illegal status, churches and synagogues, veterans and other nonprofit groups, came to depend upon bingo for raising funds to carry on their good works. The authorities had long looked the other way when charitable organizations set up games a night or two a week. They drew auditoriums full of mostly working-class women for a night out—and the chance to win hundreds of dollars by betting that the cards they were issued would have the right numbers in the right places at the right time.

In 1954, the game of bingo was made legal in New Jersey, after the question had been put to a vote of its citizens. At the same time, a movement began in New York State to crack down on games of chance, especially bingo. The bingo squeeze was precipitated when the police commissioner received complaints from Protestant groups staunchly opposed to gambling that professionals were running some of the games, and that children were being allowed to play. PROTESTANTS MAP POLICY ON BINGO. The complaints were sent down the chain of command in the five New York boroughs, where police officers were expected to crack down on professional gamblers but continued to turn a blind eye toward those games that raised money for schools, hospitals, and other worthy causes.

Deputy Chief Inspector Louis Goldberg, head of Brooklyn's Morals Squad, who had a reputation for arresting fireworks salesmen on the Fourth of July, took the complaint to heart and began raiding bingo games being played in churches and synagogues. Goldberg was accused by proponents of leading a crackdown on the game. He was rebuked for his action, his superior declaring that games falling into the category of "amateur status" could proceed, but Goldberg soon renewed his drive to enforce the letter of the law against games in Brooklyn. Shortly thereafter, he was charged with insubordination for not informing his superiors of his intentions to go after the games, and he was demoted to captain. Before that could take effect, he tendered his resignation after thirty-six years on the police force.

Goldberg's crusade lasted only three weeks, but bingo became an election-year issue in New York, and Democratic and Republican candidates alike vowed to make the game legal in the state, at least on a local option basis. The incumbent governor, Thomas E. Dewey, a Republican who had been opposed to legalized gambling of all kinds, called for a plank in the party platform and had backed a state referendum on the issue after a particularly busy weekend of Goldberg's police raids on bingo games in progress. Each political party wanted to capture the votes of the bingo bloc. One politician was quoted in a *Press* headline as saying, 'AS QUEENS GOES, SO GOES N.Y.'

The publicity having made it clear that they were breaking the law, the churches, synagogues, and veterans groups canceled games and concentrated their energies, though quietly, on making the recreation legal. CHARITIES AND CHURCHES AGREE TO END BINGO. The New York Catholic Archdiocese and the Brooklyn Diocese, under whose jurisdiction our parish fell, were mum on the issue, denying that they had ordered games stopped. To do so would have been an admission that they had not ordered the cessation of the illegal games before all the flap. In any case, the basement of Sacred Heart School was to remain dark on Saturday nights, at least until after the election, in which the Democrat Averell Harriman became governor. Three years later, in 1957, New York State voters would fully endorse legalization of bingo, thus allowing local referenda the following year. In the meantime, bingo was revived.

The games had resumed under the cloak of an appeals court ruling that had found the game to be legitimate as long as the players were charged an admission fee for entertainment, rather than for the game itself. Some churches provided the entertainment by interrupting bingo games every twenty minutes or so with some recorded music. Not amused, the bingo players sat silently through the music, wishing no more to listen to it than they did to the refrigerator cycling on and off at home. The entertainment took up time that could have been spent gambling, and the latter gradually won out, as a *Press* reporter discovered:

'I Played Bingo, Spelled G-U-E-S-S'

I played bingo in Queens last night, only it wasn't called bingo.

At Mary Immaculate Hospital in

Jamaica they call it "Guess." But it's not
much different from good old-fashioned
bingo.

The "guessing" part of the game comes
when someone makes bingo. The winner
must first answer a question before getting a
prize.

The questions are not very hard. One of
those they asked last night was "who won
the second game of the 1955 World Series?"

Church basements became so overcrowded with bingo players
that the overflow sat in classrooms and listened to the numbers
called over the school public address system. Some children, coming to school the morning after a bingo night, found their classrooms in disarray, the floor littered with cigarette butts.

In the wake of Inspector Goldberg's crackdown, the *Long Island
Press,* being neither nonprofit nor a charitable institution, as its
paperboys knew all too well, had introduced a bingo-like game to
fill the void. Like "Guess," it was ostensibly a game of entertainment and skill, like television's *$64,000 Question,* which scandals had
not yet discredited. The *Press*'s Bingo-Quiz Game appeared in the
Sunday paper and carried a first prize of a thousand dollars.

Since it would have been impractical to provide different-
numbered cards to every subscriber/player, not to mention that it
would raise the specter of gambling, instructions were provided on
how contestants could construct their own bingo cards for playing
the game. A matrix of five rows and five columns was used, as on a
regular bingo card, but instead of numbers between 1 and 75
arranged under the columns headed B-I-N-G-O, the *Press*'s Bingo-
Quiz card used the numbers 1 to 99, with numbers between 1
through 19 being found in the first column, and so forth. The
twenty-five numbers were filled in, along with the contestant's
name and address, on an entry blank, which was pasted on the back

of a postcard and mailed to the *Press*. Before doing so, the contestant was to make an exact copy of the numbers, in the same arrangement as on the entry form, to play the game.

Instead of numbered balls being fished out of a rotating drum, which would have made it a game of chance, the numbers to be marked on the Bingo-Quiz card were determined by answering true-false questions appropriate to the paper's readership:

> *Coney Island is not an island.* If TRUE check
> #35 ... if FALSE check #26.
> *Love in tennis means 100 points.* If TRUE
> check #48 ... if FALSE check #56.
> *Philadelphia scrapple is a word game.* If TRUE
> check #75 ... if FALSE check #77.

The game, however, must still have appeared to be a little too close to breaking the law, and so the *Press* discontinued it. Before too long a new game was instituted, with no chance of being confused with bingo. The game was Stock Market. Each Sunday a list of one hundred stocks, ranging from Alcoa Corp. to Youngstown Sheet and Tube Co., was published, along with their closing prices on the New York Stock Exchange for the previous Friday. The contestant was to "buy" two hundred shares each of five of these stocks, paste the list on the back of a two-cent postcard, and send it in to the *Press*. At the end of the week, any player who made a "profit" of at least a thousand dollars qualified for a cash prize.

The game went well for a while. NO FINANCIAL EXPERT BUT HE WINS $500 IN STOCK MARKET GAME! One week, the *Press* found it remarkable that even women could play: GALS STEAL THE SHOW IN PRESS CONTEST. But the game got into trouble when the market itself did. For weeks, the *Press*'s master list of stocks showed all negative signs in the change column. This downturn in the economy, occurring as it did while bingoish games like Guess were being introduced throughout Queens, sounded the death knell for Stock

Market. All across the borough, people wanted to play bingo, and even the Curious Cameraman was asking the man- and woman-on-the-street, SHOULD BINGO GAMES BE LEGALIZED?

With the advent of Guess and like games, in what seemed like no time, the *Press* scrapped Stock Market and, in response to reader requests, brought back a bingo game. Bingo-Lingo differed from Bingo-Quiz only in using familiar quotations instead of trivia questions to determine what numbers were "called":

> Money is the _____ of all evil.
> cause—10, beginning—11, root—18

Church-basement bingo had been largely the province of women, but the play-at-home games in the *Press* attracted a new clientele. One player, Dominick Martello, was kidded by his coworkers in Long Island City, until he won the five-hundred-dollar first prize just weeks before Christmas. BINGO-LINGO WIN-NINGS WILL BUY 'THE BIGGEST CHRISTMAS TREE.' He said, "The boys I work with thought it was a big joke, but I guess I've showed them." FATHERS SHARE TOP BINGO-QUIZ CASH.

My father, who enjoyed games of chance, did not play the stock market. But he did begin to play Bingo-Quiz and Bingo-Lingo in the paper and then, like increasing numbers of men, real bingo in the basement of Sacred Heart School on Saturday nights. He attacked the game with the gusto and intemperance with which he attacked anything that involved numbers and chance. Instead of just playing the three cards that were provided in exchange for a contribution at the door, he doubled his bet and got six cards, expecting also to double his chances at winning. Sometimes he played a dozen cards at once, in total silence.

The game was nerve-racking, because a gust of wind from an open door or any careless movement of the hand or bumping of the table could shift the pattern of beans, cardboard squares, or other markers on the card, leaving the player frantically trying to put them back in place before the next number was called. As with any technological system, we can imagine that evolutionary changes came to be introduced to address such problems. Heavier coins became popular markers, but they provided too obvious a reminder of what the game was all about. One clever bingo player began to use plastic tiddledywinks to cover the numbers called, and soon opportunistic camp followers sold more hard-edged plastic disks at the door. These were less likely to be blown off the card by the wind, but they still were subject to being displaced by someone's shifting knee or, on occasion, the thumping fist of a frustrated player who was stuck with an unlucky card. When the "cards" began to be gathered into pads of light, disposable newsprint, the players could check off the numbers permanently with a pencil or other marking device. This also meant that a card could be used for one game only, but that suited most players fine, since they had a chance to start each new game with a card luckier than the last.

In spite of the condition of his toolbox, my father was a stickler for detail. He was also a sucker for gimmicks, and so any new device offered to help him organize or speed up his game he purchased without hesitation. Among the things hawked at the door by entre-preneurial bystanders were oversized clipboards supplemented with rubber bands that held many pads of bingo cards in place. Since the newsprint cards were no longer covered with movable markers, they did not have to be played in a horizontal position, and someone using a clipboard could lean back in his chair and scan bingo cards as if he were sitting in an easy chair reading a book and checking off interesting passages. But marking the newsprint cards with a regular black-lead pencil ripped the paper and made progress toward bingo difficult to see. Soon, soft colored pencils became the things to have. But colored-pencil points broke easily. In addition, it took time to peel the paper wrapping off the self-sharpening pencils, as it did to use the new special bingo-pencil sharpener. Pointing a pencil could cause a series of numbers to be missed, and so my father acquired a fistful of longer-pointed grease pencils that he carried to bingo.

The next improvement in the marking system was thick

crayons, which not only did not break easily but also made a bold colorful mark that couldn't be missed. Finally, in the ultimate bingo bag of specialized equipment were the liquid markers—called daubers, dabbers, dubbers, and variations on such words—that required only to be tapped on a number to cover it with a blotchy circle of red ink. This meant that there was not the wasted wrist motion of checking, so that a dozen or more cards could easily be scanned and marked before the next number was called. My father carried his paraphernalia in a canvas shopping bag that in its disorder looked like his toolbox. But he was fastidious about his game, and he sometimes won big at bingo, which made him quite happy. Still, he seldom, if ever, remained ahead of the game. He seemed to think he had a better chance with the games in the newspaper.

The Bingo-Quiz and Bingo-Lingo games in the *Press* could be played without any special equipment, requiring only the general knowledge that was in one's head. My father prided himself in his general knowledge, learned on his own in the School of Hard Knocks, as he was always at pains to point out. He had been a star pupil in grammar school, winning medals for his scholarship, but by virtue of his being the oldest child, high school was not an option, and college not even a dream. His choices were two. He could work in the coal mines, which were killing his father, who came home each evening and coughed for thirty minutes at the dinner table before being able to eat. Or he could leave the hills of Pennsylvania and find a job in a big city. His city of choice was New York, which he hit just before the Great Depression hit it.

My father was a quick study, and he advanced to a clerical job in a brokerage house, which meant plenty of overtime to handle the paper damage left behind by the financial crash. In time the paperwork was in order, though, and then there was little more for the likes of him to do on Wall Street. He went to night school at Erasmus Hall and later attended the Academy of Advanced Traffic to learn how to read freight tariffs and rate shipping bills. The work, which required the assignment of the appropriate government-

The father at work

regulated rates to each freight shipment, was perfectly suited to his temperament, and he excelled at it. The Peter Principle kept bringing him offers to move into sales and management, but he preferred to keep his nose in the tariff books and run the numbers to the bottom line.

He brought his job home with him, in that he was always looking at the labels on cans and boxes, noting where the peas and the cereal came from. No doubt, in his mind he was rating a truckload of them from the factory to Long Island City, where they could be distributed to neighborhood stores in communities like Cambria Heights. Reading labels led to reading the fine print everywhere, for he believed that no fact was without its potential use someday. It was with the same attention to detail that he approached games of chance and choice.

With real bingo increasingly available in a social setting, Bingo-Lingo ran its course in the *Press*. That is not to say that the paper did not offer new opportunities for my father to use his mind. One of the most challenging and frustrating of the newspaper contests was Coinword, a diabolical form of crossword puzzle. The game appeared on page 2 of each Monday's paper, heralded on the front page by the value of the accumulated jackpot, usually just beneath the "*Press* Picks" for Aqueduct, Belmont, Saratoga, or wherever the horses might be running at the time. My father saw the *Press* too late at night for those to be helpful or of much interest to him, but he did more than note the new game.

Coinword looked superficially like a crossword puzzle, but its pattern lacked the usual diagonal symmetry of a straight crossword and its preponderance of black squares were marked with dollar signs. Each week's puzzle was printed within dotted lines that also enclosed spaces for the name, address, and phone number of the contestant, who was supposed to clip out the completed puzzle, paste it on the back of a postcard, and send it in to the *Press*. The phone numbers to call to subscribe to the paper were noted at the bottom, where they would no doubt be read by players like my father, who didn't want to miss any advantage hidden in the fine print.

The puzzle was printed partially filled in, giving the Coinword player the illusion of a head start. A typical Coinword clue read, "Something taken on a train." This clue for 26 Across corresponded to a four-letter word, the last three letters of which were already there: _RIP. But was the answer TRIP or GRIP? In a legitimate crossword puzzle the intersecting word would provide additional help, but no such assistance was available in Coinword. The first letter of 26 Across was in a cul-de-sac bounded by dollar-signed curbs. The answer, in other words, was essentially a guess between two equally arguable possibilities.

Each Coinword puzzle had about two dozen independent clues, which meant that the contestant—and that is how the rules described the player—had repeatedly to choose between at least two equally probable answers. It was like flipping a coin, and everyone should have known from experience the odds of guessing correctly the outcome of two dozen successive flips. Each Coinword choice represented a bifurcation between the road to two thousand dollars and a dead end. Needless to say, there were few winners, and each week that the jackpot went unclaimed it increased in value, as heralded on the front pages of the papers I delivered. The word COINWORD, being centered in the headline, always ending up prominently isolated on the folded paper. Winners of the contest were the subject of news stories. COINWORD'S NOT TOUGH! 39 SOLVED THE PUZZLE.

Each new Coinword was accompanied not only by the solution to the previous puzzle but also by an "explanation" of it. It was here that the madness of the game was truly revealed. Why WOUND and not HOUND or POUND was correct in last week's 2 Across was explained by the *Press* this way: "You 'might' (but not inevitably) WOUND a friend by plying him with too much advice, especially on sensitive matters of health. That you are HOUNDing him with advice is already implied in the clue words 'frequent advice.' POUND would require 'at' to fulfill the meaning here."

My father studied these explanations and argued with some of them. But they were the official answers and so were to be studied to gain insight into the ways of the puzzle. There were patterns, my father insisted, and he noticed that there were also word choices that were repeated now and then. He reasoned that in time the Coinword puzzle makers would, like creators of real crossword puzzles, have to use words and clues that had been used before.

Theoretically, there could come a time when the words a puzzle used would mostly if not entirely be words that had been encountered previously, and so it should be possible to prepare for that time by keeping a file of all the words that had appeared in the puzzles.

Billy and I had built a desk of sorts in our basement. The top of the desk consisted of the butcher-block counter removed from the kitchen corner to allow the Chambers stove to be moved into that less obtrusive place. This move in turn had made room for a new refrigerator, thus making more room for the kitchen table and chairs. The desk was installed behind the wall that my brother and I constructed to screen off the oil burner and wash tubs from our model-train layouts, which were in what had come to be called the train room. The desk's working surface was positioned at the right height for someone sitting on the bar stool that had been borrowed from the train room. The bar now served mainly to hold my mother's and aunt's pickles and preserves.

On that desk, my father set up the old Remington, a supply of three-by-five index cards, and some discarded file drawers that he had salvaged at his job. Characteristically, he had saved all the Coinword puzzles and explanations, and he began to work down through the pile, typing each solution word on a card with the clue and explanation below it. With twenty or so key words per puzzle and almost a hundred puzzles to work through, he ended up with about two thousand cards as his starting point. He added to the accumulation each week by typing up new cards from the answer to the last week's puzzle, and this became his principal occupation at home, his files having expanded to capture the knowledge base in a similar puzzle that appeared in the *Daily News.* My mother encouraged his new activity because it kept him from going to the bakery on Saturday mornings.

Like a scholar in his study, when engrossed in his work my father was oblivious to his surroundings. With his back to the washing machine and laundry tubs, and with the oil tank and furnace at his elbows, he bowed his head before the awkward framing of two-by-fours erected with broken-handled hammers and bent nails by two young boys. My father typed out explanations that he fully believed were the canonical truth. He derived pleasure from the increasing number of drawers of index cards, whose edges grew dark with smudged newspaper ink and soft with use. He created his own music, hunting and pecking in his two-fingered typing style, and he created his own atmosphere, smoking George Washington, Granger, or Prince Albert tobacco in his pipe. ("If you have Prince Albert in a can, why don't you let him out?") Before him on the desk was his universe, and he was pleased with it.

He began to work each new puzzle at the desk, looking through his files to see if a candidate word had been used before. Once in a while he did encounter some repeat clues and words, and when he did he filled in the answer with confidence that his chances to master that week's Coinword had been greatly increased. Unfortunately, he discovered, the clues were seldom *exactly* the same, and increasingly it became evident that the answers and their explanations were capricious. Nevertheless, he stuck to his system, needing to believe that he had an advantage in beating the odds. It never happened.

How much is a boy like his father? I certainly played cards for nickels at family gatherings, and I flipped baseball cards and pitched pennies behind the *Press* office. As an adult I have gambled in social settings, playing the slot machines as part of the Las Vegas experience, and once the horses as part of the racetrack. I have never bought a lottery ticket, nor do I feel that I need to experience the sensation. I have not played bingo in churches or entered contests in newspapers. I certainly have no records of winning numbers or words.

But I am more like my father than I would have admitted as a child or a young man. I learned from him the pleasure of reading product labels and fine print, ready to be taught the most obscure fact about the most obscure thing. (What other influence brought

me to see the world of engineering in a pencil or a paper clip?) I
also learned the pleasure of making lists of unfamiliar words to be
looked up in a dictionary or of 45-rpm records of songs with simple
sentiments to be enjoyed. If my father could tell me why it was
more appropriate to take my GRIP rather than a TRIP on a train, I
would be able to tell him what song was on the flip side of "Silhou-
ettes," by the Rays. It was "Daddy Cool," and, timed at 2:43 and 2:40
respectively, this was one of the longest pairs of songs then on the
Cameo or any other record label.

I also read the fine print associated with the Church, which gave
mixed signals about a lot of things, as it had about gambling. Unlike
PS 147 and the other public schools that I knew, all of which had
large and high-fenced schoolyards contiguous to the school, Sacred
Heart's schoolyard was across the street from the classroom building and had a relatively low fence. The yard also was rather long
and narrow, not like the conventional squarish shape of a real
schoolyard.

Each Sunday, the schoolyard doubled as a parking lot for
churchgoers, which made it unavailable to those kids who went to
early mass and wanted to play stickball before lunch. When our
family drove to church, we never parked in the schoolyard, because
it so frustrated my father to have to wait in a long line for the cars in
front of him to move before he could get out. So we parked on
222nd Street, often in front of the rectory, which occupied two lots
and was fronted by one of the largest stretches of curb uncut by a
driveway in the whole area.

For a while, the southeast corner of the schoolyard had been
cordoned off as workmen used jackhammers and shovels to remove
a section of pavement and dirt larger than the foundation of any of
our houses. When the noise interrupted the classes being held
across the street, they were given over to silent reading and study
hall. After the dump trucks carried away their last load, things got
back to normal in the classrooms, but the kids by the windows were
distracted by the pouring of a foundation and the erection of the
brick walls of a structure that in shape and size looked confusingly

like a gas station—inside the schoolyard. In time it took its final shape, a three-car garage for the priests' cars, all of which were large and black and needed to be kept out of the sun.

One of the younger Sacred Heart priests was very chummy with some of the boys I hung out with, and he often gave them rides in his car over to Elmont, where they bought Carvels. The car was a Chevy Bel-Air, and it had plenty of room for five, six, or seven kids at a time. Father Charlie, as he encouraged us to call him, always seemed distracted when driving and had to be told, "Watch out!" He seemed to want to be as young and cool as we thought we were, and he dressed in what looked like a tighter cassock, wore dark glasses, and turned his rearview mirror to a vertical position so that he could see only a slit of what was behind him on the road. This act of nonconformity seemed affected to me, and rather than attracting me to the car, repelled me, as a magnet turned the wrong way did the little Scottie dogs we bought in the candy store. PRIEST KILLED IN ACCIDENT. Once, when I was sitting in the center of the front seat, just below the mirror, I reached up to straighten it. Father Charlie repositioned it immediately, declaring that he preferred the tall, thin view. I preferred to be with kids my own age.

Every spring, a bazaar was held in the schoolyard, and for the weeks it took to set up and occupy the site we students assembled and recessed in the street. It was unofficially blocked off by traffic monitors from the seventh and eighth grades, whose only authority and protection were their small pink palms and their white traffic-guard belts. The overall plan of the bazaar had been the same for years, but after the priests' garage was built the layout had to be changed, and the aisles between the booths became narrower and more irregular.

The booths were primarily of two kinds: food and games. There were many fewer of the former than of the latter, which was fortunate, since the latter were always more popular than the former. Many of the gaming booths centered around a Wheel of Fortune in one form or another. Like an unbalanced bicycle wheel ready to be trued, the wooden wheel sat on a small table in the center of a square of narrow counters on which were painted the game board. It was not unlike the arrangements of benches in the *Press* office, but unlike there, where *Press* boys stood facing outward, here everyone stood facing inward, focused on the wheel.

One booth's game board consisted of a series of different-colored rectangles, corresponding to the colors on the wheel. Another booth's was a series of numbers, corresponding to the numbers on the wheel. Still another was a series of dice, corresponding to the dice on the wheel. The idea was as simple and as boring as the design: You put your coin on the color, number, or die you wanted to bet on, the wheel was spun, and you either lost your coin or won more. Most wheels had six or more colors or choices, and so the house—the church—always came out ahead.

There were also games of skill—toss the ring on the soda-bottle neck, toss the coin into the milk-bottle neck, toss the ball into the empty wooden soda-bottle case—whose odds of winning were more difficult to know. But they were never in favor of the player. There was only a slim chance for someone among the hundreds in the crowd to win, of course, but the money went for a good cause, and everyone was said to have had a good time. What the good cause was I never knew, and I didn't like having to squeeze myself between adults to place my bet on a favorite color or number. Nevertheless, everyone was expected to have a lucky choice on each type of game, and mine were green and 8 and the three-pipped die. I bet those choices invariably, and whenever I won I was convinced that my choice was truly lucky.

The crowds on Friday and Saturday nights were the greatest. But those were also the only nights that we kids were allowed on the grounds after dark. One Friday evening I spotted a girl who lived on my paper route. I knew that her name was Jane, because her mother had introduced us one day while I was collecting, and I thought she was the prettiest girl in Cambria Heights. She kept her hair in a ponytail and wore clothes that hugged her body. Jane was

Catholic but she went to public school, and I dreamed of dating her. I spotted her playing the colors game, and I maneuvered my way next to her—feigning surprise that we were side by side. I asked her what her favorite color was, and she pointed to the red she was playing. I put my nickel on the green beside it, and expressed great disappointment when neither of us won.

I asked Jane if she would like to play a different game, and we walked over to the numbers table. We played together for half an hour or so, winning now and then. So our handful of coins did not disappear disappointingly fast. After a while I put my left arm around Jane's shoulder and imagined that she moved closer to me. We walked around the bazaar like that for another half hour, stopping to get an Italian ice, and talking mostly about the games. I used my right hand for everything, from placing bets to holding my Italian ice, but it was my left arm that grew tired. It was tired from resting so lightly on her shoulder, levitated above it, really. My arm was at about my own chest level, but I dared not alter the position I had seen so many older boys hold for what seemed like hours. After the winning raffle ticket had been drawn, Jane asked me to walk her home, which I did. On her stoop, I asked if she was going to the bazaar the following night, and she said she was. I took that as a date and said, "See you there," not thinking to ask her if I could pick her up at her home and take her. I left without attempting a kiss, thinking there would be time for that on Saturday.

Delivering papers and collecting the next afternoon, I hoped that Jane would come to the door, but she didn't. Her mother paid me the usual amount but didn't say anything about seeing Jane and me at the bazaar the previous night. In fact, she seemed to be unusually quiet. I went home and showered and dressed and left right after supper for the bazaar, which was already crowded when I arrived. I walked all around the schoolyard but couldn't find Jane, so I stopped at the color wheel and played green a few times, losing each time. I turned to go to the dice wheel next, but then I saw Jane in the distance. I headed directly to the numbers game that she was playing. Just short of the table I saw that she was not alone. A tough-looking red-haired boy was standing next to her, and he was alternately resting his arm on her shoulder and placing bets. I turned away and walked to the other end of the schoolyard, toward the gate.

19

IKE PRAISES NEWSBOYS

WHILE MY FATHER WORKED AT cataloging Coinwords in our basement, I worked at cataloging automobile brochures and rock-and-roll records in the attic. Sharing a room with my brother hadn't worked for very long, given our divergent interests and temperaments. Billy was a collector, not a cataloger, and with such an incompatibility, we could not share the same closet, let alone the same bed. We had long outgrown the merger of our electric trains, and we had gone our separate ways. LIRR'S LAST CHOO-CHOOS TO JOIN DINOSAUR AND DODO. My mother had put some old faded bedsheets over the platforms. Bill occasionally took off the sheets and played with the trains; I left them covered. It was only when my mother called for me to help my little brother, who was being beaten up in front of the neighbor's house, that we came together—pushing the bully into the hedge and in getting away before he got out.

The attic to which I retreated was what might have been called semifinished. It was entered through a door that I figured originally opened into a linen closet with a movable ceiling panel for gaining access. Sometime in the past life of the house, the linen closet was abandoned to an attic stairway, the support of which encroached on my parents' closet. At the top of the stairs now stood the winter-clothes closet that my father and Uncle Joe had built. It had filled up with clothes of every season. The rest of the attic was under-utilized, holding mostly a scattering of boxes full of family memo-rabilia, some broken appliances awaiting repair that never came, and assorted pieces of furniture. The floor itself was finished in splintery pine, and the underside of the roof—the rafters—was covered with four-by-eight sheets of a corklike material that, whenever I brushed against it, came off like pollen onto my shirt. A radiator was located under the single window, which was a double casement in the south wall that overlooked the driveway and the Dougherty house next door, not fifteen feet away.

An extra twin bed, from the set my brother and I had used in Brooklyn and that my sister could not fit into her closet of a bed-room downstairs, had been stored in the attic. I assembled the bed and set it up just to the right of the window, the space providing barely enough room for the headboard to fit under the sloping ceil-ing. I hung a lamp on the wall above the headboard and so had the perfect place to lie and read. I used the radiator beneath the win-dow as the support for one end of an old door; a pair of orange crates supported the other end. This was my desk, and the crates my bookcases. A bureau had been moved upstairs, and it hid some of the boxes that were scattered around on the floor behind it. I had a room, or at least a space of my own into which I could retreat with books, and lists, and thoughts that extended beyond Cambria Heights.

Beside my bed was my radio, an old plastic-cased model of no memorable manufacture. The radio was so slight that it was easily knocked to the floor when I reached to turn off the alarm clock, and so its shell was cracked and broken into uselessness. Eventually I unscrewed the case from the chassis of the radio and threw the shards of plastic away, priding myself on having a piece of naked technology by my side. The tips of the tubes glowed orange, and the interleaved condenser was visibly turned when the dial was. I listened to Dodger games in the dark, save for the dim light of the vacuum tubes, and marveled at the vividness of the action in my mind's eye. Red Barber and Vin Scully described every pitcher's windup, announced every umpire's ball and strike, painted in words every batter's swing and every fielder's catch. The ball game was being played in the ether through which the radio waves traveled, and I was on my back in some otherworldly stands seeing everything as clearly as if I were in Ebbets Field rooting for the Bums.

They had ceased to be the Bums for a while after the 1955 World Series, but they had returned to their old ways the very next year:

Dodgers in Trouble . . . Again
Pennant Race Could End in 3-Way Tie
It Looks Bad for the Bums
Today Is 'If Day' for the Bums
Dodgers Win Opener
Dodgers Clinch Tie as Milwaukee Loses

The Dodgers did go on to make it the second subway series in a row, but after taking the first two games from the Yankees, the Bums let the Bronx Bombers come back with a vengeance. Don Larsen's perfect game was a crushing blow for Dodger fans, who listened to their heroes go down one-two-three, inning after inning after inning. It was devastating, humiliating, final. The Yanks did to the Bums what the Dodgers had done to them the year before: They came back from losing the first two games to win the series.

The next season was to be the Dodgers' last in Brooklyn and the Giants' last in New York. The Giants announced late that summer that they would play the 1958 season in San Francisco, and Dodger fans believed it would be only a matter of time before they heard similar news. The last game at Ebbets Field was attended by 6,702 fans, who listened to organist Gladys Goodding play "After You're Gone," "Thanks for the Memories," and other heart-wrenching tunes. At the end of the game, the fans filed out in an orderly fashion and the groundskeepers tended to the field, as if it would be used again.

The last game at the Polo Grounds was a different matter. After the final out, thousands of the 11,606 fans chased the team into the clubhouse and proceeded to rip up sod and carry away whatever souvenirs were movable. There was no subway series that year. The Milwaukee Braves took the National League pennant and went on to take the series from the Yanks. Yet even the fall of the Yankees could not rekindle hope or enthusiasm in Giant and Dodger fans.

With baseball no longer drawing me to the radio, I listened to Alan Freed beat on his phone book to the latest rock-and-roll releases. I never called in a dedication or was the recipient of one, as far as I know, but often my favorite records were played when I wished for or listened for them long enough. Like my father playing bingo always with a lucky pipe in the right side of his mouth, I wondered if my private victory was the result of some efficacious thing that I did, such as tuning the radio to WINS from right to left, instead of my usual left to right. I repeated the action ritualistically whenever I wanted to hear the Everly Brothers sing "Bye Bye Love," with their intoxicating close harmony and warbling voices.

After Alan Freed, I tuned in to WOR to listen to Jean Shepherd, with his interminable stories about life in the Midwest. He may have been telling an anecdote about fishing in a pond in Indiana, but he was really talking—my fellow listeners and I knew—about seeking success in the great ocean of life. Exactly what he was saying about life was not at all obvious to us, we just knew that he understood it all, with a patience and intensity that we could only hope eventually to match.

In spite of my weekly obligation to get up no later than three-thirty on Sunday morning to deliver the *Press,* I became a night person, looking for something to listen to on the radio in the early-morning hours. I looked with my ears by turning the dial very slowly, trying to catch the news from Chicago or a talk show from Toronto. I was not much interested in news or talk, but I was fascinated by the fact that I could hear a radio program broadcast that followed the curvature of the earth. When I heard that reception could be improved by installing an antenna, I strung copper wire all over the attic, stapling it to the corkboard. I imagined that I heard an improvement in the signal, but then I also imagined Jean Shepherd facing a blast furnace in a steel mill in Gary, Indiana, or, as he waxed philosophical, seated in a dark New York City studio talking into a round microphone about gold medals with oak-leaf clusters.

I never played my radio very loudly, and so the slightest disturbance outside my window broke the spell. Next door, the Doughertys had replaced the grass in their backyard with concrete, had erected a basketball hoop at the end away from the house, and had installed a spotlight. Many a night I waited for the dribbling to stop and the light to go out so that I could concentrate on my homework or hear the radio clearly. Unfortunately, my attic room could get very hot, and so I had to keep the window open when it was most likely that the Doughertys would seek relief from their own hot house by playing basketball late into the night. Even after they had set up their large aboveground swimming pool on the concrete basketball court, they continued to shoot baskets—from a recumbent position while floating in inner tubes. Though there was no dribbling, the aging backboard reverberated and rattled with every shot. I could neither read seriously nor listen to the radio until very late at night. The only times I felt more frustrated were when the jets approached Idlewild from the north, using a flight path directly above, and not too far above, my room. JET CRASHES AT IDLEWILD: SKIMS OVER ROOFTOPS IN JITTER ALLEY.

Other than reading, I seldom had to do homework at home, there being plenty of time in the study hall or detention room to finish whatever assignments were due the next day. Holy Cross offered a curious spectrum of courses, ranging from woodworking shop and typing to Latin and calculus, and I picked from each end of the spectrum. I say I picked, but I can't say that I chose, for I don't know what rationale there might have been for my straddling the wide line between a vocational training course and a college preparatory one.

Typing class used manual typewriters, but the Royals were

brand-new and so much quieter than our family Remington. I was
determined to learn to touch-type, so that I did not have to hunt
and peck like my father or the reporters I had seen in the Press
Building. My father said that was the way all newspaper reporters
typed, and if it was good enough for them, always working under
deadline, it was good enough for him. But I was a paperboy, not a
reporter. In any case, the course provided an excellent example of
the interrelationship between teaching and learning. Though
Brother Eugene may have said that he taught typing, he probably
no more believed it than did we. In fact we learned typing by typing. But the methodical manner and deliberateness with which we
were introduced to the keyboard surely gave our learning a structure of incomparable worth. We practiced typing exercises like
`asdf;lkj asdf;lkj asdf;lkj` over and over, until the
movement of the keys under the different fingers became automatic. When it was time for us to begin typing meaningful words,
phrases, and sentences, metal caps were placed over the keys so that
we could not see the letters printed on them. We learned to touch-
type by touching the typewriter, and it was a skill that would serve
me well as the computer keyboard became the indispensable communications tool.

Mechanical drawing was a class that should have given me my
first inkling that I would become an engineer, but when I was in the
course, and its successor course, Mechanical Drawing II, I did not
look beyond the paper taped to my drawing board. I liked the class
even before I drew a line, for in approach the course had a deliberateness and a decisiveness like no other. On the first day we were
presented with a list of supplies that we had to acquire for the next
day. Everything was available in the school bookstore, and so it was
no problem to find the exotic Staedtler B, 2H, and 4H drawing pencils; the sandpaper pad on which to sharpen them; the mechanical
drawing instruments, made in Germany, chromed and laid in a
velvet-lined case; the three-sided wooden architect's scale; the
30-60-90- and 45-degree plastic triangles; the French curve; the

T-square; and the drawing board. It was a load to carry, even just from the bookstore to the classroom. Fortunately, we could leave the paraphernalia in the back of the room, and so I did not have to carry the stuff on the bus. In fact, I would not take it home until the close of the last day of classes in the spring.

What made mechanical drawing special was the power of the instruments to make someone like me, who could not have passed the artist talent search test advertised on a matchbook, into a credible draftsman. The compasses enabled me to draw perfect circles, the T-square perfectly parallel lines, and the triangles perfectly receding lines. The ensemble gave me the power to turn the combination of everything into plans for ingenious devices. But not without practice. We drew a lot of nuts and bolts, complete with their threads, and lots of parts with holes. We were introduced to orthogonal projection, whereby we could represent in three views on a flat sheet of paper all the information that a machinist should need to make a part in three dimensions.

My enjoyment of mechanical drawing became evident in this course, as did my ability to visualize things in space. Some students were repelled by the repetitiveness of drawing threads on bolts or shingles on houses, but I found in the exercises a chance to perfect technique. It was like a typing exercise or, before that, an exercise in the Palmer method. From a blank piece of paper could spring an order of lines, as neat as if made by a machine. I agonized over the details of sharpening pencil points to perfect cones, of making inked lines meet square at corners, of making curved lines flow smoothly out of straights, of making arrowheads that didn't look like crow's feet, and of printing legends that were near perfection.

Mechanical drawing gave me a sense of satisfaction not unlike delivering papers. The repetitiveness of crosshatching a section of a machine part reminded me of the repetitiveness of folding and packing papers into a *Press* bag. Done right, with the correct amount of spacing between the lines and the papers, the seemingly disparate actions produced patterns of equally stark beauty, each as graceful in its rigidity as the sand on a beach or the leaves on a tree were in their natural disarray.

Taking mechanical drawing may have been laying the foundations for my engineering career, but delivering the *Press* had been teaching me the rudiments of entrepreneurship, an important aspect of so many engineering careers. Mechanical drawing met three times a week; delivering papers met seven. It was easily the latter activity that occupied more of my energy and time and demanded of me unrelenting discipline. But the discipline was of a less rigid kind.

As much as I admired the appearance of order in a freshly counted draw of papers sitting flat on the bench before me, I was never reluctant to reorder them by reshaping them into folded aircraft to be landed on stoops and porches. Whatever was ordered could be reordered, and in that reordering could be given a new form and function that did not in the least diminish the original— at least in a paperboy's dreams. The correctly folded paper unfolded was a fresh, familiar thing, one that could have been picked off the newsstand on the way to the subway. No matter how tightly packed, no matter how swiftly flipped, the perfectly delivered paper could be unfoliated by its master or mistress like a blossom from a bud or a gift from a beau. It was a billet-doux wrapped in its own envelope, an aerogram from Shangri-La. The working man's newspaper did not have to be ironed like a shirt creased at the cleaner's. It did not have to be untied like a parcel. It did not have to be cut from a package like a prize. It did not have to be torn from its wrapper like a piece of candy. It did not have to be chewed from its cellophane like peanuts from a bag. It did not have to be pounded from its neighbors, like a cigarette from its pack. It did not have to be, for it was.

Like a shrew brought home by the family cat, the paper appeared without fanfare. Like the cat jumping down from its perch, its arrival was announced by the single muffled thud it made landing on the rubber welcome mat. It was there when the customer went to the door. The newspaper boy was as regular as the milkman and as reliable as the postman. When everything went right, the newspaper delivered to the doormat was as fresh as the news could be in the mid-1950s.

American paperboys won praise from no less than President Eisenhower, in appreciation of their "faithful service to the public." The paperboys' friends, he noted in his message—without specifying who those friends might be—set aside one day each year to honor the boys, and he was once again joining them on this National Newspaper Boy Day in paying tribute to youthful enterprise:

Ike Praises Newsboys

WASHINGTON (UP)—President Eisenhower today praised the newspaper boys of America for their faithful service to the public.

The President issued this message addressed to the newspaper boys of the country:

"Delivering papers has been part of the early chapters of some of America's greatest success stories. From this youthful experience, requiring the industry and loyalty of each newspaper boy—and girl—I know you are gaining a sense of responsibility which will serve you in good stead for the rest of your lives."

Along with a sense of responsibility, we also were gaining a sense of perspective. Dogs got a full week of recognition; paperboys only a day. And National Dog Week was celebrated in the *Press* not with a message from the president, which was probably ghost-written in the Midwest by some official of the Newspaper Boys of America, but with drawings by James Thurber, "America's great satirist and literature's leading dog lover."

Not all paperboys developed into cynics, and so the outlooks of some of them remained as fresh as the papers they delivered each afternoon. To show its appreciation for its army of delivery boys, the *Press* ran a story under the headline IT'S NEWSPAPER BOY DAY and announced that fifty carriers would be awarded prizes ranging from a trip to the newly opened Disneyland on a TWA Constellation to a helicopter ride over Manhattan. HELP SEND CARRIER BOY TO SPAIN AND PORTUGAL. The winners were identified as carriers who had sold the most new subscriptions in a recent contest. One year, a *Press* boy was a guest on the Steve Allen television show, interviewed about National Newspaper Boy Day by Steverino himself. CARRIER BOY ON TV. The picture that ran on the front page of the paper showed the sixteen-year-old dressed in a sports jacket and tie, a sartorial condition in which few *Press* boys had ever seen any of their colleagues. Those of us who wore jackets and ties to school always abandoned them before going to the office.

Press boys delivering papers out of the circulation office next to the Tip Inn were also on occasion asked to canvass for new customers, but we were never pushed to compete for prizes, and I never heard about a contest leading to exotic trips or interviews on television. I was as competitive as the guy next to me at the folding bench or on a bar stool, but the routes in Cambria Heights were already heavily subscribed, with about two out of three houses taking the *Press*. Those houses that did not take the paper had long since been given up as hopeless.

Unfortunately, everything did not always go right either for prizewinning carriers in competitive markets or for those more fortunate of us in solid *Press* territory. The heavy Thursday paper all too often crashed against the aluminum door like an incoming plane overshooting the runway. The paper that skidded along the concrete walk had the center story under the fold reduced to ribbons, as if it had been passed through a paper shredder. The mechanical forces of gravity and friction conspired against us.

Ultimately, though, it was the weather that was the greatest enemy of the newspaper boy. The sixteen-page paper on a windy

Easter Monday was blown to kingdom come, no matter how squarely folded. The heat of summer and the cold of winter, though not particularly unkind to the papers, added discomfort to the route. COLD? JUST WAIT. Freezing rain and snow drove the paperboy to doorknobbing, which added distance and time to the route. But woe to the paperboy who gambled at beating the odds by flipping his papers under a darkening sky. The house always won. The paper was never supposed to get wet, and if it did it could be no one's fault but the paperboy's.

That is not to say that the paperboy was not forgiven his transgressions, as long as they were few and far between. One fall, the gods seemed to be especially angry with paperboys, and the *Press* itself had to come to their rescue. It had been a very wet season, with "steady, heavy, sometimes wind-driven rain" making rainfall in the first week of October over an inch ahead of the average for the entire month. In addition there was an outbreak of Asian flu, which had kept children home from school and adults home from work. And those who did remain home, especially if they were bedridden, wanted their papers more desperately than ever. Complaints prompted the *Press* to respond on the front page:

Your Press Late? Blame the Flu!

> More than a hundred of The Press' 3,000 carrier boys are flu victims. Other carrier boys, after servicing their own routes, are delivering papers for their sick friends, and some papers are unavoidably late.

Frank O'Connor and I got the flu a week apart, and we each doubled up for the other. But delivering two double routes with the flu coming on or just past was not easy. It seemed to take forever, even though in our fevered states we didn't bother to retrieve errant papers from the bushes.

It was not only subscribers who were impatient with the *Press;* merchants who were looking forward to Jamaica Days were getting increasingly nervous as the annual sales event approached. THIS YEAR'S JAMAICA DAYS BIGGER, BETTER THAN EVER. A story under the headline DON'T SAY 'HELLO,' SAY 'JAMAICA DAYS' told readers they might win five dollars by answering their phone with "Friday is Jamaica Day and so is Saturday." For the paperboy this meant that Thursday's paper was going to be a whopper, advertising the reasons shoppers should take the bus and the subway from Cambria Heights and other neighboring communities to Jamaica, their main shopping district on Long Island.

In anticipation of the trouble the paperboys would have delivering the paper, the *Press* issued a preemptive explanation on the front page of the 124-page Thursday paper:

Carrier Boys Not to Blame!

If your carrier boy was a little late with today's jumbo-sized edition of The Press, please excuse him. He had a heavy load to carry.

More than 200 tons of newsprint went into today's paper.

Today's delivery problem was also complicated because some carrier boys are still ill with the Asian flu.

If all the pages in all the copies of today's Press were placed end to end, it would form 10 space ladders to Sputnik, the Russian satellite.

In previous years, the amount of newsprint used for Jamaica Days was expressed in purely terrestrial terms. In 1956, for example, the 263,000 copies of the paper printed would have formed a bridge halfway around the world. After October 4, 1957, the reference to space and *Sputnik* were to be constant in the *Press* for the remainder of my tenure as a paperboy. The very same edition of the paper that celebrated Newspaper Boy Day and pictured the *Press* boys who would fly to Disneyland carried a banner headline that put a damper on the festivities: It announced that *Sputnik* was orbiting overhead.

Bad news for America

Though the *Press* would continue to run prominent stories about the likes of Jamaica Days and the Asian flu, the headlines about school desegregation in Arkansas were driven off the front page by the Soviets' successfully launching the first artificial satellite to orbit the earth. The space race had been won, at least the first heat of it, by the enemy, and it was a striking blow to American pride and confidence.

How could it have happened? We were the country that invented the atomic bomb. We had jet airliners taking off and landing at Idlewild, not four miles from my home. We had transistor radios and push-button transmissions. We had television. We had Lincoln Logs and chemistry sets. We had electric trains and Erector sets with electric motors. We had rock and roll. We had baseball. We had bingo. We had Black Phantoms. We had a free press and a *Long Island Press* that cost only forty cents a week, daily and Sunday, delivered. We had paperboys who grew into iron men. We had *Superman* and *Batman* and *World's Finest Comics.*

How could a Communist country with its *Pravda* and Iron Curtain and Khrushchev beat us into space? Early news stories and editorials credited Russian scientists with the feat, almost invariably neglecting to mention that the successful launch of an artificial satellite was not a scientific discovery but an engineering achievement. The words "engineer" and "engineering" crept into the reports only slowly in the wake of *Sputnik*, but it was their rising prominence, more than anything else, that would affect what I and many of my fellow *Press* boys and classmates would become. Our future, like that of our country, lay in engineering.

As the basketball-sized *Sputnik*, "Russia's little moon," orbited the earth, sightings of it transiting over America were reported to be of help to U.S. "scientists" striving to compute its precise orbit. One television viewer on Long Island described tuning in on *Sputnik*'s radio signals on Channel 4. "They went beep-beep. It was the eeriest sound I've ever heard." Within a day of the first *Sputnik* sighting, the *Press* announced, SOVIET MAY TRY FOR MOON IN 2 YEARS.

But if that was the banner headline across the top of the paper, the bottom of the page continued to carry the familiar Monday lure: $1,900 PRESS COINWORD JACKPOT. As I folded my papers, the news of *Sputnik* and what it portended was covered up by twenty-eight pages of newsprint being formed into a suborbital missile, and what came into my field of view as I placed each folded paper into my *Press* bag was not MOON but COINWORD. It was the game and Jamaica Days that dominated the news below the fold and hence the headlines that we paperboys saw repeated a hundred times each day as we folded, packed, and flipped the papers onto the same stoops and porches as were on our routes before the Soviet feat. International peace may have been threatened, but Long Islanders were not ready to give up their shopping or their gambling.

So the announcements of games and sales were the first things our customers saw, as they picked up their paper and walked into the house reading the folded news as if it were the whole. Did they leave their papers folded on the table beside the easy chair? Did they wait until after dinner to look at the news inside and above the fold?

And then what happened? Were their houses quieter, like bars in which games of guts replaced games of chance? Were their bodies more slumped in the chair, wondering what their future would be like under Russian rule?

20

EDUCATION PLAN FOR
SPACE AGE UNVEILED

IN THE FALL OF 1957, the Soviet Union may have been preparing to take over the world, but to the residents of a certain section of Queens the greatest threat to American democracy was personified not in Nikita Khrushchev but in a rookie postmaster. It was he, not the Russian leader, who was in the advance guard of tyrants. The postmaster was trying to take away our inalienable right to call our community what it had been called for as long as we had known it. As schoolchildren, we had written on the inside cover of our composition books our place in the scheme of things, after the pattern in *Our Town:* Cambria Heights, Queens County, Long Island, New York, United States, Western Hemisphere, Planet Earth, the Solar System, the Milky Way, the Universe.

Our mail seemed always to have been addressed, in abbreviated form, to Cambria Heights, N.Y., or, as if to emphasize our schizophrenic relationship with Long Island, to Cambria Heights, L.I., N.Y. The Jamaica postmaster was now claiming that it was not efficient to have mail to the fourteen different communities served by his post office addressed to anything but Jamaica, N.Y., and he instituted a new scheme to effect a change.

Mail to Brooklyn had long borne only the name of that New York City borough, not the names of its individual neighborhoods, like Flatbush, Greenpoint, or Canarsie. I had never seen a letter addressed to Park Slope, N.Y. It was always Brooklyn, N.Y. But the name of Queens, Brooklyn's sister borough on Long Island, did not appear in mailing addresses. No one got mail addressed to Queens, N.Y. Mail destined for residents of the county and borough carried the names of its communities: Astoria, Bayside, Corona.

To assist Brooklyn mail sorters in directing letters addressed to the two million people in the borough, postal zones were used. Our old address in Park Slope was Brooklyn 15, N.Y. What the new Jamaica postmaster wanted to do was make mail addressed to a dozen or so Queens communities reflect the fact that it was routed through Jamaica. Our address was to be changed to Jamaica 11, N.Y., making us a mere postal zone in a larger post office district. The *Press* noted that the Flushing Post Office delivered mail addressed to the localities of College Point and Whitestone without any demands on their residents. IF FLUSHING CAN DO IT, WHY CAN'T JAMAICA?

The debate ostensibly revolved around community pride and tradition. In fact, no homeowner in Cambria Heights wanted his neighborhood to be confused with Jamaica, where subway and bus routes began and ended, attracting hordes of commuters just passing through. It was also where Gertz Department Store anchored an avenue of stores, the way Penney and Sears would anchor malls of them in decades to come, bringing crowds of shoppers. Jamaica Avenue, readily accessible by public transportation, was definitely the place to shop, even though the elevated tracks and stations cast the street into perpetual shade and the bus terminal created an urban rather than a suburban ambiance. No one wanted to live too close to it, unless he could afford a house in the enclave of Jamaica

Estates, whose winding streets bore such un-Queenslike names as Wareham Place and Palo Alto Avenue.

Jamaica proper, with over 150,000 residents, was already the largest and most densely populated community in Queens, so why should the postmaster have needed to add us to its numbers? The commercial and transportation hub was also the home to the gargantuan Jamaica High School, whose reputation was even worse than that of Andrew Jackson. Jamaica was also where blacks lived; they did not live in Kew Gardens, or Queens Village, or Cambria Heights, and everyone knew that. Jamaica was where mothers went to shop, where fathers went to traffic court, where eighteen-year-olds went to register for war—ELVIS GETS HIS DRAFT NOTICE—and where twelve-year-olds went to get working papers. Jamaica was a place to wait on line. It was not where we lived; it was not our address.

Irate citizens enlisted their congressman to take the issue to Washington, where the Post Office Department ruled that a local postmaster could only *suggest* how mail was addressed, and communities served by the Jamaica Post Office could not be forced to subsume their identities under the single rubric of Jamaica. The idea of postal zones was a less contentious one, even though it should have been a moot point. We began to give our address as Cambria Heights 11, N.Y., though Cambria Heights and Postal Zone 11 were congruent on the map, and so the designation was redundant. It was a happy compromise, though, before the days of zip codes. Our address may have gained a superfluous number, but it certainly did not acquire a less desirable name.

Such diversions and small victories were what kept Americans on Long Island sane as they read the headlines that the *Press* boys tried their best to hide inside a folded afternoon paper that came to be read later and later in the evening. But the paper could not be left folded forever. It had to be opened for the comics, the sports, the ads, the classifieds, the contests, the obituaries, the editorials, the news. And when it was, the *Press*, like papers across the country, rubbed the customer's nose in it, over and over, day after day:

U.S. and Soviet Must Talk or Fight, Says Khrushchev
Ike Summons Cabinet on the Missile Race
'Unknown Force' Tugs at Sputnik, Scientists Baffled
Ike Calls on Free World to Form Scientific Alliance
U.S. Orders Missile Speed-up
Ike to Tour the Nation in 'Chins Up' Campaign
Apes Next, Reds Say: Hope to Land Space Dog Safely
Russians May H-Bomb the Moon
Czar Mobilizes US Science to Overtake Reds
US Developing Anti-Missile Space Bombs
Co-Existence or Death, Mr. K Warns Us
Senate Opens Missile Inquiry
Navy to Fire 1st US Moon Wednesday
Sputnik Rocket Down: US Set to Fire 'Moon'
US Satellite Test Fails: Rocket Explodes
Next Moon Test May Be Secret
US Has No Rocket Like Sputnik's
US Launches ICBM
Ike Denies Russia's Stronger
Education Plan for Space Age Unveiled by Ike:
Calls for Aid to Gifted HS Students

A paperboy approaching draft and college age could no longer believe he was immune to events taking place around the world. Like the chance of pulling radio programs in from Canada, that of missiles incoming from Russia was real. The possibility of war was real. The possibility of college was suddenly more real than it ever had been. It was increasingly talked about by teachers and counselors, especially to those of us who had demonstrated talents in math and science. I heard the bell, and I was going to answer the call. But I was too wrapped up in the daily lectures and exercises in science and math themselves to think about their applications and implications for my own life.

I folded the headlines in the *Press* over onto themselves, as if I were wrapping fish. I saw the headlines and the stories in the paper a hundred times a day, but at the same time I didn't see any of them. I did not want to see them. I didn't want to have to think beyond the next exam. I was willy-nilly following my talents, not current events.

My sleight of hand turned the paper inside out, and each day I read a hundred smaller stories about swindles, gyps, and family squabbles. The headlines about *Sputnik* and its aftermath were put to bed under the covers of the paper itself. We had to learn to beat the Reds. Increasingly, I went to bed thinking about school.

I folded my papers extra tight after *Sputnik*, lest they explode between my launching them from my armed bicycle and their landing on their intended targets. The lawns became as wide as the Atlantic Ocean, and the papers were ICBMs—Independent Carrier Boy Missiles—to be handled with care. I was accurate, but the papers landed with the thud of a dud. None did explode, but none went into orbit either. America was earthbound, and so was I. Even if I folded the papers just right, I could not change the past, hide the present forever, or affect the future. When I tuned the radio dial to hear shows broadcast around the horizon, it was not my hand on the knob but weather conditions that made the station come in. It was no longer just a talk show in Canada that was beamed toward New York but the threat of missiles from Russia. Jean Shepherd's mordant humor was real, and we were all living on a suburban lotto card, ready to be daubered into oblivion if the next ball drawn had our house number on it. BINGO!

Even if we were not killed instantly, we knew we could not escape atomic fallout. We read in the paper how, ten years after the A-bomb was dropped on her hometown of Hiroshima, the effects of radiation caught up with an athletic eleven-year-old girl named Sadako Sasaki, who was diagnosed with leukemia. She believed that she could beat the illness if she folded a thousand origami cranes, which are good-luck symbols in Japan. Sadako had folded only 644 cranes when she died, but her classmates folded enough others so that she could be buried with a full one thousand of them. The folded bird became an international symbol of peace, and in Hiroshima the Tower of a Thousand Cranes was built in Peace Park as a memorial to Sadako. It is the destination of Japanese schoolchildren carrying their origami paper birds on a pilgrimage for peace.

All those cranes no more keep the peace than Sadako's had kept her alive. And now, barely a decade after Hiroshima, in Cambria Heights and elsewhere across America, boys and girls her age were folding themselves into a fetal tuck beneath school desks and beside lockers in basement corridors. The children were not symbols of peace but of war. We had to be prepared for the blast and the fallout, prepared to be blown away like exploded papers or radiated to a crisp like a matchbook in a charcoal grill. The Russians were capable of attacking at any time.

With *Sputnik* came the winter, my fourth as a paperboy, and the experience was getting old. I was nearing my sixteenth birthday, and I was tired of the grind. I had trudged through snow deep enough to prove that I could do it with the dedication of a postman. I had carried the *Press* for almost 170 weeks, for almost 1,200 days. I had folded over 100,000 papers, but I could not smother the headlines in which Khrushchev threatened us with obliteration. As much as I closed the paper around itself like a great coat against the cold, the truth about *Sputnik* lurked inside.

I had gotten about as good as I could get at folding papers and flipping them from a moving bicycle. But there seemed nowhere else to go with those talents. I delivered the news, but it was up to my customers to do with it what they would. I could not change the news in any substantial way. I tried to fold it into origami birds of joy and peace, but when the tail was pulled the bad news inside always unfolded like the flapping wings of death. No matter how much of the paper's white border I showed, the black headlines it framed drove the message home.

I was tired, and so were my two bikes, troopers that they were. I had gone through half a dozen delivery baskets, and several sets of tires and inner tubes. Neither of my bikes had fenders or a chain

guard left, and the handlebars ended in bare sharpened tubes of
steel, ready to cut into my palms the way cookie cutters cut into
cookie dough. The seats were worn to the metal core, and the
chains had come off so many times they knew how to ride themselves back onto the sprockets.

I would see my route through Christmas, and then I would give
it up in January, as soon as a new boy could be found. I collected my
last Christmas bonus with mixed emotions, for the weather seemed
balmy and the holiday season had made the customers cheerful. I
did not tell my customers that I was leaving the route, because I did
not want to have to engage in conversation about it. I did not want
to be asked what I was going to do with my time. I did not want to
be asked if I was going to go to college and, if so, what I was going
to study. I was not yet used to saying "engineering," and I was not
sure I could explain, if asked, what it was. Besides, it was not yet a
done thing.

On my last Saturday collecting, Jane came to the door of her
house and asked me into the vestibule while she went to get the
money from her mother's purse. I did tell her that I would be quitting after Christmas, and I told her that I hoped she and I could go
out together, maybe at the next bazaar. She told me she had a steady
boyfriend now, but maybe that would change. As I left her house, I
saw him in my mind's eye, with his arm around her, his fist
clenched, his red hair blazing.

At least without my *Press* route I would not be reminded every
afternoon of him with her. I would be able to stay after school and
be photographed with my homeroom class on the front steps of
Holy Cross. I would have plenty of time to engage in after-school
activities that spring and the following year, but I would spend most
of the time playing in the intramural bowling league at the nearby
Victory Lanes. After almost three years, all the other activities at
Holy Cross had been captured by well-established cliques of over-
achievers. The bowlers were the dregs, the rejects from the junior
varsity teams and the outcasts from the clubs. We did not even
compete on school grounds. We bowled at some alley a few blocks

High school homeroom class photo; with author in back row, third from left

from school, on Tuesday afternoons, when no one else wanted the lanes. At least then I could find a pair of shoes to fit me.

I was an okay bowler, as I had been an okay stickball player and an okay handball player. Sports were like delivering papers for me: I got good enough to put the ball where it belonged, but as I could never put the papers into orbit, so I could not bowl a strike, hit a home run, or get a killer shot frequently enough to be really good. The trophy I did win in the bowling league was a generic one, with a plastic card inserted into a slot in a plastic base. It sits atop a bookcase in a closet now, dusty but not forgotten.

I was definitely not gifted as an athlete, and certainly did not consider myself gifted as a student. Good, maybe, but not gifted. My teachers and advisers saw me differently, however, especially after the National Defense Education Act was passed, with its emphatic support of science, math, and engineering students. The country needed scientists and engineers, and it needed them quickly. High school counselors across the nation were suddenly enlisted as talent scouts, looking for so many boys to direct into scientific and technical areas that they had to cast their net widely. The counselors were thinking more about my future than I was.

While I was delivering my papers in the freezing rain, my hair caked with ice and my socks sloshing around in my canvas sneakers, I did not think very much about what I was going to be when I grew up, for I had already been doing something grown-up. At the time, having a paper route was a responsibility, an occupation, a job, a profession, and a career, at least until after Christmas. If I did talk, but maybe not think, about the future, it had been when I was lounging on the parkway grass with Jim Wall, waiting to see pass our first 1955 Ford Fairlane Crown Victoria with a transparent plastic roof panel. He always knew and continued to know that he wanted to own such a car and work in a Ford dealership that sold it. I had always figured that with my knowledge of car models and the mechanical skills I had picked up at Sam's I could always work at the corner garage on Linden Boulevard.

Increasingly, I found myself sitting at a bar with Frank O'Connor, talking about girls, oblivious to the fact that we were drinking beer illegally. More and more, the conversation moved to college. We had become committed to going, but why were we going? Was it something we really wanted to do? Frank wanted to play the odds and study something practical, like business, a clear extension of what he had done on his paper route and something that contributed to the country's purpose. He asked me to persuade him not to join ROTC, but I couldn't compete with the financial argument it waged.

After *Sputnik* and the relentless headlines it had generated, I knew, even if only in a subliminal way, that engineering was in my future. I did not ask Frank to persuade me to study math or science, since those were the subjects that I was good at. In spite of my shop and typing classes, I had willy-nilly been tracked into college preparatory classes, which were listed on the left side of the report card, rather than into the industrial education and trade math, which were listed on the right. It was as if the hemispheres of my brain had been manipulated. It was as if for years I had been riding, without realizing it, a bike with a bent fork that biased the front wheel and kept steering me into engineering.

For my senior year, I took courses most engineering schools were offering to college freshmen. I took chemistry, using the brand-new laboratories just opened on the third floor of the Cross. Chemistry lab was the first class since physical education in which I found myself standing up, and mixing chemicals at the bench reminded me of my mother cooking. Working at the laboratory bench now also reminded me of folding papers in the *Press* office. But unlike with folding papers, which concealed their contents, the idea of chemistry lab was to unlock the secrets of a sample in a test tube, to unfold the compound into its component carbon, sulfur, oxygen, and hydrogen, getting the test tube full of gas to bark over the Bunsen burner. In some experiments we had to pass through hydrogen sulfide, the stink bomb of the chemistry lab, to get to our goal. The experience of doing such things, along with advanced mathematics and mechanical drawing courses, gave me a taste of engineering, which I found I liked. I took trigonometry and solid geometry concurrently with analytic geometry and calculus, fortunately not with Mr. Duncan, who did not teach such advanced courses. I liked to think that he could not.

Our math teacher was a young man with a round red face who wore round horn-rimmed glasses, white shirts, plaid ties, and sleeveless sweaters. Mr. Cappriello had no trouble with my name, and he asked me and a half-dozen other boys in the calculus class if we wanted to build an analog computer. Most of us had never heard of a computer, let alone an analog one, but we were game, for we trusted Mr. Cappriello implicitly. If he wanted us to do it, it must have been related to math, which we all enjoyed and enjoyed excelling in. It had become a game, but a game in which I wanted to do more than okay.

Because the computer group seemed to get the ideas of infinitesimals and limits and rates of change with little difficulty, the seven of us were given our heads in the class. We often worked on our homework for the next class during lectures explaining its principles, and we got special permission to work on the computer project during study hall. But we were not successful in assembling the computer from the kit, for we soon discovered that no matter how essential math might have been to understanding the theory of the machine, it took something more, something left out of the derivations, to complete the task of making one. Something a mathematician could not help us with. That extra something, I would realize only years later, was engineering. All the while, the story had been in the headlines: ENGINEERS WRESTLE SATELLITE'S 'BUGS.'

Engineering, I would learn, is neither math nor science, though it uses them as fundamental knowledge and as tools. In its most basic form, engineering is the synthesis of things, as a working computer comes out of the idea of a computer and its parts, or as a three-dimensional bicycle comes out of a flat box of its parts. Things did not come simply of the math and science with which they were understood. Rather, things came of engineering, even if the math and science were not understood.

Being an engineer is in fact a lot like being a paperboy. In theory, all a *Press* boy had to have was a route book full of house numbers and special delivery instructions, a bicycle with a big basket, and a reliable source of newspapers. In practice, he had to have stamina and resolve. And he had to have hands and a plan and the willingness to learn how to fold and how to pack and the savvy to learn when to double-fold and when to stuff. He had to have rules of thumb. He had to have an arm. He had to learn why his papers were exploding over the lawn, or why they were missing their targets. He had to analyze his failures and he had to learn from them. He had to read not the weather forecast but the weather, and he had to know when to put the papers in out of the rain.

How many papers a paperboy had to draw was math; how he delivered them was engineering. How many papers could fit in the bag was math; how many more could be fit in was engineering. How the bicycle moved with its load was science; how he managed to pedal it up a hill was engineering. How the papers were supposed to be flipped was science; how the papers were flipped was engineering. How the papers landed where they did was science; how the papers got there was engineering. How the newsprint soiled his hands was science; how he washed it off was engineering. How much a paperboy had to collect was math; when he collected it was engineering. How many raindrops danced on the head of a paperboy was math and science; how he avoided half of them on his speeding bike was engineering. And simple as the theory might be, it was never that easy in practice.

In the rush to catch up to the Soviets and to top their *Sputnik*, educators wrongly equated science and engineering, thinking of the latter as following from the former. Science and math textbooks, so the conventional educational wisdom had it, had all the theory, information, and rules an engineer needed to know to apply the laws of nature to practical problems, like building computers or launching satellites. In practice, as we found out with our math project, there was a missing ingredient, a missing equation, a missing step. The engineer had to supply these missing elements, by being an inventor, an improviser, a conjurer, a diviner. Where and how one developed all these talents was as mysterious as the question of the chicken and the egg or whether heroes are born or made, but they came more from playing with electric trains and bicycles than from playing with bats and balls. It had more to do with being a paperboy than with being an office boy. Only the understanding of all this often came long after the fact, as thermodynamics came long after the steam engine.

Many a successful businessman, reflecting perhaps in a Kiwanis Club speech on a long and successful career, has acknowledged the value of having been a paperboy as a youth, of having learned by being a little merchant what it meant to be a big entrepreneur. Engineers-turned-CEOs have tended to attribute their career success also to having played as children with Erector sets and electric trains and chemistry sets and having taken their bicycles and the family appliances apart. I did my share of those things, but I was not destined to become a CEO. Rather, I would become more privately entrepreneurial and, as a sole proprietor of my career, a chief without Indians. Playing with technology may give a leg up the corporate ladder, but not everyone wishes to climb it.

How many of my classmates, friends, and fellow paperboys knew as they approached the end of high school what, if any, ladder they wished to climb I cannot say. Those of them who did talk of jobs and careers at that stage in their lives talked of them pragmatically. Frank liked figures, fiscal as well as female, and he was as drawn to columns of numbers as he was to a good pair of legs. He did what he set out to do. He studied business administration in college, became a CPA, married a local girl, moved to the Midwest, and had lots of kids. Ed, his bad eye closed shut, studied philosophy and became a Washington bureaucrat, monitoring defense contracts. Jim, who liked the nuts and bolts of cars, became attached through them to the service department of a Ford dealership in Nassau County. He continued, as far as I know, to live with his mother in Cambria Heights.

As graduation approached, I and my classmates donned the white dinner jacket provided by the diocesan school photographer and posed for our senior portraits. I looked the way the photographer directed me, showing off my fixed teeth and looking into the lens of the future.

With an aptitude for math and science, I was directed by Brother Adviser into engineering school as deliberately as I had been tracked into college preparatory courses. I had willy-nilly become a student, and so I would apply myself to the task with the same assiduousness as I had to learning how to ride a bicycle and how to fold and flip a newspaper. I would become a paperboy of sorts again, but I would deliver a different kind of paper on a new route. I would deliver homework and midterm and term papers to customers who were my college teachers, and I would work for

For the senior yearbook

grades as I had worked for tips. In time, I would graduate and then go to graduate school, and then go back to school again, as a teacher. I would fold my dissertation into professional papers and deliver them at professional meetings. I would toss transparencies onto the stoops of overhead projectors and make flip remarks at cocktail parties. I would get a ten-speed bicycle and backpedal my way to tenure.

My ambition was not so grand as to design America's answer to *Sputnik*, but I was determined to do at least as well in engineering school as I did on my *Press* route. If delivering the newspaper had taught me nothing else, it had taught me that I did not like to be embarrassed by having my missiles of news—or anything else—come apart in the air or get lost in the bushes. But, as every paper-boy knows, the hardest thing in the world to do is to fold every paper perfectly and to flip it squarely onto the stoop from a speed-ing bike. I would learn in college that I also did not like my test papers being handed back to me heavy with red ink and topped with a grade that I immediately covered with my hand. It scared me to think I might not make the grade, in college or in life.

The threat of having their address changed to Jamaica had given my parents their own scare, especially with the rumors that the neighborhood was changing. For years they lived on in Cambria Heights worrying whether their house would hold its value. They were hopeful that they could stick it out until Bill and Mary finished high school, but they were constantly watching who was moving in and out of the other houses on the block. Their weekend car rides began to range well beyond Lynbrook, far out on the Island and even north of the city.

In the meantime, the blue spruce trees grew together and had to be cut back just to grant the mailman access to the slot in the front door. The branches of the trees closer to the house brushed against the windows in the slightest breeze, and larger limbs thumped upon the roof during windstorms and rested heavily upon it when laden down with snow. The hedges around the front lawn had grown higher and fuller, making the driveway impossible to negotiate without the car being scratched. Increasingly the car was left out on the street.

In the garage, my bicycles rested against the yard tools, the tines of the leaf rake entangled in the wire net of a rusty delivery basket. The tires were flat and the spokes were loose. After giving up my paper route, I had not ridden either bike in over a year. The Schwinn that I had assembled so lovingly just five years earlier was practically unrecognizable as one now. My Black Phantom was a shadow of its former self, its chrome fenders and its accessories gone. It was still recognizable by its spring fork, but that too had begun to rust. Along the back wall of the garage, years of old newspapers were piled high. They were worth no more than a dime a hundred, and so they remained unbundled and leaning away from where my father parked the car.

The house that my parents worried about so had filled up with the detritus of childhood. Closets were stuffed with old clothes.

Plastic models of cars and planes sat on the bar in the basement, gathering dust. Electric trains sat under dusty old sheets draped over the platforms. My BB guns remained hidden in the garage, forgotten. A boy's toys had yielded to a student's books. My attic fortress, built with boxes of old comics, baseball cards, car magazines, train catalogs, rock-and-roll records, and paper route receipts, was where I retreated now not to play but to read, trying to make sense of it all.

Acknowledgments

Except for a seven-week hiatus early in 1956, I delivered the *Long Island Press* pretty much continuously from August 1, 1954, through January 25, 1958. Headlines used as chapter titles and interspersed throughout this memoir have been taken verbatim, though sometimes curtailed, from editions of the *Press* published during the period of my tenure as a paperboy.

This is still a work of memory, not exact history, and others' memories may serve them differently. My family will recognize much here, but they might wonder about more. The names of all my friends and teachers are of my own creation, and their characters are composites. Distinct faces and traits merge and morph over almost a half century in the mind; distinct places and events likewise coalesce and fragment. Place and street names are real, to ground the story in geographical and political fact, but the same cannot be said about the names and locations of places of business. Chronology, where liberties have not been taken for narrative advantage, is only as reliable as my recollection aided by the newspaper files.

Though issues of special significance may be preserved in attics and basements on Long Island and elsewhere, complete files of the

Long Island Press were hard to come by in the late twentieth century. The Sunday "*Sputnik* issue" of October 6, 1957, is missing even from the standard microfilm edition. I am grateful to the Levittown Public Library for letting me use its microfilm files of the *Press* through Interlibrary Loan. This admirably cooperative institution also enabled me to consult hard-to-find sources on the American newspaper carrier boy, which served to confirm my recollections about the nature of the enterprise and document it.

Libraries that were unstintingly receptive to my Interlibrary Loan requests and that provided excellent resources generally are Duke University's William R. Perkins and Aleksandar S. Vesic libraries and Bowdoin College's Hawthorne–Longfellow Library. At Duke, I am especially indebted to Eric Smith, Dianne Himler, and Linda Purnell, for their persistent pursuit of the *Long Island Press* and my other unusual requests, and to David Ferriero, the director of Duke's libraries, for introducing me to Bowdoin's library director, Sherrie Bergman. She most graciously extended full borrowing privileges to me while I worked on this book in Maine.

I found useful reference materials in the wonderfully open and accommodating reading rooms of many institutions, including the New York Public Library. Among the materials that I used there and in other libraries and found to be most helpful in refreshing my memories of the 1950s were the *New York Times Index,* and microfilm files of the *Times* and other newspapers. In writing this book, I have also found the World Wide Web to be an invaluable source of information on trivia, arcana, and general culture. The search engine Google proved extremely helpful, and *Newsday*'s web site, with its pages on the history of Long Island, was a joy to find.

A conventional bibliography not only is inappropriate for a book like this, but also would be a stylistic nightmare to compile. Nevertheless, among the books that I should mention having consulted often and relied upon frequently for a reality check on my recollections of mass, length, and time are my Uncle Joe's copy of *Hagstrom's Pocket Atlas of the City of New York: Five Boroughs;* Henry

Bonner McDaniel's dissertation, *The American Newspaperboy: A Comparative Study of His Work and School Activities;* and the Newspaper Boys of America *Handbook for Newspaper Boys.*

While I was planning this book, Dan Lewis and Sue Hodson, curators at the Huntington Library, visited me in Durham and went through scores of boxes of my manuscripts, correspondence, and general memorabilia. Pronouncing the material suitable for their collections, they assured me that they thought my past might be worth preserving for the future, and this encouraged me to continue what I had already begun.

Duke University granted me a sabbatical leave to work on this book, and Dean Kristina Johnson of the Pratt School of Engineering supported my exploration of how being a paperboy prepared me for becoming an engineering student and, ultimately, an engineer. The encouragement and support I have received from the leadership of Duke and Duke Engineering for this and my various other writing endeavors over the past dozen or so years have been a most satisfying aspect of my career at the university.

Doron Weber championed this project at the Alfred P. Sloan Foundation, and I am grateful to him and to the foundation for supporting my travel back to Cambria Heights, Queens, Long Island, and enabling me to complete this book with a refreshed memory. The foundation's support also assisted me in locating and processing the photographs to complement the text. Among those who searched their archives for contemporary illustrations were Annette Thompson of the Bicycle Museum of America and Kathleen Roche of the Hagstrom Map Company.

I am grateful once again to my editor, Ashbel Green, who at the outset of this project gave me a reading list of contemporary memoirs so that I might study the genre. He also gave me sound advice on how I might make the manuscript of this one better. I am grateful too to the many editors and designers at Knopf who took the manuscript and turned it into a book, especially to the production editor, Melvin Rosenthal.

I am thankful to many members of my family for their help,

even if unintended for this end. My mother, my brother, and my sister, in addition to aiding my memory, preserved the artifacts that have helped me be more specific in my recollections than I might otherwise have been. My late father, as this memoir attests, showed me by his example how to look closely at things and how to create the lists that helped me remember them.

Watching my children, Karen and Stephen, growing up rekindled in me memories of my own childhood. Finally, and certainly not least, I am grateful to my wife, Catherine, who in the summer of 1999, through the thick of the Friday-afternoon traffic heading out to Long Island, drove with me to Cambria Heights so that I could cruise my old paper routes and test my memory of the place. As navigator and photographer, she accompanied me again in February 2000 through the locales of the book, so that I might check its representation of the geography. Catherine has also once again been my first reader and closest critic, and I am thankful to her for encouraging me to bring this book to fruition.

Arrowsic, Maine,
and Durham, North Carolina

THE BOOK ON THE BOOKSHELF

As writing and literacy advanced over the last two thousand years, the development of the book was seemingly inevitable. As books grew more common, the question of how to store them became more pertinent. But how did we come from sheets rolled on spools to the ubiquitous portable item you are holding in your hand? In *The Book on the Bookshelf*, Petroski answers these and virtually every other question we might have about books as he contemplates the history of the making and storing of books—from the great library of Alexandria to monastic cells to the Library of Congress.

History/Books & Reading/0-375-70639-9

ENGINEERS OF DREAMS
Great Bridge Builders and the Spanning of America

In *Engineers of Dreams*, Petroski explores the engineering—not to mention the politics, egotism, and sheer magic—behind America's great bridges. It is the story of the men and women who built the St. Louis, the George Washington, and the Golden Gate bridges, drawing not only on their mastery of numbers but on their gifts for self-promotion. It is an account of triumphs and ignominious disasters (including that of the Tacoma Narrows Bridge, which twisted apart in a high wind). In this engaging book, Petroski lets us see how bridges became the "symbols and souls" of our civilization, as well as testaments to their builders' vision, ingenuity, and perseverance.

Science/Engineering/0-679-76021-0

THE EVOLUTION OF USEFUL THINGS

How did the fork acquire a fourth tine? What advantage does the Phillips-head screw have over its single-grooved predecessor? Why does the paper clip look the way it does? What makes Scotch tape Scotch? In this delightful book, "the poet laureate of technology" [*Houston Chronicle*] takes a microscopic look at artifacts that most of us count on but rarely contemplate. At the same time, he offers a convincing new theory of technological innovation as a response to the perceived failures of existing products—suggesting that irritation, and not necessity, is the mother of invention.

History/Science/0-679-74039-2

REMAKING THE WORLD
Adventures in Engineering

Feats of engineering have changed our environment in countless ways, big and small. *Remaking the World* focuses on the big: Malaysia's 1,482-foot Petronas Towers as well as the Panama Canal, a cut through the continental divide that required the excavation of 311 million cubic yards of earth. It tells the stories of the personalities behind the wonders, from the jaunty Isambard Kingdom Brunel, designer of nineteenth-century transatlantic steamships, to Charles Steinmetz, oddball genius of the General Electric Company, whose office of preference was a twelve-foot canoe. This spirited book is a celebration of the creative instinct and of the engineers whose inspirations have immeasurably improved our world.

Science/Engineering/0-375-70024-2

TO ENGINEER IS HUMAN
The Role of Failure in Successful Design

How did a simple design error cause one of the great disasters of the 1980s—the collapse of the walkways at the Kansas City Hyatt Regency Hotel? How did an oversized waterlily inspire the magnificent Crystal Palace, the crowning achievement of Victorian architecture and engineering? These are some of the failures and successes that Petroski examines in this wonderfully literate book. More than a series of case studies, *To Engineer is Human* looks at our deepest notions of progress and perfection, tracing the fine connection between the quantifiable realm of science and the chaotic realities of everyday life.

Science/Technology/0-679-73416-3

VINTAGE BOOKS
Available at your local bookstore, or call toll-free to order:
1-800-793-2665 (credit cards only).